THE SPECTRE OF BABEUF

THE SPECTRE OF BABEUF

Second Edition

IAN BIRCHALL

Haymarket Books
Chicago, Illinois

© 1997 and 2016 Ian Birchall
Previous edition published in 1997 by Palgrave Macmillan

This edition published in 2016 by
Haymarket Books
P.O. Box 180165
Chicago, IL 60618
www.haymarketbooks.org
info@haymarketbooks.org

ISBN: 978-1-60846-605-4

Trade distribution by Consortium Book Sales and Distribution, www.cbsd.com.

This book was published with the generous support of Lannan Foundation and
Wallace Action Fund.

Cover design by Eric Kerl.

Printed in the United States.

To the French strikers of 1995, true heirs of Babeuf

Contents

Chronology

1760	23 November	Babeuf born at Saint-Quentin.
1773–75	approx.	Working on Picardy canal.
1777–78		Apprentice *feudiste*.
1782	13 November	Marries M.-A.-V. Langlet.
1785	November	Begins correspondence with Dubois de Fosseux.
1789	14 July	Storming of Bastille.
	October	Publication of *Perpetual Land-Register*.
1790	October onwards	Babeuf publishes *Le Correspondant picard*.
1792	17 September	Babeuf elected to *conseil général* of Somme.
1793	21 January	Louis XVI executed.
	May–October	Babeuf in Paris, working in food administration.
1793–94	December–July	Babeuf in prison.
1794	28 July	Fall of Robespierre.
	3 September	Babeuf launches *Journal de la liberté de la presse*.
	5 October	*Tribun du peuple* launched.
1795	February–October	Babeuf in prison.
	31 October	Establishment of Directory.
1796	28 February	Closing of Panthéon Club.
	30 March	Establishment of 'secret directory'.
	10 May	Babeuf and comrades arrested.
	9 September	Grenelle mutiny.
1797	20 February	Opening of Vendôme trial.
	27 May	Babeuf executed.

Preface to the
Second Edition

I first became interested in Babeuf at the time of the celebrations of the bicentenary of the French Revolution in 1989. The "revisionist" school of François Furet [see chapter 9] was in the ascendant. On the left there was a general tendency to defend the classic Marxist accounts of the Revolution by Lefebvre and Soboul [see chapter 8]. While the work of these historians contains much material of value, and many fruitful insights, it draws heavily on the French Republican tradition, seeing the Revolution (in Clemenceau's words) as a *bloc*, and stressing its overall historically progressive nature.

I found this perspective unsatisfactory. I had been greatly impressed by the work of Daniel Guérin, who showed how there had been an embryonic working class active in the French Revolution.[1] In Marx's words, I considered that in this bourgeois revolution the bourgeoisie had "played a most revolutionary part",[2] but that at the same time it had been, from the very outset, an exploitative class. Babeuf, who developed the first revolutionary socialist programme and the first revolutionary socialist organisation, seemed to me central to an understanding of this contradiction.[3]

---

[1] D Guérin, *La Lutte de classes sous la première république* 2 vols, Paris, 1946; revised version 2 vols, Paris, 1968. Abbreviated English translation *Class Struggle in the First French Republic: Bourgeois and Bras Nus, 1793-1795*, London, 1977.

[2] *Communist Manifesto*, in K Marx and F Engels, 1975ff., *Collected Works*, London, 1975ff, VI, 486.

[3] I was denounced by Alex Callinicos for my "enthusiasm for the ultra-left critics of the Jacobins"; letter to *Socialist Review*, March 1989.

I began to study Babeuf's extensive writings and the way he had been perceived by successive generations of historians and socialists. Throughout the nineteenth century Babeuf remained a shadowy presence, but it was only after the Russian Revolution of 1917 that historians such as Maurice Dommanget and Victor Dalin began to give us a full picture of this remarkable man [see chapter 8]. As I read more widely I found some of my preconceptions confirmed; others I had to modify in the light of evidence.

I completed the book in time for 1997, the bicentenary of Babeuf's execution. Unfortunately, the only publisher I could find, Macmillan (now Palgrave), produced an edition so expensive that only academic libraries could afford to buy it. I am therefore extremely grateful to Haymarket Books for producing a second edition which will have a much better chance of reaching the audience I originally aimed at – activists, students and all who take an interest in the history of the socialist and working-class movements.

I still stand by all the main arguments and analyses presented in this work. Indeed, if anything, I should now be somewhat harder on the French Republican tradition, because of the way it, and especially the ideal of secular education (*laïcité*), has been used to defend Islamophobic policies. So, in introducing the second edition I should merely like to note a few of the new contributions which have been made since 1997 to our understanding of Babeuf's so-called conspiracy and its place in history.

Some of the most important work on Babeuf has come from the French scholar Jean Marc Schiappa. In my book I drew heavily on his short study *Gracchus Babeuf, avec les égaux*.[4] But now we have a much fuller analysis in *Les Babouvistes*.[5] Here Schiappa undoubtedly breaks new ground. In his preface to the book the historian Michel Vovelle hails it as marking "a turning-point in the understanding of Babouvism".

The book is based on Schiappa's doctoral thesis, and draws, among other sources, on the study of 20,000 police files in the National Archives. By the remorseless accumulation of detail, he shows the true extent of Babouvist organisation, and makes clear, in the words of Vovelle's preface, that the conspiracy was not an "accident" or an "insignificant epiphenomenon". Moreover, Schiappa is not just a conscientious researcher; he

[4] Paris, 1991.
[5] Jean Marc Schiappa, *Les Babouvistes*, Saint-Quentin 2003. See also my review in *Revolutionary History*, 8/4 (2004).

is also an active socialist, and the whole work is infused with a sense that he is recovering an important part of the authentic socialist tradition.

Schiappa demonstrates that, contrary to the impression often given, the conspiracy was not a purely Parisian affair. In fact it was "an attempt, very often a successful one, to build a communist organisation on the whole national territory". Schiappa backs up the assertion with close analysis of different areas of France. He is scrupulous not to claim a more substantial implantation for the conspiracy than can be demonstrated, and admits that the picture across France was extremely uneven. Thus the departments of Nord and the Pas-de-Calais in northeastern France could legitimately be described as "bastions of Babouvist activity"; these were the areas most threatened with foreign invasion, there was a substantial and impoverished proletariat. This area was also Babeuf's own native region, where he had been active in the early years of the Revolution. But there was also substantial Babouvist influence in the southeast, organised around two main axes: one running along the Rhône from Lyon to Marseille through Avignon and other towns, the other running along the Mediterranean coast from Béziers and Montpellier to Toulon and Nice. In Marseille, he argues, "Babeuf's friends, numerous and well-organised, formed a real political tendency with its own newspaper". Certainly the geography of Babouvism shows great weaknesses as well as strengths, but the overall picture is impressive. After all, in 1848 and in 1871, the militancy of Paris was largely isolated (there were communes is several provincial cities, but none lasted more than two or three days).

Moreover, Schiappa draws out the links between the Babouvists and the emergent working class in revolutionary France. Drawing on the approach developed by Edward Thompson in *The Making of the English Working Class*, Schiappa shows that during the revolutionary decade there was the significant development of a wage-earning class which began to act in its own class interests, using its own characteristic means of struggle. There were significant concentrations of workers in both Paris and the provinces. Thus there were 2,400 workers in the Toulon arsenals and 800 workers from these arsenals and elsewhere in the area were reported to have gathered to hear readings from Babeuf's journal.

Schiappa cites industrial disputes around particular problems posed by the revolutionary decade. In Dunkirk, workers demanded to be paid in bread rather than in the highly unstable currency of the time. At Sèvres workers voted for a day off every seven days rather than just once in the ten-day week imposed by the new revolutionary calendar. The strike weapon was widely deployed, often with a high level of consciousness. Schiappa cites a letter sent by printers to two strikebreakers which informs them that their names can be made public, so that they will find it difficult to get work in the future, but since they are young and inexperienced they are being given a warning before the threat is implemented.

Babeuf and his followers were well aware of the problems of wage workers. What is much more dubious is whether the Babouvists played any significant role in instigating or organising strike action. But even if they were unable to do so, it is still clear that Babouvism was linked to the ideas and interests of an emergent class. Writing of strikes after Babeuf's arrests, Schiappa goes so far as to claim: "It is probably the first time in history that there is a correlation between workers' strikes and the communist endeavour."

Schiappa also confronts the widespread argument that the main impetus behind Babouvism came from former Jacobins who had been ousted from power after Thermidor. Certainly there were links between Babeuf's organisation and the former Jacobins (he needed allies), but Schiappa makes it clear that the Babouvists always stood firmly for their own principles, and placed no excessive trust in their allies. As Darthé put it, the former Jacobins "don't want democracy, they want aristocracy for themselves and nothing more". The Babouvist demand for the abolition of private property was a fundamental point of division on which there was no compromise. The language of socialism had not been developed as yet, but terms such as "common happiness" were widely used to indicate a society without private property. Babouvist literature bore the slogan "Liberty, Equality, Common Happiness", with the final term in larger characters.

Finally, Schiappa provides a great deal of detail about how the Babouvists actually organised. The conspiracy was caught between contradictory pressures; state repression enforced clandestinity, yet the politics of Babouvism required popular involvement. But despite persecution, the centre succeeded not only in distributing propaganda but in receiving reports of its impact. For the Babouvists, the "party" did not aim to act on behalf of the people, but rather to show the people "where and how" it should go. Schiappa is quite honest about the weaknesses of the conspiracy, and shows how, to a considerable extent, these derived from objective circumstances. As he puts it, the Babouvists "wanted to be like fish in water, but, quite simply, there was no more water left". But although historians generally refer to it as a conspiracy, it was in reality a broadly based popular movement.

Babeuf recognised the importance of a newspaper as an organiser. Schiappa has studied in detail the list of subscribers to Babeuf's paper, *Le Tribun du peuple*, both in Paris and in the provinces. While this gives us important indications of how the organisation functioned, it is inadequate. Some key figures were not subscribers and some subscribers were inactive. Moreover, *Le Tribun du peuple* was both expensive and difficult to read. Many subscriptions were on behalf of whole groups of supporters. Cafés provided an important location for meetings, speeches and readings from journals. They were also places for singing; songs were an important part of the Babouvist propaganda machine, especially for reaching those who could not read.

Schiappa is thus able to correct the judgements of historians from all parts of the spectrum. He undermines the claims of RM Andrews that the conspiracy had little support and made no real impact [see chapter 4]. As he points out, Andrews has the advantage of hindsight, from which it is easy to sneer at the "amateurism" of the Babouvists, but such an approach fails to appreciate the situation of real human beings confronting the real difficulties of their own time. Schiappa also challenges the views of Communist historian Albert Soboul who underestimated the originality of Babouvism. Thus Schiappa shows clearly that Babouvism was not marginal or accidental, not the work of a few eccentrics; it was an integral and significant current within the French Revolution.

A number of other books have tried to draw out the relevance of Babeuf for the twenty-first century. Jean Soublin, best known as a historical novelist, has written *Je t'écris au sujet de Gracchus Babeuf* [I'm writing to you about Gracchus Babeuf].[6] It consists of a series of five letters, addressed to an undefined young person, whom we may assume to be politically uncommitted, yet in "revolt against the world". The first four letters are followed by short essays on the various dilemmas posed by the concept of equality.

Soublin opens his book by noting the similarities between 1797 and the present, both marked by a contrast between the wealth of gilded youth and the poverty of starving beggars. Hence, he assumes, Babeuf

[6] Villelongue d'Aude, 2001. See also my review in *Historical Materialism* 11/1 (2003).

can speak to us directly. But Soublin is at his weakest when dealing with Babeuf's ideas. Since he fails to situate Babeuf historically, he vacillates between two extremes: on the one hand he applies Babeuf directly to the present, then, observing that things have changed over two hundred years, he reduces Babeuf to a set of anodyne platitudes. In the end all he has to offer is a phrase he attributes to Rousseau: "Let everyone have enough and nobody too much" – a formulation so elastic that even the mildest reforming politician could adopt it.

Yet the book is not without value. Soublin's enthusiasm shines through every page of the text; if he convinces even one or two readers to make a serious study of Babeuf, his effort will not have been in vain.

Philippe Riviale's earlier study of Babeuf[7] is discussed in chapter 9. His more recent book *L'impatience du bonheur: apologie de Gracchus Babeuf* [Impatience for Happiness: A Defence of Gracchus Babeuf][8] follows similar lines. Riviale claims to be independent of all schools of historical interpretation, and rejects both the right-wing attempt to belittle the importance of Babeuf and the left-wing orthodoxy that saw him as a "precursor" of later socialists. Riviale ignores the work of previous historians, and dismisses "erudition" with contempt. His aim is to liberate Babeuf from abstract historical schemes and to allow him to speak in his own voice. Consequently he has provided us with a valuable anthology of Babeuf's writings.

Riviale is certainly right to insist that Babeuf must be understood as a person of his own time, grappling with the unresolved problems of his own age and not merely putting a message in a bottle for the future. Yet in rescuing Babeuf from the mechanical accounts of left historians, Riviale tends to cut him off from the historical process. And in stressing Babeuf's originality, Riviale often unfairly downgrades the contributions of Babeuf's fellow conspirators, such as Maréchal, Darthé and even Buonarroti.

Thierry Guilabert's "unauthorised biography" of Babeuf is a peculiar work. Guilabert stresses that he is more interested in people than in ideas, and claims that it is only today, when Babeuf is no longer claimed by Communist historians, that it is possible to write an honest biography of him. In fact his short account of Babeuf's life is largely accurate, but it is based on well-known published sources, and, for example, makes

[7]   *La conjuration*, Paris, 1994.
[8]   Paris 2001. See also my review in *Historical Materialism* 11/1 (2003).

no mention of Schiappa's work on the base of support for the conspiracy. Indeed, Guilabert seems to consider that the conspiracy made little impact. Likewise he considers that Babeuf's ideas were not significantly original. What is left is an account of a man whom Guilabert describes as "a 'Tribune of the People', a friend, a defender, a fighter who was a bit naïve and too self-confident, but always sincere".[9] In other words, a nice person, but little more. Guilabert makes no contribution to our understanding of Babeuf's historical importance.

Two important studies have extended our knowledge of Babeuf's influence on the developing socialist movement of the nineteenth century. The first comes, again, from Jean Marc Schiappa, who has given us a biography of Buonarroti, described as "inoxydable" [rustproof].[10]

Born in Italy in 1761, Buonarroti was profoundly influenced by Rousseau and other eighteenth-century thinkers, but he became politically involved only after arriving in Corsica, where in April 1790 he embarked on his career as an activist by launching his own weekly newspaper. He arrived in Paris in the spring of 1793, a convinced Jacobin. After Thermidor, when Robespierre was overthrown, the crucial development took place. Imprisoned in 1795, he met Babeuf. As Schiappa notes, the Paris prisons at this time were "real schools of political confrontation and education". He soon became a close and trusted ally of Babeuf, and played a leading role in the unsuccessful conspiracy of 1796. Buonarroti was never as profound or as original a thinker as Babeuf, though he was a fluent writer. But his talent was above all as an organiser, and he complemented Babeuf in the frenetic activities of the short-lived attempt to organise an insurrection against the post-Thermidor regime.

After the Vendôme trial and Babeuf's execution, Buonarroti went to prison and then spent many years in exile in Geneva and later Brussels. Babeuf's movement had been broken, and it would be three decades before a recognisably socialist movement would begin to reemerge. But, as Schiappa's research shows, many of the individuals who had been around Babeuf continued to be active in one way or another. Buonarroti was constantly attempting to regroup such activists. In particular his

---

[9] T Guilabert, *Gracchus Babeuf: biographie non autorisée*, Saint-Georges d'Oléron, 2011, in particular p. 241.

[10] J M Schiappa, *Buonarroti (1761-1837): L'Inoxydable*, St-Georges d'Oléron, 2008. See also my review in *Revolutionary History* 10/3 (2011).

History of Babeuf's Conspiracy[11], published in 1828, passed on the social-ist ideas developed by Babeuf to those who would go on to make the revolutions of 1848. Without Buonarroti's tenacity and self-sacrifice that continuity might have been lost.

Schiappa's biography will be of value to all who want to understand the early history of our movement. Nonetheless it leaves unanswered questions, notably about the differences between Buonarroti and Babeuf. Babeuf was a convinced atheist while Buonarroti believed in a supreme being. Buonarroti was an uncritical admirer of Robespierre, whereas Babeuf, while working with Robespierrists, had a much more nuanced appreciation of Robespierre's contradictions. And Buonarroti does not seem to have shared Babeuf's passionate commitment to the equality of women. There is still more to be said about Buonarroti. But Schiappa's research provides an invaluable foundation on which future studies can be built.

The full significance of Buonarroti's contribution becomes clear from Alain Maillard's closely researched study of "neo-Babouvism" in the years before 1848.[12] He traces the emergence of French communism in the 1840s, not as an inexorable movement towards a predetermined goal, but as a complex, messy and frequently contradictory process.

Without Buonarroti, things would have developed differently. Without a Babouvist heritage to draw on, communism would have developed more slowly, and as a result the events of 1848–51 might have taken a somewhat different shape. And it was to those events that Marx devoted his finest historical writings; had they evolved differently, the whole Marxist synthesis might have had a somewhat different shape.

Maillard gives an extensive account of the organisational forms adopted by the neo-Babouvists. He draws out the central importance of the press; as he points out, in the 1840s the term "party" did not have its present meaning, but represented a current of opinion expressed through a paper. But long years of repression imposed clandestinity on the revolutionary left, and in turn clandestinity imposed hierarchy; in Buonarroti's secret societies only a small minority of senior members knew that the ultimate aim was communism.

[11] F Buonarroti, *Conspiration pour l'égalité dite de Babeuf*, Brussels, 1828; English translation *Buonarroti's History of Babeuf's Conspiracy for Equality*, London, 1836.
[12] *La Communauté des égaux*, Paris, 1999. See also my review in *Historical Materialism* 11/1 (2003).

Maillard's book makes an important contribution to the history of socialism. It demonstrates that modern socialism did not originate by Karl Marx founding a science inside his own head (a fantasy so evidently absurd that only self-congratulatory intellectuals could believe it). It developed in a long, slow and often contradictory fermentation in the heads of thousands of individuals, a few rescued from oblivion by historians such as Maillard.

In this context I should make a small correction to my original book. In chapter 6 I claim that the figure of Kersausie, to whom Engels attributed the organisation of the June 1848 rising in Paris, was a significant example of the continuity, via Buonarroti, between Babouvist organisation and the later movement. Closer examination has shown that although Kersausie was a remarkable figure, his alleged role in June 1848 is a myth perpetuated by those who have accepted Engels' account of events too uncritically.[13]

One important organisation encouraging study and research about Babeuf and his associates has been Les Amis de Gracchus Babeuf (The Friends of Gracchus Babeuf). This was formed in 1993 by a number of inhabitants of Saint-Quentin, many of them local historians or activists in the labour movement. (Saint-Quentin was Babeuf's birthplace, but it was only in 1989 that the municipality named a square after the great revolutionary.)

On 16–17 October 1997, Les Amis called a conference in Saint-Quentin to mark the bicentenary of Babeuf's execution. It reflected the international interest in Babeuf, with speakers from Russia, USA, Brazil and Britain as well as France. Although a number of academic historians presented papers, the conference was held quite independently of any academic institution. The various papers dealt with aspects of Babeuf's life and thought – his involvement in the campaigns against taxation in Picardy; the social and political base of the conspiracy in 1796, not just in Paris, but throughout France; the importance of Babeuf's ideas and example for the development of French socialism between 1797 and 1848, and so on. The papers were subsequently published in book form.[14]

---

[13] See I Birchall. "The Enigma of Kersausie", *Revolutionary History* 8/2 (2002), available at https://www.marxists.org/history/etol/writers/birchall/2002/xx/kersausie.html.

[14] *Babeuf et les babouvistes en leur temps. Actes du colloque (16-17 octobre 1997)*, Saint-Quentin, 2000. My own paper made a minor correction to my book. In chapter 6

The association now has an international membership and publishes an annual bulletin, containing unpublished documents and short articles relating to Babeuf and those associated with him, and to historians who have worked on *babouvisme*, as well as reports of conferences and debates. For further information see the association's website.[15]

It is also worth mentioning that there is a useful collection of documents on Babeuf and the conspiracy in English translation on the Marxists Internet Archive.[16]

Not surprisingly, most of the recent work on Babeuf has been in French. In the English-speaking world, perhaps the most important development has been the inclusion in the *Cambridge History of Eighteenth-Century Political Thought*[17] of a substantial essay by Michael Sonenscher on "Property, Community, and Citizenship", which gives a central place to Babeuf. That Babeuf should be taken seriously as a political thinker, and not just as an activist and conspirator, can only be welcomed. Sonenscher relates his ideas to those of several other eighteenth-century thinkers, among them Rousseau, Morelly, Mably and Helvétius. There are many insights here which could profitably be developed by other historians.

Yet in the end Sonenscher's account is somewhat disappointing. While it is valuable to see Babeuf in context, Sonenscher's approach tends to play down the originality of Babeuf. As he writes: "What now seems so odd in Babeuf was not quite so far from the eighteenth-century intellectual mainstream as it was once made to seem in nineteenth- and twentieth-century historiography."[18] In particular he relies rather too heavily on Babeuf's invocation of "those other levellers" (Rousseau, Mably, Helvétius and Diderot) in his speech at the Vendôme trial. But as we know from Buonarroti, this was all part of a defence strategy which claimed that Babeuf's ideas were commonplaces of eighteenth-century

I claimed that Southey's recollection from thirty-four years before was the only basis for the claim that Babeuf and Wollstonecraft met during the latter's time in France. I subsequently discovered a letter from Southey to Coleridge written in 1800, where he recounted a dinner with Wollstonecraft shortly before her death in 1797 at which she had spoken of her admiration for Babeuf.

[15] See the Les Amis de Gracchus Babeuf website, http://amisgracchusbabeuf.monsite-orange.fr/index.html.

[16] "Gracchus Babeuf (1760–1796) and the Conspiracy of the Equals (1796)," Marxists Internet Archive, http://www.marxists.org/history/france/revolution/conspiracy-equals/index.htm

[17] Eds. M Goldie and R Wokler, Cambridge [UK], 2006, pp. 465-94.

[18] Sonenscher, article quoted, p. 494.

philosophy, and therefore did not merit the death penalty. Sonenscher has little to say of the documents of the conspiracy, especially the *Draft Economic Decree* (written by Buonarroti but the product of collective discussion), where Babeuf's originality most clearly emerges.

Henry Heller's short study of the French Revolution vigorously rejects revisionism and seeks to demonstrate that the years after 1789 saw "a capitalist and bourgeois revolution". In particular Heller notes the role played in the revolutionary process by hundreds of thousands of wage workers. Drawing heavily on Jean Marc Schiappa's *Les Babouvistes*, Heller shows that Babeuf had significant working-class support, that working-class agitation was widespread throughout France in the period leading up to 1796, and that Babeuf's followers "played a surprisingly significant part in structuring this agitation". However, Heller also argues that circumstances made Babeuf "an advocate of a rather unattractive equality of scarcity rather than of abundance". As I try to argue in chapter 10, things were not quite so simple.[19]

Neil Davidson's monumental study of bourgeois revolutions gives Babeuf only a few passing mentions. But though it is not one of his central preoccupations, he does affirm clearly that "Babeuf was the figure who more than any other embodies the transition from Jacobinism to socialism".[20]

In 1957, shortly before his death, the great historian Georges Lefebvre wrote: "The last word has not been said about the Conspiracy of the Equals."[21] Despite the important studies that have appeared since 1997, this remains true. There is still much more to be discovered and analysed about this remarkable individual and the social movement which he headed.

One important resource that has as of yet not been sufficiently exploited by historians is the documentation on the Vendôme trial of 1797. We have both the official stenographic record and the reports produced by Babeuf's supporter Hésine.[22] There is a wealth of material here that casts light on the various individuals who were drawn together into Babeuf's organisation. A full analysis of the trial, the testimonies of the defendants

---

[19] H Heller, *The Bourgeois Revolution in France 1789-1815*, New York & Oxford, 2006, in particular pp. ix, 115, 116.

[20] N Davidson, *How Revolutionary Were the Bourgeois Revolutions?*, Chicago, 2012, in particular p. 103.

[21] Preface to F Buonarroti, *Conspiration pour l'égalité dite de Babeuf*, Paris, 1957, Vol. I, p. 16.

[22] See the "Bibliographical Note" at the end of this book for full details of these.

and the tactics adopted by the defence would significantly advance our understanding of the personalities and their ideas.[23]

In 1997 the archaeological society of the Vendôme area celebrated the bicentenary of the trial by holding a conference, the proceedings of which were subsequently published.[24] The report is a fascinating document, with pictures and diagrams of the courtroom and the prison, and illustrations showing the clothes and furniture of the time. There were also contributions by a number of historians, including Philippe Riviale, Michel Vovelle and Claude Mazauric. Of particular interest are two papers by Didier Lemaire. One deals with the evolution of Babeuf's position in the course of the trial and the contradictions that this entailed; the other deals with the attitudes of the inhabitants of Vendôme to the trial, many showing a sympathy for the defendants which did not go so far as to become active solidarity. But it is clear that there is much more work to be done on the records of the trial and their implications for an understanding of Babeuf.

Secondly, a theme which has been neglected or downplayed in most of even the best studies of Babeuf is his understanding of the oppression of women. It is on this point perhaps as much as any other that Babeuf differentiated himself from the mainstream of the revolutionary left. As is well-known, the Jacobins, with their base among small craftsmen for whom the family was a unit of production, distrusted political activity by women and eventually closed down the women's clubs. And it was the Jacobin position that dominated the French left for the following century and a half. Despite the brave efforts of some remarkable individuals such as Marthe Bigot in the early French Communist Party, France saw no militant struggle for women's suffrage comparable to that which took place in Britain; and when French women did get the vote, a quarter of a century later than their British and American sisters, they owed it first to the Vichy Constitution, and then to General de Gaulle rather than to the efforts of the political left.

Yet the *babouvistes* in the *Draft Economic Decree* made it quite clear that "Every French person of either sex who makes over all his or her

[23] See also Ian Birchall, 'The Vendôme Defence Strategy', *British Journal for Eighteenth-Century Studies* 20/2, 1997, and Didier Lemaire, 'Babeuf et le procès de Vendôme', in *Babeuf et les babouvistes en leur temps*, Saint-Quentin, 2000.
[24] *Bulletin de la Société Archéologique Scientifique et Littéraire du Vendômois*, 1999, pp. 19–123.

property to the fatherland, and devotes his or her person and labour to it, is a member of the great national community. . . . The great national community is administered by local governors chosen by its members, in accordance with the laws and under the direction of the supreme administration" [Appendix E]. Thus women would have full rights of citizenship. This may be explained partly by Babeuf's passionate commitment to the principle of human equality and partly by the fact that some of his support came not from the artisan and shopkeeper milieu, but from unskilled workers, many of whom were women. The interrelationship between socialism, class struggle and women's emancipation remains a subject of controversy two hundred years later, and a fuller study of Babeuf's thinking on the question could help to illuminate the roots of the debate.[25]

But in the end it is Babeuf's burning zeal for equality that is the most significant thing about him. Babeuf stands at the very beginning of the socialist project, and he made equality a moral and economic imperative for that project. The abandonment of that imperative has been a key factor in the decline of mainstream socialism as a political force. When I came into left politics over fifty years ago, the right wing of the British Labour Party, which rejected nationalisation and common ownership, nonetheless insisted that its aim was to move towards a greater degree of equality in society.

Today in Britain, the USA, France and many other countries, income inequality has been growing; the neoliberals encourage the process, the social democrats are terrified of offending the rich. In such a world Babeuf can remain an inspiration.

Of course there are problems with Babeuf's quantitative concept of equality. Marx's slogan, "From each according to his abilities, to each according to his needs",[26] is a more demanding formulation. Yet there too the definition of need can be problematic, and Babeuf's insistence on equality may serve as a corrective.

Within his lifetime Babeuf was confronted with those who insisted that the Revolution had gone far enough and was now finished. The argument has recurred in many forms in our own time – the "death of

[25] My own article "Babeuf and the Oppression of Women", *British Journal for Eighteenth Century Studies*, 20/1, 1997, only scratches the surface.
[26] *Critique of the Gotha Programme*, in K Marx and F Engels, 1975ff., *Collected Works*, London, 1975ff, XXIV, 87.

socialism", the "end of ideology", the "end of history". Babeuf's response was a simple one – "if the revolution were finished . . . then the poor could live".[27] It is as true today as it ever was.

Ian Birchall
June 2016

---

[27] Ami des lois, 9 frimaire, an IV [30 November, 1795], cited *Le tribun du peuple*, No 36, 20 frimaire, an IV [11 December, 1795], p 111.

1
Introduction

Nothing is ever lost.

Victor Serge[1]

. . . while I wanted to be both a historian and a revolutionary, the latter part of my task is the more important, and the other must give way to it if necessary.

Gracchus Babeuf[2]

On 26 May 1797, after a trial at Vendôme lasting three months, Gracchus Babeuf and his comrade Augustin Darthé were sentenced to death. They immediately stabbed themselves with improvised daggers made of sharpened brass wire;[3] they failed to kill themselves and were patched up for execution. The next day they were taken to the guillotine; Darthé succeeded in picking his wounds open, and was carried to his death with blood pouring from him.[4] Babeuf's last words were of his love for the people.[5]

Why did the French state find it necessary to impose such a bloody end on Babeuf and Darthé? The legal technicalities were tortuous (see Chapter 5), but the prosecutor Viellart made clear their real crime when he accused them of wishing to destroy the 'right of property, the chief and universal basis of social order'.[6] The words 'socialism' and 'communism' were not yet in currency, but when Babeuf and his associates spoke of 'common happiness' and 'true equality' they meant something recognizably the same as what later socialists have fought for.

Babeuf was not the first to dream of a world without private property. But he did not confine himself to dreaming; he organized politically for the realization of his dreams. As Béatrice Didier wrote, 'if he had merely described a happy, egalitarian and republican island, nobody would have convicted him'.[7]

Lenin (himself to be a victim of the process) described how, after their deaths, great revolutionaries are converted into 'harmless icons'.[8] Yet Babeuf has proved singularly resistant to such conversion. There are few roads and squares named after him, and in many histories of the Revolution he gets no more than a cursory paragraph. His name was rarely mentioned during the festivities that marked the bicentenary of the Revolution in 1989.

Within the socialist tradition Babeuf has been more enthusiastically accepted. When Trotsky drafted the Manifesto of the newly founded Communist International in 1919, he invoked 'the heroic endeavours and martyrdom of a long line of revolutionary generations from Babeuf to Karl Liebknecht and Rosa Luxemburg'.[9] There is more written documentation on Babeuf than on any other individual participant in the French Revolution, and scholarship in France, Russia and Italy has built up a picture of the remarkable thinker and activist who died on that May morning in Vendôme two hundred years ago.

But in the English-speaking world Babeuf has remained marginal. Only three full-length books on Babeuf have appeared in English this century. The first, Belfort Bax's *The Last Episode of the French Revolution*,[10] was the only one to approach Babeuf from a committed socialist point of view; it will be discussed briefly in Chapter 7. The second, David Thomson's *The Babeuf Plot*, was short and added little that was new; Thomson conceded that Babeuf had 'passionate sincerity and integrity of purpose', but dismissed the political tradition emanating from Babeuf as 'crude, doctrinaire and . . . inadequate'.[11]

The third, R.B. Rose's *Gracchus Babeuf*, was a very different matter. As a biography, Rose's work was honest and thorough, bearing comparison with the best work in French. It was generally sympathetic and saw Babeuf as 'a democrat and revolutionary of considerable stature and some personal nobility'. Yet its analysis of Babeuf's socialism was weak; Rose concluded that Babeuf may have 'anticipated the insights of utopian socialists like Charles Fourier and Robert Owen, but hardly those of Karl Marx and Josef Stalin'.[12] Yet on Rose's own evidence, Babeuf was in no sense a utopian, and further study of socialist history might have revealed that Owen and Stalin had rather more in common with each other than either had with Marx.

My book is based on rather different premises. The recent dramatic collapse of the state-directed economies of the Eastern bloc has been paralleled by a slower but equally catastrophic decline of traditional social democracy, marked by an abandonment of principle and a remorseless slide into corruption. Some have welcomed this as the 'death of socialism'. For others, like myself, the death agonies of Stalinism and reformist socialism offer the exciting opportunity of rediscovering a genuine socialist tradition based on the principle of the self-emancipation of the working class. It may therefore be of relevance to go back to the very start of that tradition, to the man who may legitimately be called the first revolutionary socialist, Gracchus Babeuf. (Rose subtitled his study 'The First Revolutionary Communist'; because of the historical associations of the word 'communism' with Stalinism, I prefer the term 'revolutionary socialism'.)

A study of Babeuf reminds us that revolutionary socialism was born in revolutionary struggle, not in the contemplations of a philanthropist or a fanatic. Revolutionary socialism is not a finished doctrine, but something in constant evolution; as Alex Callinicos has written: 'Classical marxism is not a monolith, a seamless robe. Its gaps . . . too-hasty answers created the space in which vulgar marxism emerged.'[13] There is no script for the transition to socialism written in advance, so that the agency of revolutionaries would consist of no more than reciting their lines on cue. We write the script as we go. Since the future of socialism remains to be invented, there may be some value in studying someone like Babeuf who had to invent so much from scratch.

I am not a *babouvologue*, as the French now call specialists in the field; I have based my assessment on published primary and secondary sources. The works of Dommanget, Dalin, Mazauric, Schiappa, Legrand and Rose are frequently cited in the text, though my debt to them is broader than simply the acknowledged points.

What the book aspires to be is an essay in what is often called 'the history of ideas', an attempt to show the originality and significance of Babeuf's thought and practice. Yet I have a problem with the term 'history of ideas', now current in many universities. 'Ideas' have no history; only human beings have histories. This is an attempt to show how human beings formulated and appropriated ideas in the process of making their own history.

For some this account will be seen as guilty of anachronism. It has been widely argued, notably by Quentin Skinner, that concepts such as 'freedom' or 'socialism' cannot be traced historically because they have radically different meanings in different ages, and thinkers of each period are trapped inside the language of their own time.

I reject this approach. As I hope to show, Babeuf, though living in conditions vastly different from our own, was fighting a battle in the same war that has mobilized millions of the oppressed in the course of the twentieth century. As one who has been active in left politics for many years, I have been repeatedly struck by the resemblances, in both aspirations and activities, between Babeuf and his successors two hundred years later.

But I also reject the teleological account that sees Babeuf as merely a staging-post on the way to Marxism, awarding him marks out of ten according to how completely his thinking coincides with that of Marx. Babeuf must be seen in his own terms, a man groping towards new understandings, sometimes confused, sometimes lurching violently from one position to another, but responding inventively to rapid change.

The book falls into three sections. Part I, 'The Emergence of a Revolutionary', offers an outline of Babeuf's life and development. As far as possible I have tried to let him speak in his own words.

Part II, 'The Condescension of Posterity' (the phrase is E.P. Thompson's),[14] tries to trace historical interpretations of Babeuf over the last two hundred years. Historians have their own histories, and it is by inserting Babeuf into those various histories that we can see how he has been used in the construction of various pictures of the revolutionary past, designed to obstruct or advance the revolutionary present. I thus hope to have made a small contribution to the continuing debate about the interpretation of the French Revolution.

In Part III, 'Babeuf's Socialism', I have tried to draw out the main themes of Babeuf's political thinking. Babeuf contains no blueprint for socialism in the new millennium. But his grappling with the concept of equality may provide food for thought for those dissatisfied with the anodyne platitudes of 'ethical socialism'. Babeuf appropriated the ancient Romans for his purposes, and we can appropriate Babeuf for ours. If socialism is about the self-emancipation of the working class, then its history is precisely the slow, messy process of liberation from the concepts of the old order and the formation of a set of values that can transcend the old society to found a new one.

Many people have made it possible for me to write this book. The writings of Daniel Guérin and Maurice Dommanget first enabled me to disentangle the history of the French Revolution from the orthodoxies of both left and right – their work is discussed in Chapter 8. Norah Carlin, Keith Flett, Paul McGarr, Martine Morris and Malcolm Pratt made valuable comments on a first draft. I gave papers on Babeuf to the London Socialist Historians Group, to a conference on 'Alternative Futures and Popular Protest' at Manchester Metropolitan University, and to the SWP's Marxism 96, learning much from the discussions. Staff at the British Library, London Library, French Institute, Middlesex Polytechnic Library and the Bibliothèque Nationale helped me locate material. Thanks, too, to Daniel Birchall for computing advice, to Karen Hoult for support and encouragement, and to Paul Foot for writing an article which first convinced me that this book was necessary.[15] The final formulations are my own responsibility, and all translations are my own except where a published English version is cited in the notes.

A Note on Time and Money

The revolutionary calendar, established in 1792, divided the year into twelve months of thirty days each, with an additional five *jours sans-culottides*. The twelve months were called: *vendémiaire, brumaire, frimaire, nivôse, pluviôse, ventôse, germinal, floréal, prairial, messidor, thermidor, fructidor.* Thus 22 September 1792 became the first of *vendémiaire* Year I. Many important dates of the Revolution, especially the events of *thermidor* Year II, were commonly referred to by the names of the new months. Wherever possible I have used the Gregorian calendar. This is not from any lack of revolutionary enthusiasm, but to make it easier for a modern reader to trace the sequence of events.

The standard unit of currency during the Revolution was the *livre*, divided into twenty *sous* (or *sols*); six *livres* made a *louis*. In 1789 the average male urban worker earned 24 *sous* per day, the average agricultural wage-worker 20 *sous*. Women got 15 *sous* or less.[16] Consumption patterns were totally different; on the eve of the Revolution many workers spent over 80 per cent of their wages on bread alone. In 1961 Edgar Faure estimated that a 1789 *livre* had a purchasing power equivalent to 205–220 modern francs (old francs, before the de Gaulle currency reform). Since living standards had risen roughly ninefold, he estimated that an equivalence could be established by multiplying by 2000; thus a worker earning 200 *livres* per year before the Revolution was comparable to one earning 400 000 francs around 1960.[17] The Revolution led to rapid inflation, aggravated by the introduction of paper money (*assignats*), which depreciated catastrophically. In early 1796, according to Buonarroti, prices were doubling in a single day.[18]

PART 1

The Emergence of a Revolutionary

2
'Born in the Mud'

'I was born in the mud.' This was the first sentence of the *Memoirs* that Babeuf began to write when imprisoned in Paris in December 1793.[1] Unfortunately he never continued them beyond the first paragraph.

Babeuf was born on 23 November 1760 in Saint-Quentin, in the province of Picardy in northeastern France, in what is now the *département* of Aisne. He was christened François-Noël – later in his political career he changed his name, first to Camille, then to Gracchus (see Chapter 3).

Babeuf always spelt his name thus in his many political writings. However, the spelling Baboeuf was used in some documents from his childhood, and by other members of his family.[2] In the many documents produced by the authorities at the time of his trial in 1796–7 the spelling Baboeuf was almost always used; and that spelling was commonly employed by historians who had spent more time looking at documentation produced by his enemies than at what he published himself. Spelling was less firmly fixed in the eighteenth century, but misspelling may not have been wholly innocent. The French word *boeuf* means ox, and the authorities may well have been happy to imply the assimilation of a dangerous revolutionary to a farmyard animal. (Likewise Carlyle compared the Chartist working class to a 'dumb creature in rage and pain'.[3])

Picardy in Babeuf's youth was a region of intense social upheaval and conflict. The political explosion of 1789 was the culmination of a long process of social and economic change at a molecular level. The old regime was crumbling; new social and economic relations were growing up within it. The young Babeuf could observe around him, on the one hand, communal practices inherited from the past, and, on the other, the first signs of a new industrial society.

Like the rest of France, Picardy was still overwhelmingly an agricultural area. But the region had its own particular traditions, as Georges

9

Lefebvre has stressed in his account of the genesis of Babeuf's communism. In a system comparable to British open-field agriculture, the arable land of a village, consisting of many long narrow strips, would be divided into three sections according to a system of three-yearly crop-rotation. One section would be devoted to wheat, the second to crops sown in spring such as oats and barley, and the third would be left fallow. The communal herd of cattle would graze on the fallow land, and after the harvest on the other sections also. The fields remained open, with no fencing permitted. There were also common lands and ponds and sometimes common rights to forests. As a result all the peasants of the village had to respect the common rotation, ploughing, sowing and harvesting at the same time. Such practices undoubtedly encouraged habits of co-operation and a collectivist mentality among the peasants.[4]

Yet these traditional patterns were already under threat in the late eighteenth century. Land was being concentrated in the hands of rich farmers who often drove smaller tenants from their land. As a result the employment of wage-labour to cultivate the land became more common. There was often bitter resistance to attempts by landowners to evict tenants and replace them with new tenants at higher rents.[5]

While agriculture was still the basis of the economy of Picardy, a growing number of peasants were unable to survive by cultivation alone. Pierre Goubert showed that in the middle of the eighteenth century, three quarters of the peasants in Picardy were obliged to supplement their income as day-labourers or artisans, especially in weaving.[6] Picardy had become one of the major textile regions of France, with around a quarter of a million people involved in wool, cotton and linen manufacture.[7]

Most of this work still took place in the homes of the workers, in the villages more than in the towns. But it had become an integral part of the regional economy. As Maurice Dommanget pointed out, factory production existed before 1789. There were 'large factories of a capitalist type' in Saint-Quentin, Amiens, Beauvais and Abbeville, with 'a proletariat vegetating in horrific poverty, subject to the strictest discipline, to rigorous obedience and to despicable fines and sometimes being required to live in barracks reminiscent of the conditions of North American slaves'. There were strikes and other disturbances in these factories during Babeuf's life-time; he can hardly have been unaware of these developments.[8]

THE SPECTRE OF BABEUF   11

Capitalism was rapidly penetrating Picardy in the second half of the eighteenth century, and with capitalism came its inevitable accompaniment, the working class. Obviously this class still differed greatly from the later industrial working class, and Dalin described it as a 'preproletariat'.[9] The social relations of a new epoch were beginning to emerge.

Babeuf's father, Claude Babeuf, was born in Picardy in 1712, the son of a peasant. In a letter of 1788 Babeuf gave a sketch of his father's life, telling how he joined the army in 1732:

> His education was very neglected, for he had scarcely emerged from childhood when, boiling with courage, burning with zeal for the good of his country, anxious to contribute to the glory of his King, in short, filled with the highest feelings of what is known as patriotism, he enlisted in a fine cavalry regiment.

His patriotic feelings did not survive very long, for in 1738 he deserted; and as Babeuf put it:

> he engaged afresh, in the service of an enemy sovereign, the loyalty that he had betrayed in the case of his own king, after having sworn so solemnly to keep it under all circumstances.[10]

This was only the beginning of a career of desertion and vagabondage that lasted at least seventeen years. He benefited from an amnesty in 1755,[11] and had returned to France by 1758 when he married Marie-Catherine Anceret, some twenty years younger than himself.

For the sons of peasants in the eighteenth century, the army played a role akin to that of recruitment into factories a century later. It tore them away from the narrow confines of a locality, and introduced them to collective discipline and life. Despite the poverty of his upbringing, the young Babeuf had access, through his father's experiences, to a wider world and this undoubtedly helped to develop his remarkable curiosity and intelligence.

On his return to France, Claude Babeuf became an employee of the tax-collecting administration, earning between 19 and 20 *livres* per month. Babeuf blamed the 'deep poverty' of his family for the fact that his mother could not supply the basic needs of her children.[12]

We know much less of Babeuf's mother than of his father; she suffered the fate of most lower-class women in pre-Revolutionary France – ignorance, poverty, hard work and constant child-bearing. She was probably illiterate,[13] and between her marriage in 1758 and the death of her husband in 1781 she bore thirteen children.[14]

Babeuf never went to school. He attributed this to his father's vanity, saying that 'although he only knew how to read and write very badly, he got it into his head that he would be his children's only teacher'. Advielle claimed that Claude Babeuf taught his son Latin and German; certainly it seems probable that he acquired some knowledge of Latin in his youth.[15]

Babeuf claimed that his own 'fortunate gifts' came from 'nature alone', and that he soon had no difficulty in getting the better of his tutor.[16] But he was probably overstating the case when he suggested his father could not read and write well. We know from his later work that Babeuf wrote fluently, and had a firm grasp of French grammar (including the imperfect subjunctive); his writing was vivid and imaginative, though his sentences were sometimes too long and lacked elegance; he read voraciously on a range of literary, historical and scientific subjects. It is not very plausible to attribute these skills entirely to 'fortunate gifts' of nature, and we must presume that his father had some success in communicating basic skills. More significantly, he seems to have awakened in his son an intellectual curiosity that led him a long way from the mental world of his childhood.

The peculiarities of Babeuf's education produced a very uneven development of his intellectual capacities. To begin with, he responded well to his father's teaching; at the age of eight he was regarded as something of a prodigy.[17] But as his knowledge progressed, he became increasingly weary of his father's obsession with 'sieges, battles, duels', and irritated by the way he gave value only to things he had himself seen while 'he despised all the officers who were not of his own time, the towns he had not seen, and so on'. Babeuf was already developing the broader grasp of history which was to characterize his mature thinking; the immediate response was disobedience. Despite the punishments he received, 'I shook off the yoke, and became the greatest little rascal you can imagine'.[18]

The result of this adolescent rebellion led to the next crucial stage in Babeuf's development:

> For some years they had to let me live in this state of anarchy, if I may use the term; in the end, both to teach me a lesson and to lighten somewhat

the burden of extreme poverty which was afflicting my parents with their large family during very hard times, they made me go and earn my living working on the Picardy Canal, where the excessive harshness of manual labour gave me cause to think; my conclusion, in short, was to find some way of earning my keep with less difficulty.[19]

The Picardy Canal was an extension of the canal joining the Somme and the Oise, which had been completed in 1738; the building of this canal had been an event of considerable significance for the region, for when it was completed it became possible to send grain from Picardy directly to the Paris market.[20] The new extension was to join the canal to the river Escaut, and was carried out under the direction of the Duke of Choiseul and the engineer Laurent; it was financed jointly by the government and the local region.[21] Arthur Young, a British traveller in pre-Revolutionary France, observed the building of this canal.[22]

The extension of roads and canals was a vital part of the establishment of a modern economy in France. When Babeuf went to work on the canal, around the age of fourteen, he was participating in the economic process that was to bring France to revolution. As Henri Cavaillès pointed out, the improvement of the transport system meant not only a better circulation of goods, but also a better circulation of ideas – the new roads and canals carried subversive books and journals as well as royal decrees and commodities to market.[23]

Babeuf came too soon for the machinery which made possible the great canal-building achievements of the nineteenth century such as Suez or the Manchester Ship Canal – steam dredgers, cranes, and so on. One estimate is that without such machinery those canals would have required twenty times the amount of labour and twenty times as long to build.[24] The building of the canal must have required a huge mass of labour – some skilled artisans, but mostly unskilled labour provided by beggars, members of peasant families seeking to supplement their incomes, and such like. The Languedoc Canal, built in the late seventeenth century, required some 8000 workers,[25] and building methods had changed little by the time Babeuf was working on the Picardy Canal. Canal building provided one of the biggest concentrations of wage labour in eighteenth-century France, a living anticipation of the nineteenth-century proletariat.

In the absence of written documentation, Babeuf's biographers have neglected the experience of work on the canal, giving it at best a few sentences. But it would be wrong to underrate the importance of this experience for the growing boy. Babeuf was introduced not only to the harshness of manual labour and work discipline, but to a large concentration of proletarians.

Estimates of how long Babeuf worked on the canal vary from three to six years;[26] (according to Vignon, construction was suspended at the end of 1775).[27] By 1778 he had found the profession that was to take him back to the more intellectual pursuits of his childhood. He became apprenticed to Henri Joseph Hullin at Flixecourt, a market town of some 705 inhabitants, where he was to learn the profession of *feudiste*.

To be a *feudiste* was a thriving trade in the last decades before the Revolution. The old aristocratic landowners were making a final effort to assert their power in a society that was changing beneath their feet. One way of doing this was to re-impose feudal rights over the peasantry which had fallen into disuse. To establish precisely what these rights were required the services of the *feudiste*, who would search through old documents in order to provide the landowner with a legal statement of his entitlement to exploit. To survive in the profession the young Babeuf obviously needed to draw on all the resources of his limited education – a good grasp of the French language and basic arithmetic – as well as acquiring a knowledge of law on the job.[28]

In his first year Babeuf was not paid at all, but he ate at table with the Hullin family and Hullin's wife did his laundry every six weeks. By about 1781 he had managed to learn enough to start seeking independent employment, and by 1783 he had set himself up in business in the small town of Roye.[29] Now began the one period of relative prosperity in Babeuf's life. Ten years on from having toiled in the mud of the Picardy Canal he was himself an employer, with up to twenty clerks working for him.[30] Such success was short-lived; in the period immediately preceding the Revolution business declined, and by 1788 he had only eight employees.[31]

Babeuf's professional success was obvious proof of his intelligence and competence; we may presume he had also mastered the art of politeness. But we also know that he was not happy with the social order of which he had become a servant. Maurice Dommanget quoted an unpublished document where Babeuf spoke of himself in the third person:

He groaned continually at seeing how, by the perpetuation of established abuses, idleness, indolence and debauchery were able to live in luxury on what they extracted, in a thousand different forms, from the sweat of the wretched inhabitants of the countryside . . . Not being able to remake a world he had found ready made . . . cast into a world of injustice based on foolishly respected traditions, he was able only to take note in the strictest manner of what had to be necessary until a revolution came to strike dead all usurpations in the name of equity.[32]

The resentment that Babeuf felt towards his noble clients can be seen in his tortuous relations with the marquis de Soyécourt. Initially, in approaching the marquis Babeuf was full of the required politeness, expressing his 'respectful homage', but when Soyécourt first expressed dissatisfaction with the *feudiste's* work, and then failed to pay, the tone of Babeuf's letters changed markedly, and eventually he was reduced to seeking justice through the courts.[33]

A gut feeling of resentment may be an essential part of what goes to make up a revolutionary, but it is only a part. Among the archives Babeuf found not only anger but understanding. Years later, as a revolutionary journalist in Paris, he declared: 'It was in the dust of the aristocratic archives that I discovered the terrible secrets of the usurpations by the noble caste.'[34]

He had expanded on this in *Le Scrutateur des décrets*, a short-lived paper he published in Picardy in 1791. Here he argued that neither the historian nor the man of letters could understand so well as the *feudiste* the 'monstrously extortionate history of the institution of the *cens* [feudal rent]'. If, he argued, the *feudiste* could reconstruct in imagination the means whereby the landowners established their domination, then

he will show that it is not true, as has been impudently claimed for a long time, that the landowners had subjugated the entire human race before the establishment of the *cens*; that they alone had succeeded in possessing immense territories; that all the other classes of men were propertyless, and that they had become so thanks only to the goodwill of the children of the sun. He will show that it was only over a long period of time that these demigods succeeded in exploiting the properties of those who laboured and cultivated; that it was only done by outwitting some, by successively threatening, flattering, intimidating and corrupting the others, by taking advantage of some and leading others into error, by forging documents and by taking perverse foresight so far as to get children to sign documents which were not to be used for the present, but which would be carefully preserved to exploit a later generation which was no longer in a position to challenge their legality.[35]

From these insights into the origins of particular forms of exploitation, Babeuf was slowly groping towards an understanding of the origin of property as such; in a letter of June 1786 he wrote:

In my capacity as a *feudiste*, I could not fail to know how the majority of large estates were formed and came into the hands of those who possess them. The most ancient titles are almost all nothing but the ratification of enormous iniquities and vicious robberies. It was law enforced with sword and torch in hand on peasants, those who tilled the fields, and who, to save their skins, abandoned to their robbers, along with the soil they had brought into cultivation, their own persons, which they no longer knew what to do with. These simple people became serfs, like the herd of cattle which they had raised but which no longer belonged to them.[36]

Having made himself economically independent, Babeuf took on the additional responsibility of a family. On 13 November 1782 he married Marie-Anne-Victoire Langlet, born in 1757. His wife and children were to be drawn into deep poverty and many hardships in the course of Babeuf's revolutionary career, but the family always maintained a deep sense of mutual trust and affection. Both his wife and his eldest son took an active role in the conspiracy of 1796. Rose (quoting a phrase of Boris Pasternak's) described Babeuf as a pure incarnation of the 'revolutionary extremist . . . narrowminded to the point of genius'.[37] But all the evidence that we have of Babeuf's family life shows him to have been a man of powerful emotions, deeply attached to those nearest and dearest to him. If anger at social injustice was one component that went to make up the revolutionary, then passionate affection for his fellow human beings was another.

Before her marriage Babeuf's bride had worked as a maid in one of the local *châteaux*. Doubtless she had little formal education, but the claim that she was illiterate is mistaken. When she was arrested in 1796, Babeuf protested in his paper[38] that 'this dangerous conspirator cannot read and write'. This was a tactical attempt to win public sympathy and outrage rather than an intellectual put-down; Babeuf knew well enough that his wife could read and write for he corresponded regularly with her whenever they were separated. A number of her letters survive, and though the spelling is erratic, the expression is clear and fluent enough.[39]

In Rose's view:

> How far she really understood her husband's revolutionary ideals is another matter. Marie-Anne was barely literate in 1782 and remained so . . . Babeuf . . . is completely and strangely silent on the question of the education of his wife. Theoretically a believer in the intellectual equality of women, he was clearly unconvinced of the intellectual equality of the one woman closest to him.[40]

This patronizing misrepresentation bears little relation to the facts. Babeuf's correspondence shows that he communicated his developing political ideas to his wife whenever they were separated; we can only presume they discussed them when they were together. Some of his most interesting political letters were addressed to his wife, for example the discussion of revolutionary violence written from Paris in July 1789 (see Chapter 3). Madame Babeuf was a courageous and dedicated woman who deserves a biography in her own right. If we set her political involvement alongside Babeuf's deep interest in the problems of child-care, it can be seen that as a couple they were well in advance of their time.

Between 1783 and 1797 she bore Babeuf five children. The two eldest were named Sofie and Emile, after the main characters in Rousseau's *Emile*, an educational treatise in the form of a novel. Unlike Rousseau, who abandoned his own children, Babeuf found time and enthusiasm to devote to his children's education. He was an affectionate parent but a strict one, who expected high standards of his children, and imposed firm discipline on them.

The most powerful testimony to Babeuf's character as a parent comes from the sad story of his first-born, Sofie. In July 1787 Sofie, nearly four years old, fell onto the fire, despite the presence of a fire-guard, and was badly scalded with boiling water. She suffered from the effects for some months and in November, following the attentions of what Babeuf referred to as an 'ignorant and murderous' doctor, she died. Babeuf's grief was profound:

> I have lost everything . . . My dearest possession, my sole possession, the one possession which could enable me to enjoy the others, has been

cruelly snatched from me! O grief, my daughter, my tender child, my dear
daughter, my idol, my everything . . . You are gone![41]

There is a bizarre story linked to Sofie's death. Babeuf apparently cut
the heart out of the corpse, ate part of it, and wore the rest in a locket
on his chest.[42] It was an odd mixture of superstition and materialism,
indicative of the way that Babeuf's view of the world was developing.
Without hope that his daughter's soul might achieve immortality, he was
seeking to preserve the object of his affections by fusing his body with
the remnant of hers.

Babeuf's profession and his family life both contributed to the formation of the character of a revolutionary. But in themselves anger, love
and the contents of the archives were not enough to produce an original
revolutionary thinker. What made this possible was the fact that Babeuf
was heir to a whole century of radical philosophy.

For one who never enjoyed any formal education, Babeuf had a remarkable capacity for intellectual activity. He devoured books throughout his
adult life, and his writings reveal a remarkable range of references. Yet,
as a self-taught thinker, he never studied any subject systematically. For
most of his life his access to bookshops and libraries was necessarily
limited, and his reading was often determined by the books that chanced
to fall into his hands.

Babeuf was in a sense 'overqualified'. He had the ability and the culture to play a leading role in society, but the existing order had no place
for him other than as a minor functionary, servicing exploitation by the
parasitic rich. Though lacking formal education he belonged in some
ways to that social group of whom Danton was to say, 'The old regime
drove us to revolution by giving us a good education without opening
any opportunity for our talents' (a sentiment echoed by many unemployed graduates two centuries later).[43]

Babeuf knew the work of such political theorists as Machiavelli and
Thomas More, while heroic Roman figures such as Brutus, founder of
the republic, and the Gracchi, advocates of the agrarian law to distribute
land to the poor, were a moral and political inspiration to him throughout his life; in all his political writings he held up the model of Roman
values.

But his most important reading came from the philosophical movement of his own century. The Enlightenment was a rich and complex

movement, but a few principles ran through it. Reason and the evidence of the senses were to be trusted before authority and tradition; the 'revealed truths' of religion were to be challenged. Scientific knowledge provided the basis for human betterment; human society was progressing towards a better and more enlightened state. By the 1780s these ideas had spread widely among the literate middle classes, and the great philosophers had found many imitators. It was an exciting time to be discovering new books and new ideas. Babeuf knew his Voltaire, and quoted from him lines that seemed to question the whole structure of existing society:

> Les mortels sont égaux, ce n'est point la naissance,
> C'est la seule vertu qui fait leur différence.
> (*Mortals are equal, and it is not birth but virtue alone which distinguishes between them.*)[44]

He knew something of the empiricist philosophy of Locke, which had been the foundation of the French Enlightenment; and he was also aware of developments in political economy – he read Adam Smith and such French economists as Linguet (a critical economist and advocate of tax reform) and Necker (a reforming finance minister in the last years of the monarchy).[45]

But reading was not enough; Babeuf aspired to make links with other enlightened thinkers. One possible route to this aim was freemasonry. In the late eighteenth century freemasonry was still a radical movement, committed to philanthropy and the propagation of enlightened ideas. Babeuf apparently applied twice to become a freemason; one letter of application survives, in which he referred to freemasonry as 'a school of morality, of virtue, of honour and of all kinds of good sentiments'.[46] His first application was rejected and it seems likely he never became a freemason. One reason was a simple question of class; the enlightened middle classes might wish to use freemasonry for their own emancipation, but they had no desire to open the doors to those like Babeuf, who were trying to rise out of the mud. Freemasonry at Roye was dominated by the Billecocq family of prosperous lawyers, with whom Babeuf was to have more than one brush.[47]

Babeuf had rather more success with the *académie* of Arras. The *académies* which had existed in many French towns since the time of Louis XIV were forums for the discussion of literary, philosophical and scientific questions; they held meetings, circulated correspondence and organized essay competitions. Increasingly in the later eighteenth century they became one of the means whereby the radical ideas of the Enlightenment percolated through to a significant section of the middle class. In the 1780s the Arras *académie* recruited mainly from the *moyenne bourgeoisie* – doctors, lawyers and the like – though its membership included a number of nobles.

In 1785 the *académie* of Arras elected as its secretary a man called Ferdinand Dubois de Fosseux (one of the defeated candidates was Robespierre). Dubois conducted an extensive correspondence with many people in the area; in his seven years as secretary he sent 13 856 letters and received 7749. This was achieved using a system whereby his secretaries reproduced the same letters to a number of correspondents with the addition of a few personal sentences to each. Babeuf was probably not aware of this and thought that Dubois was taking more of an interest in him than he in fact was.[48]

Dubois belonged to the moderate wing of the Enlightenment; he was a Deist and a believer in private property, but he had a strong belief in human equality, and was particularly interested in the social status and education of women.[49] For reasons of class Babeuf could probably not have become an active participant in the *académie*'s work. But the correspondence with Dubois was of immense importance for him. Dubois sent him books and stimulated his interest in a variety of topics. It was in the correspondence with Dubois, much of which survives, that Babeuf made the transition from a voracious but passive reader to an active writer.

The correspondence reveals just what a lively curiosity and intelligence Babeuf had developed. He jumped from one subject to another with ease, referring to electricity and magnetism, and the classification of different forms of gas. In one letter he moved from the constitution of the sap of plants to an essay on the necessity for inventing new words. Despite his lack of schooling he was confident about grammar, and presumed to suggest that one of the texts sent him by Dubois contained an incorrect tense of the subjunctive.[50]

The French Enlightenment was not a monolithic movement. Like the society that produced it, it was riddled with contradictions. In broad terms the Enlightenment can be seen as expressing the world-view of the emerging bourgeoisie, anxious to rid itself of the fetters imposed by monarchy, aristocracy and church. But that bourgeoisie was both an oppressed and an exploiting class; while it sought its own place in the sun, it was not anxious to open the gates too wide for those below, the great mass of peasants and artisans, and the embryonic class of wage-earning workers, on whose continuing labour its own privileges depended.

Voltaire summed up perfectly the world-view of this middle group in society. He fearlessly denounced the corruption, abuses, brutality and injustice that were endemic in the old regime, but at the same time continued to believe that monarchy was the best form of government and scorned the belief that the peasantry could ever rise from its humble status in society. He denounced savagely the absurdities and pretensions of priests and popes, but insisted that a belief in a creator was essential to social order; as he argued in *Histoire de Jenni* (1775), if atheism spread among the lower orders, no-one's purse would be safe.

One crucial influence on Babeuf was Jean-Jacques Rousseau. Rousseau's work was extensive and contained many inconsistencies; I shall not attempt to deal with the complex question of what Rousseau 'really' meant, but merely set out how he must have been perceived by a contemporary such as Babeuf.

Rousseau was both a product of the Enlightenment and one of its most penetrating critics. In two *Discourses* written for the *académie* of Dijon, one on the contribution of the arts and sciences (1750) and the other on the origins of human inequality (1754), he undermined some of the basic assumptions of Enlightenment thinking, and in his *Social Contract* (1762) he set out a theory of the sovereignty of the people which was to have an enormous influence on subsequent democratic thought.

One of the central tenets of mainstream Enlightenment thought was a belief in progress. Through reason and science humanity could come to know more; such knowledge, slowly but surely, would improve the human condition. Rousseau, whose *Social Contract* began with the inspiring phrase 'Man is born free, and everywhere he is in chains',[51] directly challenged this assumption. In the original state of nature, he argued, human beings had been free, equal and virtuous; the growth of a more complex society, the development of 'arts and sciences' – that is, of culture, science, technology and luxury – had not led to the betterment of the quality of human life but rather to its corruption.

The revolutionary implications of Rousseau's thought were clear. If the Voltaireans were right, then humanity would advance slowly, without any need for a fundamental change in the social order. For Rousseau, on the other hand, there was no slow automatic progress; if there was to be change, it would have to mean a clean break with the existing order.

But there was also a profound contradiction within Rousseau's thought. Human beings were naturally good; the evils of the present age had arisen because people had been corrupted by society. But since society is a human product, how had naturally good beings been depraved by their own creation? In Alasdair MacIntyre's words: 'If I can purge society of corruption by appeal to universally valid moral principles to which either every heart or every mind or both must give testimony, then how can society ever have become corrupted in the first place?'[52]

Rousseau had no adequate explanation of how inequality had come into existence; consequently he had no concrete proposals for putting an end to it. He believed that human beings could arrest the deterioration of their society; but to do so would involve an act of the will, a moral stand. There was no particular reason why the eighteenth century was a better time for such an act than the twelfth or the twenty-third. Thus Rousseau lapsed into his own kind of reformism. When, as the author of the *Social Contract*, he was invited to draw up constitutions for Corsica and Poland, his proposals fell far short of the radicalism of his theoretical work. (Corsican society was to be divided into three classes, while Poland would retain a king, albeit a non-hereditary one.) Above all, there was in Rousseau no encouragement to the oppressed to resist. (In 1791, when Le Chapelier moved his notorious law banning workers' organizations, he did so with a copy of Rousseau's *Social Contract* in his hand.)[53] Rousseau remained a utopian thinker, in the Marxist sense that he envisaged a goal, but could not identify the concrete historical agency that could achieve it.

The exact extent and chronology of Babeuf's knowledge of Rousseau remains a matter of debate.[54] Babeuf was certainly familiar with Rousseau's *Discourse* on the origins of inequality by 1786, when he quoted it in an essay for the *académie* of Arras.[55] And he undoubtedly read the *Social Contract*,[56] but he may not have done so before 1789, since the work achieved wide circulation only after that date.[57] But regardless of exactly what he read and when he read it, Babeuf was undoubtedly influenced by what Mazauric has called 'the diffuse Rousseauism transmitted by the media' that was current in the late eighteenth century.[58] Babeuf is unthinkable without Rousseau, yet it is quite wrong to see him merely as an uncritical disciple of Rousseau. His thought was not a development out of Rousseau's, but marked a sharp break with it. Even on the question of child-rearing, he tempered his admiration of Rousseau with the recognition that he was a 'maker of purely ideal systems'.[59]

Babeuf's thought began from the unresolved contradictions in Rousseau and sought to go beyond them, to move forward from utopianism to a theory of revolutionary practice. In a manuscript of the 1790–1 period, Babeuf dealt sharply with the limitations of Rousseau's thought, and tried to explain them in terms of Rousseau's own experience and the class perspective he represented:

> Rousseau saw nothing but Geneva, thought, reflected and conjectured only for Geneva . . . That gives rise to the idea of a small farmer, intelligent, hard-working, thrifty by necessity, who would like to see the destruction of all large estates . . . He thinks he has managed to discover all that is necessary for the prosperity of his little field, his little meadow, his little vineyard, his little farmyard; all the rest seems to him to be not only unnecessary but monstrous and destructive of prudent cultivation.[60]

Babeuf's attitudes differed sharply from Rousseau's hatred of luxury and his rejection of the idea of human progress. As he wrote in a letter of 8 July 1787:

> But Jean-Jacques claims that all the acquisitions of human history have only made us less happy than we were in the first state of nature, and as a result, he seems to want to send us back there, to obtain for us the greatest well-being that we can enjoy.[61]

There were other eighteenth-century thinkers, more radical in many ways than Rousseau, who helped Babeuf develop his understanding of society. One was the abbé Mably, author of a number of works of political philosophy. Mably vigorously deplored the inequalities that characterized modern France, and showed their roots in the forms of property that existed. Like Rousseau, he hated luxury and sought to limit inequality by imposing a maximum on how much individuals might own.

More significant was the rather more shadowy figure of Morelly, author of the *Code of Nature* (1755). During the eighteenth century this work was attributed to Diderot, and Babeuf quoted it at his trial to show that communist ideas had been held by a man now reckoned to be one of the great philosophers of the century.

Morelly put the abolition of private property at the centre of his perspective: 'Where no property existed, none of its pernicious consequences could exist.' Without property, he asserted, no human being would seek domination over others.[62] He believed sociability was rooted in nature; but he had a more optimistic view of history than Rousseau, believing that the progress of civilization had brought benefits to humanity. In his proposals for an ideal society he argued that science should be given total freedom (though philosophy should be banned). He laid down detailed proposals for a centrally planned economy.[63] Sadly he spoiled the impact of his proposals by the frank admission that 'unfortunately . . . it would be impossible to form such a republic in our day'.[64] Babeuf may not have read Morelly until after 1789; but while a Morelly specialist such as Wagner may see Babeuf's knowledge as superficial,[65] it is clear that Morelly's work made an important contribution to Babeuf's development. Inasmuch as he offered an alternative to Rousseau that was non-ascetic and did not reject progress, he undoubtedly helped to form the framework within which Babeuf developed his ideas.

One utopian work which Babeuf did know of before 1789 was the grandiosely entitled *The Precursor of the transformation of the whole world by means of well-being, good education and the prosperity of all men*,[66] written by the lawyer Nicolas Collignon.[67] This was merely a short pamphlet advertising a more substantial work in eight volumes. It sketched out, with considerable enthusiasm, the details of a wholly non-ascetic utopia. All citizens were to be provided with free food and clothing (detailed menus were included), high quality housing (with running water!) and schooling. Collignon even proposed league tables for doctors; those who cured most patients would receive rewards and promotion; those who cured least would be demoted and eventually struck off. Collignon laid down various conditions before he was prepared to reveal *how* the new world was to be ushered in, one of which was a guarantee of an income of a million Polish florins. Not surprisingly the full work never appeared.

Babeuf never saw Collignon's pamphlet, but he got extensive reports of its contents from Dubois de Fosseux.[68] Whereas the latter seems not to have taken Collignon very seriously, Babeuf was greatly impressed by the promise of a non-ascetic egalitarianism. In July 1787 he wrote enthusing about Collignon, who, he believed, had gone further than Rousseau.

> It seems to me that our Reformer [Collignon] does more than the Citizen of Geneva [Rousseau], whom I have sometimes heard described as the worst sort of dreamer. In fact he dreamt well, but our man dreams better. Like him he claims that since men are absolutely equal, they must not possess anything privately, but enjoy everything in common, so that at birth no individual is more or less rich, or less well considered than any of those who surround him. But far from sending us back, as Rousseau does, to exist thus, amid the woods, satisfying our hunger under an oak-tree, quenching our thirst at the first stream we come to, and sleeping under the same oak-tree where we got our food, our Reformer gives us four good meals a day, dresses us very elegantly and gives each of us fathers of families charming houses worth a thousand *louis*. This means he has succeeded in reconciling the pleasures of social life with those of natural and primitive life.

Significantly, Babeuf expressed one major reservation: 'How I love the general Reformer. It's a great pity that he has not explained what means will achieve his end.'[69]

Babeuf's thinking was not complete before 1789; it still needed the whiplash of revolution and counter-revolution. But as we can see from his criticism of Collignon's failure to outline the means to the end, Babeuf had already begun to grope beyond utopianism. For him the unity of theory and practice was always to be central to his thinking. So Dommanget had good grounds for claiming that by 1787 Babeuf had already 'passed beyond the stage of purely utopian socialism'. As he pointed out, Babeuf never indulged in the depiction of an imaginary ideal society.[70]

Babeuf had not broken completely with his predecessors. Like Rousseau he constantly referred to the state of nature. But in a letter of June 1786 we can see him beginning to work his way beyond the categories of his contemporaries. He rejected the idea of going back to a hypothetical state of nature: 'Go back up the ladder of the ages of humanity, at each rung there is an additional error, but descend the ladder, and on each rung there is an error less.' In trying to reconstruct the course of human history Babeuf was tentatively moving towards a materialist account, putting the fact of labour at the centre of the picture:

The law or the obligation of labour is therefore correlative to the natural right of man which in the beginning could only be exercised by means of labour. Then no human being, unless he was a child, an invalid or an old man weighed down by years could obtain anything without effort and exertion . . .

So society wants the right to live to have a sanction. What can the means of this sanction be? The means that nature taught us, labour.

Here there is the germ of a materialist account of human history. But it is only the germ. When he attempted to explain the origins of property Babeuf did not get much further than Rousseau:

Property as such is only a translation of the right to live . . . The appetite for property is the most intrusive thing, the thirst for gold is not a more ardent nor a more detestable passion. When this appetite is awakened, it becomes overexcited and is enthused by everything it takes possession of: property under its influence is like a spreading patch of oil.[71]

On this account greed is somehow inherent in 'human nature', and equality becomes either impossible or the product of some inexplicable and ahistorical moral impulse.

Babeuf had not transcended the limits of eighteenth-century utopianism before 1789; indeed, to suggest that an individual could have done so in the confines of his own skull would be rampant idealism; he learnt to be a revolutionary by participating in revolution. But his course within that revolution was very different from that of a Mirabeau or a Danton, or even of a Marat or a Robespierre. To explain that we need to see that his starting-point had been different from theirs.

Just how far Babeuf had developed by 1786 is shown by a long – and only recently discovered – letter to Dubois de Fosseux. This contained some striking considerations on the land question. Babeuf discussed at length the establishment of *fermes collectives* (collective farms). The Russian historian Dalin gave great importance to this text, pointing out that such authorities as Georges Lefebvre had claimed that Babeuf had never gone beyond a communism of distribution to a recognition of the need for collective production.[72] However, care is needed with the term. Babeuf was certainly talking about the collective organization of agricultural production, an interesting and original concept for the 1780s. But the collective production he had in mind was something like a peasant co-operative, and patently had nothing in common with the collective farms that Stalin imposed on the Russian peasantry. Babeuf set out in some detail how a collective farm might operate:

> The farm continues to be a whole, but it is no longer exploited by a single tenant; what I replace him by is a group of workers in proportion to the size of the piece of land, and gathered together under the same contract to get the most out of it.

Babeuf argued that collective working would improve efficiency:

> everyone watches himself so as not to be caught out in error or for carelessness or clumsiness: among equals, people know that the master's eye is everywhere and nowhere. If one of them falls ill, nothing suffers, neither his wife, nor his children, nor the farm, for then they all work with redoubled energy, and each one is happy to take on a slight increase in work; no accident, not even death itself, slows or stops anything.

Babeuf recognized that his proposals were not for the immediate future:

> I am not so presumptuous as to believe that the system of collective farms will be adopted immediately; it is too remote from accepted practice, and we have all too often the opportunity to observe that habit is an almost incurable illness. But any idea that is intrinsically good, however badly it may have been initiated and received, ends up by being the object of serious attention . . .

Babeuf firmly rejected the idea of the *loi agraire* (agrarian law, dividing up of the land) which was much discussed in the early years of the Revolution:

> The division of the land, an absurd operation, could be carried out only amidst bloodshed following a terrible upheaval: if it ever took place, it would condemn each person to isolation, that is, to impotence, and necessarily what had been destroyed one day would begin again the next. The agrarian law, understood as distribution of the land in equal portions, would deny all the skills which agriculture itself has had to recognize in its own interest, it would abolish every other profession except that of farmer; it would waste both space and time.[73]

The same letter contained a remarkable passage on the oppression of women (see Appendix). It is striking to see Babeuf, despite having had no contact with any of the enlightened feminists of the period, putting forward ideas which would still have seemed radical more than a hundred years later:

> The husband should no longer be a master, and the wife a slave. As husbands or fathers, our ancestors claimed too much authority . . . What must emerge from a conscientious and enlightened study of woman is that this half of the human race is destined to be the equal of the other; in the interaction of society, the importance of one sex is no less than that of the opposite sex.[74]

Babeuf's belief in the equality of women, and his insistence that the differences between the sexes were rooted in education, not nature, set him apart from almost all the other thinkers of the revolutionary period – including many of his fellow-conspirators – who stuck much more closely to Rousseau's belief in the subordination of women.[75] It is not simply chance that Babeuf's considerations on women and collective farms should come in the same letter. By proposing collective production he was breaking with the model of the family as a unit of production (which was to be central to Jacobin thinking). It was this, as well as his deep commitment to human equality, that enabled him to envisage the true equality of women.

Babeuf's letters reveal many other themes in his increasingly radical thinking. Before Malthus, Babeuf saw a problem with population growth, but his response was somewhat more sanguine than the English reactionary's: 'science, which is progressing every day, will doubtless teach us how to save ourselves from an excess of population without throwing new-born children into the water . . . '.[76] His revolutionary sentiments got clear expression in the letters:

> as long as we haven't razed to the ground a building which is inappropriate to the happiness of the bulk of humanity in order to begin it again on an entirely new basis and in perfect harmony with the demands of their free and complete development, then everything will remain to be destroyed and done again . . . [77]

He referred more than once to the evils of slavery and colonialism:

> it is we alone who have transmitted into another hemisphere the terrible vices which degraded our own, and it seems that we are not inclined to abjure any of them and banish them from our own society except on the condition that we go and tarnish with them a land which hitherto had

preserved, in its extreme simplicity, all the innocence and purity of the first ages.[78]

In 1789 Babeuf published his first book, *The Perpetual Land-Register* (Le cadastre perpétuel).[79] The book grew out of both Babeuf's work as a *feudiste* and his more general social speculations. The aim was to show how a land-register could be compiled for the purposes of taxation in such a way that it could be easily and permanently updated. The subject may seem obscure and technical, but it responded very much to the concerns of the time. The demand for fairer and more efficient taxation was at the very heart of the first stage of the French Revolution, and many of the *cahiers de doléances* (lists of grievances and demands compiled at the start of the Revolution) contained the call for land-registers to be established.

The title page of the book did not contain Babeuf's name, although he was the main author; but it did carry the name of his collaborator, J.-P. Audiffred, who had invented a new device for land-surveying, the *graphomètre-trigonométrique*. The work aimed to catch the new mood of 1789, and was dedicated to the National Assembly and dated 'Year 1789 and the first of French freedom'.

The main claim of the work was the topical one that it would provide a fairer basis for taxation, but the most interesting parts of the book are those where Babeuf strayed from his immediate purpose and engaged in more general considerations. In the introductory chapter he set out some general proposals for state spending which actually prefigure a modern welfare state, in particular the demand for a free health service:

> That a national fund for the subsistence of the poor should be established.
> That doctors, apothecaries and surgeons should be paid wages out of public funds so that they can administer assistance free of charge.
> That a system of national education be established, of which all citizens may take advantage.
> That magistrates be also paid wages out of public revenue, so that justice can be done free of charge.[80]

Babeuf made no secret of the fact that he believed taxation should redistribute from rich to poor. Perhaps under Rousseau's influence, he argued that nature sets limits to total consumption, and that therefore equality involves levelling down; 'for nature, thrifty with her gifts, only produces more or less what is useful for all the beings she creates; and some people cannot enjoy superfluity without others lacking what is necessary.'[81]

Despite its more limited focus, the *Perpetual Land-Register* can be seen as continuing the social thinking that had begun to reveal itself in the correspondence with Dubois de Fosseux. But in 1789 people had other things on their minds; at a time when the whole world seemed to be changing, a book with 'perpetual' in its title did not appear very plausible. By January 1790 the authors had received payment for only four copies. Babeuf had little time for disappointment. A new phase of his life had begun.

3
Advancing Revolution

For Babeuf, the Revolution of 1789 opened enormous possibilities, putting into practice ideas which had previously seemed to be mere abstract speculation; it also posed enormous political and practical problems. Nineteenth-century historians such as Cabet and Marx were able to distinguish between a 'bourgeois' or 'democratic' revolution on the one hand and a 'socialist' revolution on the other. No such distinction was available to Babeuf. Already before 1789 he had formulated a rather vague ideal of a society based on perfect equality. He perceived the Revolution as a process unfolding in the direction of that equality. How far and how fast it would unfold he could not know: his concern was to push it as far as it would go. At each stage of the Revolution, individuals and groups would proclaim that the revolution had gone as far as necessary and that the time had come to call a halt. Babeuf's stormy and erratic evolution was that of one who carried on pushing until the very end.

In 1788, Louis XVI, faced with insuperable economic difficulties, summoned the Estates General, hoping this would let him off the hook; the effect was to raise the people's expectations that some, as yet ill-defined, change in their conditions of life would come about. The Third Estate was not a united mass, but deeply riven by conflict and contradiction; these contradictions began to be apparent from 1789 onwards.

On 14 July a crowd of Parisians stormed the Bastille, aiming to seize gunpowder and to disarm the fortress's cannons. Most of the crowd were small artisans and wage-earners; but there were also wealthy employers, among them Pierre-François Palloy, who in 1789 had a fortune of some 500 000 *livres*. That evening Palloy assembled some two hundred employees on the site of the prison, anxious to secure the money and glory that would come with the contract for demolishing the hated edifice.[1]

In the crowd women were singing, gloating that nobles who used to call them scum would now have to pay their share of taxes. The song was by the poet Sylvain Maréchal, who would become one of Babeuf's fellow-conspirators. Present too was a law student called Augustin Darthé; within ten years he would die alongside Babeuf.[2] Babeuf himself arrived in Paris on 17 July, to pursue the publication of the *Perpetual Land-Register*. His literary and professional ambitions were soon caught up in the whirlpool of revolution.

When the Russian Revolution began in 1917, Lenin and his comrades had behind them nearly two decades of fierce debate about the nature of the coming revolution. Babeuf and his contemporaries were in uncharted territory (though there are passing references to Cromwell and the English Revolution in Babeuf's writings). Babeuf had to observe, to analyse and to act all at the same time, to invent his own future as he lived it. From the outset he welcomed every stage of the Revolution, yet remained deeply distrustful of the motives of many of those involved. In all his considerations, the theme of equality was central.

In the dawn of the Revolution Babeuf expressed great admiration for the moderate Mirabeau. But when Mirabeau stated that there were three orders in society – 'beggars, thieves and wage-earners' – Babeuf published an eight-page pamphlet in reply. He began lyrically, welcoming the Revolution: 'this attractive equality which has so fortunately returned to you, accompanied by her sister, Freedom, as loveable as she is.' But he expressed ironic indignation at Mirabeau's retention of a division into three orders, concluding : 'By obliging the beggars to work, we shall make wage-earners of them; and if the thieves do not hasten to follow their example, we shall punish their crimes.'[3] On 14 July 1790 he noted his disillusion with Lafayette: 'I admired this man when I saw him at a distance; now I've seen him close up, I abhor him; he is a pernicious man who is strangling the country in his hands.'[4]

A question which now became central for Babeuf's development was that of violence. Before 1789 he had not, of necessity, given much thought to the transition to an equal society; now the question of revolutionary violence confronted him directly. In a remarkable letter to his wife, written nine days after the fall of the Bastille, Babeuf described his reactions to the outbreak of Revolution:

I don't know where to start when I write to you, my poor wife; it isn't possible to be here and have clear ideas, my mind is so agitated. All around me there is such upset and such fermentation that, even if you're a witness of what is going on, you can't believe your eyes. In short, I can only give you an overall account of what I've seen and heard. When I arrived, everyone was talking about a conspiracy led by the count of Artois and other princes. They intended to do nothing less than to exterminate a large part of the Paris population, and then to reduce to slavery all those in the whole of France who would have escaped slaughter only by putting themselves humbly at the disposal of the nobles, holding out their hands without complaining for the chains prepared by the tyrants. If Paris had not discovered this terrible plot in time, that would have been it; never would a more horrible crime have been consummated. So people have resolved to take a striking revenge for such perfidy as has never been seen in history; they are determined and they will spare neither those primarily responsible for the conspiracy, nor their followers. The executions have begun, without satisfying a resentment that is all too justified. The fury of the people is far from having been appeased by the death of the governor of the Bastille and the demolition of that infernal prison, by the death of the *prévôt* of the merchants, by the forgiveness which Louis XVI came to beg from his subjects, by the recall of M. Necker and other former ministers, by the sending away of new regiments and troops; the people needs different forms of expiation. They want, it is said, to see some thirty more guilty heads roll. M. Foulon was due to replace M. Necker, and four days ago pretended he was dead, having a log buried in his place. Yesterday M. Foulon was arrested, taken to the town hall, and hung as soon as he was brought down from there. His body was dragged through the streets of Paris, then torn to pieces, and his head was carried on a pike to the *faubourg* Saint-Martin, to await and go before M. Foulon's son-in-law, M. Bertier de Sauvigny, the *intendant* of Paris, who was being brought from Compiègne, where he had been arrested, and who tomorrow will suffer the same fate as his father-in-law. I saw the father-in-law's head pass by, and the son-in-law following behind, escorted by more than a thousand armed men; like this, exposed to the public gaze, he was brought right through the length of the *faubourg* and the rue Saint-Martin, amid two hundred thousand spectators who insulted him and rejoiced with the troops of the escort, who marched to the beat of the drum. Oh! how this joy distressed me! I was at the same time both satisfied and unhappy, I said all the better and all the worse. I understand that the people is doing justice, I approve this justice when it is satisfied by the destruction of the guilty, but is it possible today for it to be done without cruelty? Punishments of all sorts, quartering, torture, breaking on the wheel, burning at the stake, the whip, the gallows, executioners all around, have given us such bad morals! Our masters, instead of civilizing us, have made us barbarous, because they are barbarous themselves. They are reaping and will reap what they have sown, for all this, my poor wife, will, it seems, have terrible consequences: we are only at the beginning.[5]

Some historians, notably Jaurès (see Chapter 7), have quoted this passage to try and make Babeuf into some sort of pacifist. That is a one-sided view. Babeuf understood the necessity of revolutionary violence only too well. Later that year he wrote that 'men who are hungry cannot be very peaceful'. And in another letter to his wife dealing with a bread shortage he wrote: 'This scarcity was caused by an aristocratic plot. They took one of them to the gallows . . . and that restored supplies to some extent.'[6] But if Babeuf was no pacifist, he was also free of any love of violence for its own sake. There are few figures in the socialist tradition – Rosa Luxemburg is the outstanding example – who share Babeuf's ability to combine a recognition of the necessity of violence and an awareness of the horror of violence.

Babeuf remained in Paris till October, knowing that his own life was at a turning-point; if feudalism was disintegrating, there was not much future for a *feudiste*. Yet he was happy to see the old order go. He wrote to his wife: 'I'm glad to support all these changes; I'm even quite happy to lend a hand to bring about the change that will upset my own cooking-pot; egoists will call me mad, but never mind.'[7]

The outbreak of the Revolution transformed Babeuf from a revolutionary thinker into a revolutionary activist – a journalist and campaigner. There was a swarm of new publications in 1789, and Babeuf soon recognized the significance of Marat, a revolutionary journalist who provided him with a model. He was briefly employed to write for a London journal called *Courrier de l'Europe*; though we have drafts of some of his articles, it appears none was published – and he never received any payment.[8]

In his articles for London, we see Babeuf becoming aware of a whole range of other questions thrown up by the Revolution. He noted the proposal to make the right to vote dependent on paying a certain level of tax, and recorded Robespierre's speech in favour of universal suffrage.[9] He was conscious of the problem of food supplies; more than three years before the *maximum*, he argued for the imposition of price controls.[10] He

was impressed by the large numbers of women taking part in demonstrations, and he advocated tolerance of Jews, saying it was time 'to shake off
the fanatical prejudices which for so long have made this peaceful people
the unfortunate victim of persecutions by all sects'.[11] Another theme
was to remain important for him, that of press freedom. He argued that
censorship should be kept to a minimum; if other craftspeople could
put their products freely on the market, why not those whose craft was
writing?[12]

In May 1790, Babeuf was arrested and taken to prison in Paris, where
he was held for some seven weeks. While there he planned the first issue
of a newspaper to be launched in Paris, the *Journal de la confédération*.
This had only three issues; the first was undated and the second and third
appeared on 3 and 4 July 1790. The first issue, dealing with political prisoners, began with an 'Appeal to the People' in which he set out clearly
his view of journalism and how it was to be distinguished from much of
the contemporary press:

> This is not, citizens, one of those buzzing announcements, like those in
> which aristocratic politics, helped by a few hired hacks, took pleasure in
> giving you a thousand false alarms, which soon made you accustomed,
> as your enemies had foreseen and desired, to receiving all warnings as
> scaremongering, so that you were no longer on your guard for anything.[13]

Having failed to make an impact on Parisian journalism, Babeuf
returned again to Roye, where he attempted to launch a new publication, *Le Correspondant picard*. Unfortunately no copies survive, although
we have some of Babeuf's rough drafts for articles. The paper was not
a success; initially he had hoped for a circulation of one thousand, but
the first issues had a print run of 500. He made great efforts to build up
his journal, even circulating village priests. A list of 28 addresses where
one could subscribe was published.[14] Babeuf aimed to use the journal for
local issues and campaigns, and also to link these to general questions of
political principle. But *Le Correspondant picard* lasted for only five issues.
It was succeeded by *Le Scrutateur des décrets*, which appeared as number
six. This was a bulky issue of nearly 70 pages, but again was the only
issue. By 1791 Babeuf's career as a journalist seemed in ruins.

The first three years of the Revolution Babeuf spent mainly in Picardy.
Here he became involved in the many processes of change initiated by
the Revolution. The eradication of privilege meant a long hard struggle,

in the course of which the old privilege-holders would fight their ground tenaciously, and new privileged layers would begin to emerge.

One key issue was taxation. The unjust taxation system had been one of the problems that provoked the Revolution, but its demolition was not a simple job. Babeuf played a leading role in a campaign in support of local inn-keepers against the tax – *aides* – on drinks; these complex, multiple taxes were particularly unpopular with producers, retailers and consumers.[15] He drafted petitions and personally promised to lead armed resistance against troops if they tried to enforce payment of *aides*.[16] A local priest read out Babeuf's petition from the pulpit as part of his sermon.[17] He wrote an article protesting violently against the arrest and imprisonment of those who had been accused of destroying customs barriers.[18]

Babeuf also led local peasants in a campaign against the *champart*, a tax in kind whereby local lords took a certain proportion of the peasants' crops – say one sheaf in twelve, or more. The peasants claimed with some justice that this right had expired with the Revolution, and Babeuf was active in urging them not to hand over the crops to the lords. He supported the right of citizens to share the common land;[19] increasingly he came into conflict with the 'village cocks', the wealthier farmers who tried to drive the small tenants off the land and began to employ wage-labour.[20]

Another campaign was on the question of fruit-trees. Traditionally the local landlords had been allowed to plant trees on common land and along paths, retaining the right to the fruit. At the outset of the Revolution peasants began to seize the fruit. Babeuf reported one case where the local landowner, M. de la Rochefoucault, had ordered trees to be felled. Since he was a National Assembly delegate, it was felt that he was aware of new legislation planned on this matter, and that he was trying to forestall its effects. The local population mobilized to physically prevent him selling off the trees; Rochefoucault responded by bringing a troop of supporters on horseback to enable him to sell some of the trees.[21]

There were also a number of conflicts over cultural issues. In October 1792 Babeuf went to see Desforges' play *Le Sourd ou l'auberge pleine*, a comedy in which a *gentilhomme* army officer gets the girl at the expense of a buffoonish *bourgeois*.[22] He drafted an open letter to the actors complaining that they expected him to laugh at seeing a poor wretch – 'my equal in rights' – molested by rogues. He enquired: 'Don't you have plays of the sort that never grow old? Almost all Molière is still relevant for us.'[23] In a period of revolution the theatre could hardly be an enclave of pure art; far from being a philistine, Babeuf was recognizing the theatre's political importance. His reference to Molière (scarcely a revolutionary) showed that he was not trying to impose narrow political standards on the theatre. In another incident Babeuf played a role in ensuring the removal of tapestries bearing the monarchical symbol of the *fleur de lis;* they were distributed to the poor only after having been dyed to remove the hated emblem.[24] If this seems bizarre to a modern reader, it might be compared to the way in which swastikas were eradicated in various parts of Europe after the end of Nazi rule.

While immersed in the day-to-day activities of the Revolution, Babeuf did not lose sight of fundamental issues. He was continually engaged in consideration of issues affecting the shape of a future society which as yet he perceived only dimly. The two crucial questions were democracy and property.

France was just emerging from absolutism and making its first experiments with a form of democratic government. Despite the absence of historical reference points, Babeuf made acute criticisms of the development of democratic institutions that in many ways retain relevance two centuries later. Two themes recur in his writings from this period. Firstly, that democracy does not consist in the single act of electing a representative, but in the regular supervision and accountability of those elected. And secondly, that democracy must always be related to economic power; democracy cannot co-exist with economic inequality.

Already in 1789 Babeuf had observed with concern that Prévost, the deputy from Roye to the Estates General, was one of the most conservative among the representatives of the Third Estate. Babeuf tried to get up a petition to demand the recall of Prévost, but the powerful Billecocq family (who had prevented him becoming a freemason) took action to ensure that he could not collect enough signatures.[25] The right of recall had been proposed before the revolution by Mably,[26] and was a widespread demand of the Paris sections in 1792–3; it was a principle which was to be of central importance in the Paris Commune of 1871 and in the Russian *soviets* of 1917.

In 1791 Babeuf worked closely with Jacques-Michel Coupé, who became one of the local delegates to the Legislative Assembly. In particular he sent Coupé two letters in which he set out his views on democracy. In the first of these, dated 20 August 1791, Babeuf examined how democratic institutions could be made fully accountable to the people. He insisted that all political debate be as public as possible;

> All questions of general interest must be dealt with in full assembly; no more committees, they are centres of intrigue and secret meetings where factions draw up their plans to kill freedom, and plot together about how to carry them out.

Hence he urged that the Assembly be constantly open to petitions coming from the masses. Later he enquired what could be done to discipline deputies who failed to carry out their promises. Rather than simply set up a procedure for the right of recall, he proposed the establishment in each constituency of seven 'curators of liberty', who would have the responsibility of keeping the deputy under close scrutiny, and if necessary would be able to withdraw his mandate.[27]

From the beginning Babeuf was deeply hostile to the principle that the right to vote be limited by property qualifications. In November 1790 Babeuf drafted an article for *Le Correspondant picard* in which he argued fiercely that the old class system was giving way to a new one based on money:

> In France, under the previous regime, three orders were recognized: nobility, clergy and the third estate . . . But in France, under the new scheme of things, there is not a single order, as they are trying to make the masses believe; we can see four arising on the ruins of the old three: the order of *patards*, that of the *écu*, that of the *pistole* and that of the *marc*. Of these four new orders, gentlemen, it may be that yours, that is, the order of the *marc*, is not the only one which has any real substance, but at least it is impossible to hide the fact that ours, that is the sad order of *patards*, has none at all. Excluded from public employment, deprived of the right to participate in the election of our leaders and of any part in deliberations on matters of common concern, in a word victims of more contempt than the insolence of the rich ever dared to pour on unhappy virtue: it is quite impossible for us to delude ourselves any longer about a phantom of freedom, in the existence of which only those who have robbed us of our rights would like to make us believe.[28]

[The *patard* was a small, virtually worthless coin; the *écu*, worth three *livres*, represented the sum of three days wages which had to be paid in tax by those admitted to the primary assemblies; the *pistole* (ten *livres*) was the ten days wages to be paid in tax by those admitted to the electoral assemblies; while the *marc* (around 52 *livres*) was the tax qualification for those seeking election to the National Assembly.]

He concluded with a threat:

> We who are humbly lined up in the order of *patards* declare, once again according to the charter of the Rights of Man, article 6, that the law is the expression of the general will; that where we see no general will, we see no law; and as there can be no general will when all citizens do not have the right to express their particular wills, we protest against the nomination, made without our participation, of all public officials, against any usurpation of our natural and inalienable rights, against any insidious law that challenges our social privileges. And until we have regained possession of them, we declare ourselves to be exempted from the slightest duty towards the fatherland that rejects us, exempted from all military service, exempted from any taxation, direct or indirect, and if that does not suffice, we shall also exempt ourselves from using the labour of our hands for anyone who does not belong to the order of the *patards*.[29]

If Babeuf's three years in revolutionary Picardy were a period of intense activity, he nonetheless found time to continue his reading. Indeed, the notes he took during this period – known under the title of *Philosophical Glimmers* (Lueurs philosophiques) – show a process of intense intellectual development going on. Babeuf was always striving to grasp the totality of the revolutionary process as well as intervene at strategic points.

It is in this context that we should see his attitude to the 'agrarian law'. In 1794 in Picardy the former priest Croissy was executed for advocating the agrarian law; obviously it was a question that threw into relief the basic contradictions of the Revolution.[30] But the 'agrarian law' meant different things to different people; to some it meant a complete equal division of the land among the population; to others it was less radical, a restriction on the private exploitation of public land, with the surplus made available to the poor. In the discussions of the time the two concepts were frequently confused.[31]

Already in 1786 Babeuf had rejected the agrarian law in favour of common ownership of land, and this was the position he was to defend at the time of the conspiracy, though in the Preface to the *Perpetual Land-Register* he speculated about the possibility of dividing the land equally, giving each of France's six million families eleven *arpents* (acres). If during the early years of the Revolution he appeared to support the agrarian law, it was doubtless because he welcomed any popular demand that moved in the direction of equality; in any case it would be foolish to seek complete consistency on the part of a young man who was responding to the contradictory pressures of an unprecedented historical situation.

Babeuf had no plans for returning to Paris. But in the course of his duties as an elected official, Babeuf had to deal with a dispute about ownership of a farm, and following discussion with one party he struck out the name of a purchaser on an official document and replaced it with a different name. There was no question of any personal advantage to Babeuf – his motive was undoubtedly revolutionary sympathy for the oppressed.[32] But technically it was a serious case of forgery, which could have landed him with a lengthy jail sentence. Babeuf had made enough enemies to ensure that he would be held to account for the very letter of the law. He decided not to risk the verdict of the courts and fled to Paris in February 1793.

The next seventeen months were to see the most radical phase of the Revolution, with the rule of the Jacobin-dominated Convention. It was a period of military danger abroad, civil war in the Vendée and bitter factional strife in Paris. The Jacobin leaders were determined to defend the gains of the Revolution, to ensure that the monarchy and its privileged hangers-on should not make any return to power, and that the French nation should be able to defend itself against enemies from within and without.

Jacobinism represented the interests of small property-owners, and the ideal society envisaged by Robespierre and Saint-Just would have been one in which every family owned its own patch of land or small workshop. But when it came to it the Jacobins were part of the bourgeoisie and they defended its interests against the propertyless. While they were happy to destroy the economic and political power of the Catholic Church, they followed Voltaire in believing that religion was necessary to preserve social order – hence the charade of the Festival of the Supreme Being. Even more important, they were firmly committed to the principle of private property. The Constitution of 24 June 1793 (never implemented) abolished all property qualifications for voting and established universal – male – suffrage. It stated that 'the aim of society is common happiness', and that 'all men are equal by nature and before the law'. It also stated quite clearly that 'the right of property is that which belongs to every citizen and entitles him to enjoy and dispose of as he likes his goods, his income and the products of his labour and industry'.[33] On 19 March 1793 the Convention voted almost unanimously to impose the death penalty on anyone who advocated the agrarian law. At a time when the government was making concessions to the *sans-culottes*, the purpose was to assure those who had bought noble and church lands confiscated by the state that their property rights were safe.[34]

The Jacobins found themselves fighting on two fronts. Not only did they have to resist the counter-revolution, but they also had to deal with the demands coming from the common people of Paris and other cities, the *sans-culottes*. These demands were expressed by mass demonstrations and at times by rioting, forcing the Jacobins to accommodate popular feeling to some extent. The central concern was food, especially the price of bread.

But the *sans-culottes* were not able to put themselves forward as a coherent alternative to Jacobin rule. Firstly, because their leaders – notably Hébert, a journalist and advocate of economic controls, guillotined in March 1794 – did not have any developed alternative policy. And secondly, because the *sans-culottes* did not represent the interests of a particular class, but rather contained different class interests within their ranks. Many of the most militant *sans-culottes* were small self-employed artisans, who were quite happy with the Jacobin defence of private property. Others were wage-earning workers. The working class had neither the size nor the organization to make an independent bid for power. But it cannot simply be written out of history. A number of strikes took place, and the government was forced to take repressive measures against workers; in the arms workshops there was a ban on communication between workers in different shops.[35] All the *sans-culottes* welcomed the imposition of a *maximum* on prices, since they had a common interest in the availability of cheap food. But when the *maximum* was extended to wages it meant an effective wage cut for many workers who had pushed up wage levels in the context of a war economy. By attacking the emergent working class, the Jacobin government was cutting away the branch that it was seated upon.

The developments in Paris initially filled Babeuf with an almost incredible optimism; on 17 April he wrote to his wife:

This is exciting me to the point of madness. The *sans-culottes* want to be happy, and I don't think it is impossible that *within a year*, [my emphasis] if we carry out our measures aright and act with all necessary prudence, we shall succeed in ensuring general happiness on earth.[36]

Babeuf had to negotiate his own way through the jungle of revolutionary Paris. He did not join the Jacobins because he found their membership too *bourgeois* and the subscription (36 *livres*) too high.[37] Initially he became involved with a dubious character known as Fournier the American, who gave him financial support; in return Babeuf wrote pamphlets and assisted Fournier with his project of forming a 'legion of the liberators of the peoples'.[38] In one pamphlet[39] he attacked Marat for failing to fight for 'the prosperity of the indigent class'.[40]

Babeuf had little connection with the *enragés* (the term is untranslatable, since it means not simply enraged but infected with rabies). They – notably Jacques Roux and Jean Varlet – represented the anger and resentment of the poor of Paris, who felt that they had not received from the Revolution the benefits to which they were entitled. In none of the many surviving texts by Babeuf is there any mention of Roux's name,[41] though Babeuf must have known of the bread riots in which Roux played a leading role. While it is legitimate to see Babeuf's conspiracy as the political successor to the *enragés*, there was no continuity of personnel; by 1796 Roux was dead and Varlet had withdrawn from politics.

Babeuf located himself clearly to the left of the Jacobin regime. He was critical of the *maximum* on food prices from its first introduction, not because he was opposed to the principle, but because the price was too high; the *maximum* had been based on the already high price of com, and should be lowered 'to a price all can afford'.[42] In a letter to the *sans-culotte* leader Chaumette, Babeuf claimed that

the popular class has in fact had the thought . . . that until now it has only been made to struggle and get excited for clichés, since the words revolution, liberty, equality, republic, fatherland have not changed its way of life for the better (a thought the unfortunate results of which cannot be concealed, I mean apathy, demoralization, general irresponsibility, which are the despair of the small number of citizens who have preserved their full energy).[43]

Babeuf's standpoint was also influenced by the fact that in May 1793 he got employment in the *Commission des subsistances*, the body that administered the Paris food supplies. This was an important experience for Babeuf, and certainly contributed to the vision of an equal and planned society that he was to develop. For the first time he saw food supplies, not from the point of view of the rural food producers, but from that of the urban consumers. He became aware of the poverty of the urban masses, and this awareness changed his conception of social change. At the same time he was able to exercise his very considerable organizational skills and to have the sense that he was actually participating in the official machinery, thereby influencing the course of events from within.

Babeuf's superior in the food administration was a man called Garin, a firm defender of the *maximum;* while the minister responsible, Garat, was trying to undermine the implementation of the *maximum.* Since Babeuf supported the principle of the *maximum,* even though he believed it had been set too high, he sided with Garin. Not only as part of his job, but out of political principle, Babeuf wrote pamphlets in Garin's name defending his policies. At this very time Jacques Roux was making Garin one of the main targets of his attacks. This undoubtedly helped to widen the political gulf between Babeuf and the *enragés.*

Babeuf was later to claim that there had been a 'conspiracy' to starve Paris in 1793, and that he personally had played a key role in saving the city.[44] He was doubtless dramatizing both the nature of the threat and his own role; but his experience of food supply administration was crucial in forming Babeuf the revolutionary.

Before the end of 1793 the affair of the forgery had caught up with him. In August he had been sentenced in his absence to 20 years in irons; on 14 November he was arrested and imprisoned. Released briefly in December, he was re-imprisoned and sent from one jail to another, and eventually returned to Laon in Picardy. Fortunately he had friends who campaigned tirelessly for his release, among them the poet and future conspirator Sylvain Maréchal.

Prison in the late eighteenth century was not a pleasant experience; while Babeuf was never used to a comfortable life-style, the deprivation of liberty was a heavy penalty for one committed to political activism. His wife stood closely by him, sending him food such as eggs and radishes. He was able to correspond with his family, and devoted great attention to encouraging the education of his elder son, Emile. He also continued reading; Maréchal sent him a copy of his atheist poem *God and the Priests*, and Babeuf made the young Emile (aged eight and a half) read this too.[45] Eventually on 18 July 1794 Babeuf was released.

He returned to Paris, but ten days after his release came a momentous turning-point in the course of the Revolution. Robespierre, Saint-Just and their allies were deposed and guillotined in a *coup* known by the name of the month when it occurred – Thermidor.

The defeat of the Jacobins flowed from their growing isolation. The rule of Robespierre and Saint-Just was proving too radical for many of the bourgeoisie, who believed that the promised constitution favouring small property against large was a threat to their hopes of gain from the Revolution. Meanwhile the support of the most radical of the *sans-culottes*, and especially of the wage-earning proletariat in Paris, was slipping away from Robespierre.

The next two years saw a decisive shift of power. France faced deep economic problems, and the new regime's policies ensured that the main burden fell on the most deprived. Unemployment grew rapidly; the *maximum* was abandoned in December. Food shortages sharpened the differences between rich and poor; and the privileged were confident enough to flaunt their wealth; in a telling passage Michelet described the experience of a child in Paris just after Thermidor hearing for the first time rich people being called 'master' as they left the theatre looking for a carriage.[46]

The radical Constitution of 1793 (never implemented) was scrapped; the new Constitution limited the right to vote to those wealthy enough to pay taxes (and to those who had fought in the army). In October 1795 governmental power was vested in a five-man 'Directory'. Throughout France a 'White Terror' was unleashed, in which thousands of Jacobins were arrested and imprisoned.

Three political groupings now emerged: those prepared to go along with the new regime, those who stood by the principles of Jacobin rule, and the *neo-hébertistes*, organized in the Electoral Club (with which Babeuf was associated), who aspired to the values of the 1793 Constitution.[47] Nothing so simple as a left-right division existed.

In retrospect it is clear that Thermidor marked the point at which the Revolution began to be rolled back. But at the time things were not so clear-cut. The Committee of Public Safety was open to criticism from the left – for its often arbitrary and indiscriminate use of Terror and for its neglect of the interests of the most deprived layers of society – and many of the Thermidorians initially used left rhetoric. It was a complex, historically unprecedented situation; small wonder that even a keen political brain like Babeuf vacillated politically.

Babeuf initially welcomed Thermidor wholeheartedly; at the same time he finally realized his journalistic ambitions. In September 1794 he launched the *Journal de la liberté de la presse* (journal of press freedom). This was more or less a daily paper – twenty-two issues between 3 September and 1 October. Babeuf saw the question of press freedom as inextricably linked to the democratic process; only through a free press could the population exercise its right of supervision and pressure on its elected representatives. He quoted from the 1793 Constitution the principle: 'Every citizen has the right to contribute to the formation of the law.'[48] He also quoted the first article of the 1793 Constitution at the head of various issues: 'the aim of society is common happiness.'

Babeuf believed his paper should reflect what he called the 'thermometer of public opinion' (an image he was to return to during the conspiracy). He aimed to make the paper a 'letter box for those who watch over the fatherland, and a public platform for free energetic men who love principles'. In thus encouraging correspondence he claimed to be following the example of Marat's *Ami du peuple*.[49]

Babeuf saw his duty to be a constant critic: 'I am far from finding anything laudable in the actions of those who govern us, but even if something could be discerned which is appropriate to the rule of freedom, would it be my duty to adulate those in power?'[50] The *Journal de la liberté de la presse* had eight pages; despite the use of correspondence Babeuf wrote most of it himself. In one of his pamphlets Babeuf mocked the Jacobins for their unintelligible jargon, which was not understood by the *sans-culottes* of the Saint-Antoine suburb, a traditional centre of popular agitation.[51] Yet his own style can hardly have been easy for a *sans-culotte* audience; his sentence structure was complex, he frequently invented new words and made many references to ancient history.

In the early issues Babeuf tried to analyse Thermidor and the new regime which had issued from it:

> We did indeed make a revolution five years ago; but we must have the good faith to recognize that since then we have allowed a *counterrevolution* to take place; and this latter event dates precisely from the time when we permitted the first encroachments on the freedom of opinion, whether spoken or written. 10 Thermidor marks the new date since when we have

been working for the rebirth of freedom . . . It cannot be denied that
there now exist in the Republic two clearly defined parties, one in favour
of the maintenance of the Robespierre government, the other advocating
the re-establishment of a government based exclusively on the eternal
rights of man . . . We have already openly declared that we are of the
latter party.[52]

Such was the level of hostility that he reported that Jacobins with sticks
had attacked sellers of his paper and destroyed copies of it.[53]

Many historians sympathetic to Babeuf have been puzzled and even
embarrassed by this phase. But Babeuf's critique of Jacobinism in power
was carefully considered and based on points of principle. Babeuf was
deeply committed to democratic accountability and freedom of opinion,
had a profound antipathy to violence, and was concerned for the fate of
the economically weakest. On all these points Jacobinism had seemed
to fall short. Babeuf's criticisms deserve to be taken seriously and not
simply excused as confusion. At the same time there is no doubt that he
seriously underestimated both the social achievements of Jacobin rule
and the severity of the threat to the Revolution that had made it necessary. The poor soon came to look back on the 1793–4 period as almost a
golden age in comparison with their later misery. The whole question of
revolutionary dictatorship was something that Babeuf still had to grapple with over the following two years.

It is also true that Babeuf had brief connections with both Fréron,
an ex-Jacobin who became a pillar of the Thermidorian right, and with
Fouché,[54] later to be Napoleon's police-chief. But both associations were
brief and he subsequently denounced both publicly.[55] There is no evidence that his political independence was seriously compromised.

What Babeuf gained from the experience of Thermidor was a greater
understanding of the complexity of the revolutionary process. Although
he had been aware from the beginning that there were forces that wanted
to slow down the Revolution, he had thought it enough to push the
movement forward as fast as possible. Now he was seeing that the movement could go backwards as well as forwards, and that revolutionary
rhetoric did not always coincide with revolutionary practice.

Babeuf attempted to define Robespierre's role. In the months after the
fall of the Committee of Public Safety, Babeuf attacked Robespierre in sav-
age terms. He wrote scathingly of his 'bloody court', and rather implausibly

held Robespierre – 'the moving spirit of the whole confusion' – personally responsible for government policy in the Vendée; he condemned the Convention for having put itself entirely in Robespierre's hands:

> Robespierre alone was stronger than all the members [of the Convention] . . . it had descended to this point of degradation and cowardice . . . it no longer thought except through its master . . . it wanted all that he wanted . . . it approved everything without saying a word, for fear of the rough whip it had had the shameful weakness to put into his hands.[56]

Babeuf aimed to make a balanced assessment of Robespierre. On 3 September, in the very first issue of his paper, Babeuf tried to set out a dialectical view, distinguishing two Robespierres:

> For example, this Robespierre whose memory is so justly abhorred, Robespierre in whom it seems we should distinguish two persons, that is, Robespierre the sincere patriot and lover of principle up to the beginning of 1793 and the ambitious Robespierre, a tyrant and the worst of scoundrels after that date: this Robespierre, I say, when he was a citizen, is perhaps the best source for great truths and forceful arguments for the rights of the press. It is with the weapons he left behind that I shall begin the fight against the sophisms of today's reasoners.

He praised Robespierre's declaration of rights of 15 March 1793:

> a marvellous antidote against the poison of Condorcet and his gang. All this is well-known and still in print. It is equally true that our declaration of rights, though it isn't perfect, is still sublime, even though it is Robespierre who gave it to us. We shall esteem and admire the work, and forget who was the maker; or else, as I have already said, we shall distinguish in Robespierre two men, Robespierre the apostle of freedom and Robespierre the most infamous of tyrants.[57]

In an article a few months later, Babeuf made an assessment of how Robespierre had held power, comparing him to his successors:

> His method, the very opposite of that of today's regulators, consisted in obliging the minority to agree that everything was not going too badly, while the masses were not complaining. The masses were not aroused, since they did not lack the most necessary goods, there was plenty of work available and the remuneration of all workers was advantageous. By this means it was possible to stabilize the tyranny; perhaps even it was

the only way of doing so, since the majority of citizens naturally prefer peace and quiet, ask only to keep out of public affairs and live peacefully in their homes: as soon as people get a pleasant and comfortable life, they are happy to accept the rule of whoever preserves the situation, and they easily close their eyes to the violation of great principles . . . [58]

Here Babeuf saw clearly that the economic situation of the masses would ultimately determine their political action.

In the period after Thermidor Babeuf really began to establish himself as a writer. He published two short pamphlets attacking the defeated Jacobins. He handled the satirical style well enough, but he did not feel it was what he was suited to. In the first pamphlet, *The Loser Pays*, he lamented that 'it is necessary to adapt to French frivolity in order to get read', and argued that the story of the Jacobins was at least 'tragicomic':

I don't agree in finding this story of the Jacobins purely amusing. It may be as far as individuals are concerned; but it is perhaps alarming with regard to principles. We should distinguish these two points carefully. Let us enjoy ourselves, if we wish, with some jeering about the misfortunes of certain individuals; but let us demand and defend principles with courage. [59]

The second pamphlet, *Journey of the Jacobins to the Four Comers of the Earth*, began with an irreverent parallel between 'Jesus the crucified and Maximilien the beheaded'. While Jesus brought down the Holy Spirit in the form of tongues of flame, Robespierre's spirit took the form of 'guillotine blades, grapeshot . . . and explosive fuses, striking images of the various destructive means which the religion of blood has already used and plans to use again to establish its rule'. [60]

Babeuf also wrote a longer work, *The War in the Vendée and the System of Depopulation*, published to coincide with the trial of Carrier, responsible for many of the worst atrocities in the civil war, who was guillotined in December 1794 (by a bizarre coincidence his defence lawyer was Réal, who was to defend Babeuf at Vendôme). It was a harsh indictment of the violence deployed against the counter-revolutionary rebels in the Vendée. Babeuf denounced the killing of pregnant women and children at the breast; he condemned the mass drownings and the 'republican marriages', where a couple – often a priest and a nun – were stripped naked, tied together and thrown into the water. [61] It was not a sentimental or pacifist account; Babeuf nowhere denied the need for revolutionary violence, but simply argued that the violence in the Vendée was excessive and unjustified.

He pointed out that Carrier's methods were not the most effective way of defending the Revolution. Thus the instruction to kill all brigands in fact meant slaughter of all inhabitants, since there was no way a soldier could distinguish a brigand from a non-brigand (just as in Vietnam US troops saw all 'gooks', including 'friendly' ones, as enemies). As he pointed out: 'burning the cottage of a country-dweller is breaking the strongest link he has to society, it means forcing him to retreat into the woods and making him a brigand out of necessity.' Instead he proposed an alternative strategy for fighting the counter-revolution. Patriots who were both ardent and 'wise and discreet' should have been sent to preach enlightenment, followed by written proclamations and civic festivals designed to win support for the Revolution.[62]

Rather more dubious was Babeuf's analysis of why the slaughter in the Vendée took place. He gave Robespierre and his allies credit for wishing to follow Sparta and Rousseau in establishing equality of property, but he accused them of acting on the basis of a deliberate calculation. They believed, he claimed, that France's agricultural resources were not sufficient to allow the entire population to enjoy an adequate standard of living; therefore it was necessary to destroy a proportion of the population so that the resources could be divided among the rest.

Babeuf did not share – as he is sometimes accused of doing – this 'Malthusian' belief he attributed to Robespierre. He argued: 'I do not believe as they do that the productions of French soil have ever been inferior in extent to the needs of all its inhabitants.' He added, however, that if this were the case, the answer would be for deprivation to be shared equally among all.[63]

From 5 October the paper changed its name to *Le Tribun du peuple* (the people's tribune). Babeuf believed the fight for press freedom had been won and it was possible to use his journal to broaden the struggle and campaign for 'the recovery of freedom and human rights which have been encroached upon'.[64] He explained the sense of the title in a later issue. In ancient Rome the people and the army elected tribunes whose job it was to 'watch ceaselessly' to prevent any attack on the rights of the people and soldiers (the role of the tribunes was discussed in Book IV of Rousseau's *Social Contract*). Since the French Constitution did not provide for any such institution, Babeuf hoped that his paper would

substitute in some way for it.[65] The paper appeared much more spasmod-
ically; there were just ten issues up to 1 February 1795, although several
of them were considerably larger than the *Journal de la liberté de la presse;*
there was a two-month gap from mid-October to mid-December when
no issues at all appeared (presumably while he was writing *The War in
the Vendée*).

Babeuf faced many problems in running a newspaper. Some copies
did not reach subscribers because of difficulties with postal services, and
there were threats to ban sellers from meetings of *sociétés populaires*. He
had little money and he blamed the many misprints (which he scrupulously amended) on having to correct the proofs 'in the darkness of
a cellar, by the glow of a dim lamp'. He survived a dispute in which he
claimed to have been robbed and betrayed by his printer, Guffroy. By
January 1795 he was operating semi-clandestinely, announcing that subscriptions could be taken out 'at the office that patriots will easily find.
Aristocrats would be wasting their time trying to find it.' Yet he managed to sell enough copies to justify reprinting five issues.[66]

In the first issue of *Le Tribun du peuple* Babeuf explained that he had
changed his own name. He had abandoned some time ago the 'Christian'
names he had been given at birth, and adopted the name Camille, after
the Roman patrician general Camillus. Now he decided Camille did not
fit him; Camillus had attempted to conciliate between patricians and
plebeians. Babeuf had abandoned any such hope of class reconciliation
and decided to opt instead for the name Gracchus.[67]

The choice of name may have been inspired by his youthful reading of
Plutarch. But to understand what the name Gracchus meant to Babeuf
and his contemporaries, it is best to refer to the play *Caïus Gracchus*, first
performed on 9 February 1792, in which one of the best-known revolutionary dramatists, Marie-Joseph Chénier, adapted Plutarch's account.
When the play opens, Caius Gracchus' brother has already died at the
hands of the consul, Opimius, and the Senate. Despite the pleas of his
wife Licinia, Gracchus resolves to rebel against the Senate and calls for
an equal division of the land. But to avoid bloodshed he gives his son
as a hostage. The son is saved but Gracchus faces defeat at the hands of
mercenaries. Gracchus kills himself and the people avenge themselves
by killing Opimius, who defends the virtues of wealth and inequality in
the play. The character of Gracchus has much in common with Babeuf.

Speaking to the people, he stresses, just as Babeuf always did, that liberty and equality are not contradictory but inseparable:

> Vous avez adoré le nom de liberté;
> Elle n'existe point dans les remparts de Rome,
> Par-tout où l'homme enfin n'est point égal à l'homme
> (*You have worshipped the name of freedom; it does not exist within the walls of Rome, or anywhere where man is not equal to man.*)[68]

The honeymoon with Thermidor did not last long. Babeuf had clear principles and was quickly able to make a self-criticism. As Buonarroti put it, he was 'greater than if he had never strayed'.[69] On 17 December Babeuf told his readers:

> When I was one of the first to thunder vehemently in order to bring down the monstrous scaffolding of Robespierre's system, I did not foresee that I was helping to found an edifice which, built in a quite different way, was no less harmful to the people.[70]

From now on, attacks on the regime got ever stronger. In the contents list of number 29 of the *Tribun du peuple* Babeuf enumerated a whole list of economic and political crimes of the new regime: price rises, laws to benefit *émigrés*, sacking of patriots, revival of prostitution and superstition and many more. And in number 31 he called the new regime a 'tyranny' with its own *bastilles* and *lettres de cachet* (used by the monarchy to overrule the courts, especially to imprison).[71]

One aspect of the Thermidorian regime that made a particular impact on Babeuf was the emergence of the so-called *jeunesse dorée* (gilded youth) or *muscadins* (dandies). These young men, whose elegant appearance reflected their middle-class roots, were the strong-arm men (often carrying cudgels) of the new regime. They attempted to break opposition to the government by physical attacks on surviving Jacobins. In November 1794 they attacked meetings of Jacobins, throwing stones through windows and assaulting both men and women until the premises were closed down.[72] In many workplaces *sans-culottes* were sacked and their jobs given to *muscadins*. It would be anachronistic to describe the *jeunesse dorée* as fascists, but in some ways they do prefigure the fascist street-gangs of the twentieth century.[73]

When Babeuf saw the Thermidorian leader Fréron deliberately encouraging physical attacks on Jacobins, he had no doubt as to which side he was on: 'If you want civil war, you can have it . . . You've told your people to be ready. You've cried "To arms". We've said the same to our people. Our workers, our districts are already lined up; they're asking if it will be soon.'[74] Babeuf had had qualms about the state violence of the Committee of Public Safety. Faced with the street violence of the *jeunesse dorée*, he soon recognized the necessity for revolutionary violence.

With such open opposition to the regime, it is surprising that Babeuf stayed at liberty for so long. A warrant for his arrest was issued on 13 October, but he successfully evaded capture, and was finally caught on 7 February 1795. He remained in prison until 12 October, being moved several times, and sent for some months to Arras in the North East before being brought back to the notoriously tough Plessis prison in Paris.[75] He maintained contact with his family, and while in jail learnt of the death of his daughter Sophie, aged six (named after his previously deceased daughter), apparently as the result of eating a whole cooking-pot full of potatoes.[76]

The period of imprisonment was a crucial stage in Babeuf's development. At Plessis he met a number of those who were to be key figures in the conspiracy, including Bodson, Moroy and Buonarroti (see Chapter 4). As Buonarroti was to write: 'The widespread imprisonment of lovers of freedom and their frequent transfer from one prison to another had the advantage of enabling them to get to know each other better and to establish closer links.'[77]

Babeuf stayed in touch with the worsening economic situation of the common people. During his trial he gave a vivid picture of the situation in early summer 1795:

The majority of citizens, men, women and children, scarcely able to stand upright, staggering through the streets of Paris, walking around like unrecognizable skeletons, with pale deformed faces, fighting with the lowest animals of prey over refuse from the kitchens of the rich; leaving behind them at home the even more emaciated forms of old people, sickly children, delicate wives, reduced to such a state of weakness that they could no longer leave their miserable beds. The mother giving suck found her breast dried up, so that it no longer even gave blood instead of milk to nourish the child she had given life to. Who can say how many died in those terrible months, amidst the agonies of ghastly hunger, victims of all ages and both sexes.[78]

The people of Paris did not suffer these terrible conditions passively. On 1 April (*germinal*) and 20 May (*prairial*) there were massive demonstrations spilling over into rioting. The slogan 'bread and the Constitution of 1793' was raised, showing how the past was turning into a golden age by comparison with the present. But the risings did not have any leadership or programme, and now no part of the bourgeoisie was willing to support the *sans-culottes;* they were easily suppressed by the authorities who disarmed the people of Paris and thus consolidated their power.[79] If the Thermidorian regime was to be seriously challenged, something more would be needed.

4

The Conspiracy

When Babeuf left prison on 18 October 1795 he had less than twenty-one months of life ahead of him, of which just seven would be at liberty. His career up to that point would have scarcely merited a footnote in the history of the Revolution. But the various components that made up the remarkable final phase of his life were now falling into place.

He immediately set about relaunching the *Tribun du peuple*. A new series beginning with number 34 appeared on 5 November 1795, and between then and 24 April 1796 a total of ten issues appeared. But now a new political agenda was emerging. While in jail Babeuf had clarified his political ideas.

He now took a much more positive view of the heritage of Robespierre. He again cited the Robespierre's *Declaration of Rights*,[1] which referred to the limitation of the rights of property. (Yet article 7 merely stated: 'The right of property is limited like all others by the obligation to respect the rights of others.'[2] It would be hard to think of any legal code which did not at least formally limit the right of property thus.) But now he went much further than Robespierre. Before 1789 Babeuf had developed the view that society should be based on equality and collective ownership of property. He never renounced this aim, but said relatively little about it during the early years of the Revolution. Probably he believed that the revolutionary process, if pushed forward vigorously, would lead to something approaching the communist goal. Now he began to wrestle with the problem of how that goal related to his day-to-day agitation. He traced the idea of 'real equality' (*égalité de fait*) from Sparta through Christ to Rousseau, Diderot and Robespierre. He rejected the idea of the agrarian law, which he said would last only one day; the day after the division of the land, inequality would emerge again.[3] Elsewhere he argued that the agrarian law would turn France into a 'sort of chessboard'.[4]

To grasp the originality of Babeuf's politics it is necessary to look at his attitude to the republic. In the first issue of the new series of the *Tribun du peuple*, he argued that if we turned to the ordinary unpolitical people – not those who were tortured in dungeons, but those who starved in hovels – they would be very sceptical as to whether the whole Revolution had brought them anything; he imagined them saying:

> 'What good has the new regime done us? Oh! it does not bear comparison with the old regime. Whether despotism has a single head, or whether it has seven hundred, it is still despotism. We have experienced the fact that the royal tyranny is still worth a thousand times more than senatorial tyranny . . . Oh yes! it is impossible not to want to say it: WE WERE MUCH BETTER OFF UNDER A KING . . . '[5]

Babeuf was probing beneath the surface of the rhetorical republicanism flaunted by the Directory (the new government established at the end of October) to expose the class realities behind it.

Particularly important for Babeuf's development was the political correspondence he had had in prison with Charles Germain (see below). Between June and September 1795 some 48 letters were exchanged between them. They discussed at length the nature of an equal society and the problems of transition; Germain undoubtedly helped Babeuf to refine his views. In a letter of July 1795 Germain set out a number of important issues. He confronted the international implications of a seizure of power; initially he advocated that a regime of equality should establish 'absolute isolation' from the rest of the world, in order to pursue the transition undisturbed; however, he looked forward to a time when foreigners coming to see the new regime would be so impressed that they returned home determined to emulate the principles of equality. The most striking passage was one where Germain set out a critique of commerce and a powerful argument for a planned economy:

> Where commerce has developed it tyrannizes alongside the tyrants who support it so that it shall be their assistant. With it, under it, by it and for it, everything becomes a commodity . . . Shall we destroy industry if we use with judgement at least twice the number of workers who today are employed at random and without any kind of direction? Shall we destroy industry by organizing it, administering it, assigning to everyone their task, and letting nothing useless be undertaken, by constantly regulating

production in proportion to consumption, and putting everything in harmony . . . [6]

Germain's letter stimulated a reply from Babeuf which contained a
remarkably far-sighted passage, a critique of the market economy which
retains all its relevance two centuries later:

> Competition, far from aiming at perfection, submerges conscientiously
> made products under a mass of deceptive goods contrived to dazzle the
> public, competition achieves low prices only by obliging the worker to
> waste his skill in botched work, by exhausting him, by starving him, by
> destroying his moral standards, by setting an example of unscrupulous-
> ness; competition gives the victory only to whoever has most money;
> competition, after the struggle, ends up simply with a monopoly in the
> hands of the winner and the withdrawal of low prices; competition man-
> ufactures any way it likes, at random, and runs the risk of not finding any
> buyers and destroying a large amount of raw material which could have
> been used usefully but which will no longer be good for anything.[7]

(This hostility to competition may in some ways reflect the hostility to
commerce that was common among small artisans; but Babeuf is significant precisely because he adopted backward-looking themes and gave
them a new orientation to the future.)

After the experience of Thermidor and the risings of 1795 Babeuf
had little doubt about the necessity for revolutionary violence. He wrote
in reply to a political rival: 'Then you talk about civil war . . . as if we
didn't have it already! as if the war of the rich against the poor was not
the cruellest of civil wars! especially when the former are armed to the
teeth and the latter are without defence.' He stressed the urgency of the
situation: 'The house is on fire, and when we quite naturally speak to you
about water to put it out, you insult us and tell us that we don't need
water, but that we should talk politics.'[8]

By early 1796 Babeuf recognized that a magazine and a group of
like-minded associates was not enough. The political situation under
the Directory required an urgent response. Measures to establish a
more liberal economy meant attacks on working people. Starvation
was widespread, and there were more deaths than births in Paris. Some
expressed their anger through strikes, while suicide figures rose so high
that the government forbade their publication.[9] On the right royalists
were regrouping and there was a real threat that the monarchy could

be restored. On 5 October, just a fortnight before Babeuf came out of prison, there had been an armed demonstration of 25 000 royalists in Paris. It had been suppressed by military force – under the command of General Bonaparte – but the leaders were still very much around and continued to pose a threat.

Babeuf believed that the Directory was attempting a balancing act between its enemies on left and right: 'It wants to preserve two mortal enemies, the royalists and the republicans; it wants these two parties, by maintaining a precise balance within the Republic, to ensure its peaceful enjoyment of the highest rank.'[10] He noted the royalist threat, and warned the Directory that they had more to fear from the royalists, who would put them to death as regicides, than from the republicans.[11] He was aware of the danger of precipitate or disorganized risings; the actions of *germinal* and *prairial* 1795 had helped to consolidate the power of the government.

Babeuf saw that the time for reforms was over. In a polemic against Laurent Lecointre who had advocated the restoration of the *maximum*, he argued: 'In such an extreme crisis, semi-irritants are useless: we need emetic, mercury, cantharides, lunar caustic [silver nitrate, applied to poisoned wounds]. Yes, yes, we shall administer them!'[12] He warned readers to beware of the Directory's tactics: 'The furious wolves have turned into flexible, thoughtful foxes. Don't be deceived. They are still carnivorous animals: they haven't changed their nature and they never will. Today they are drawing in their claws; tomorrow they will devour you.'[13]

Ever since coming out of jail Babeuf had been aware of the repression exercised by the Directory. He had no fixed home, but slept each night in a different place.[14] On 4 December a police officer arrived at Babeuf's home and attempted to arrest him; Babeuf resisted. The policeman chased him through the streets shouting, 'Stop thief!' A group of market porters came to his defence as soon as they heard his name, and hurled mud and refuse at the pursuing policeman.[15] Later a reward of 600 000 *livres* was offered for Babeuf, dead or alive.[16]

The problem of organization was therefore crucial. Since 1794 efforts had been made to revive the revolutionary clubs which in earlier years had served as centres for political pressure and agitation. After Thermidor various former *hébertistes* and *enragés* had formed a body called the Electoral Club. Babeuf had been involved with this and had written a pamphlet advocating organizational improvements.[17] But the club was shut down by a gang of what Babeuf called 'two hundred Eratostratus' (after the destroyer of the temple at Ephesus) who smashed up the premises.[18] While in prison Babeuf was trying to regroup supporters of what he called 'our party', as is shown by a letter to Julien de la Drôme *fils* written a few days before his release.[19]

In the autumn of 1795 a new attempt was made to form a focus for opposition to the Directory, with the founding of the Panthéon Club. This was a broad alliance; some 2000 members included critical supporters of the government as well as outright opponents. It met in a former religious building close to the Panthéon in the Latin Quarter, sometimes in a basement; Buonarroti described the setting: 'the pale torch-light, the hum of voices and the uncomfortable position of those attending, standing up or seated on the floor, brought home to them the greatness and the dangers of the enterprise, as well as the courage and prudence they needed.'[20] Buonarroti listed the activities of the Panthéon Club as reading newspapers, hearing correspondence from members, collections for distressed republicans, campaigns for the release of political prisoners and discussions on current events.[21] There was no formal structure; the participants feared that if they became too similar to the old Jacobin club, they would risk persecution. Such caution was vain; in February 1796 the Panthéon Club was closed by the authorities, with General Bonaparte personally supervising the operation.

There was now an important strategic choice to be made. A small group around Babeuf were advocating a society based on the common ownership of property, something far beyond the aspirations of even the most radical Jacobins. But they were a tiny minority. If they relied entirely on their own forces they could make no impact on the immediate situation. At best they could publish propaganda pointing to the remote future. (In 1793 Babeuf had been working on a book called *On Equality*, but he never found time to complete it.) By taking that choice they would have become just one more item in the history of utopian communism that could be traced back to the beginning of the century.

Alternatively, they could put the emphasis on immediate tasks. This would have meant dissolving the small group of 'equals' into the broader milieu of the left opposition to the Directory, the people who had made up the Panthéon Club. This contained many ex-Jacobins, people who had held positions of power or influence in the days of Robespierre, and were looking for a return to their former glory. If Babeuf had taken this option, then he would have become just another latter-day Jacobin, and his socialist ideas would have remained forever confined to his private correspondence.

The greatness of Babeuf lies in the fact that he took neither choice, but faced up to what has ever since been the central strategic problem of revolutionary socialism: how to relate the immediate day-to-day struggle to the long-term aim (see Chapter 11).

On 30 March 1796 Babeuf and his associates set up the 'secret directory of public safety'; the journalist and agitator became a conspirator. Caution must be used with the word 'conspiracy'. Historically the term is inextricably linked to the memory of Babeuf, above all because of the title of Buonarroti's book, *The Conspiracy for Equality* (see Chapter 6). But 'conspiracy' may carry a misleading impression, with connotations of clandestinity, of a small minority acting behind the backs of those they claim to represent. That the word 'conspire' did not necessarily imply clandestinity is shown by something Babeuf wrote in 1794: 'We conspire aloud, we give the greatest publicity to our conspiracy.'[22]

Babeuf and his allies had to invent their own organizational form. They had little past experience to draw on, apart from Roman history and a tradition of secret societies, especially freemasonry. Babeuf had a tendency to see conspiracies on the part of his enemies and this may have encouraged his belief in the need for conspiracy to resist conspiracy. During the Terror the term 'conspiracy' had been used almost indiscriminately to describe any anti-governmental action.[23]

From 1795 Babeuf had begun to group around himself those whose thinking was developing in a similar manner, forming the nucleus of what was to be the conspiracy. In Plessis jail Babeuf met perhaps his most important ally, Filippo Buonarroti. Buonarroti was born in Pisa in 1761 and studied law at the University of Pisa. His tutors, Lampredi and Sarti, introduced him to Locke, Mably and above all Rousseau;[24] he also encountered the work of the materialist philosophers Helvétius and d'Holbach.

At his trial in 1797 Buonarroti set out an account of how he had developed his philosophical position. 'Rousseau was my master. The principles of equality and popular sovereignty set my mind afire.' He set out the five principles of his 'moral and political doctrine', which can be summarized as follows: 1) God is silent, so we must seek moral principles in the laws of our own organization; 2) happiness is the essential condition of any society; 3) no society can deny the natural rights based on happiness; 4) happiness must be universal, so the people is sovereign; 5) every individual should participate equally in the formation of the general will.[25]

Buonarroti remained much closer than Babeuf to Rousseau; he believed in God, was hostile to materialists and *voltairiens*,[26] and was a freemason. In November 1790 he took a job in Corsica, which at that time approximated to the ideal of a republic of small property owners. There were few large landowners or landless labourers, and the practice of collective rights was essential to the pattern of agriculture.[27] This experience doubtless reinforced his belief in an egalitarian society. Buonarroti held positions under the revolutionary government in Corsica and Piedmont, and was naturalized a French citizen in May 1793. He was a fervent admirer of Robespierre, but held office for several months after Thermidor until his arrest in February 1795.

For Buonarroti the 1793 Constitution was far more than a tactical demand; as he told the court at Vendôme:

> The 1793 Constitution became my religion: I still remember with emotion . . . the great assemblies of the people consecrated by it, the impulse given to the Nation towards the abandonment of prejudices, greed and pride, and towards sweet equality, open fraternity, friendship, sincerity, compassion, nature . . . [28]

The other major intellectual figure in the conspiracy was Sylvain Maréchal. Born in 1750, Maréchal was one of Babeuf's oldest friends in Paris. He had helped him find a job in 1793, and in 1794 campaigned vigorously for his release from prison. Maréchal had already established a literary reputation before the Revolution as an author of pastoral verse and prose, and as the compiler of an almanac which has been seen as a precursor of the revolutionary calendar. In a work published in 1789 he not only advocated equality but sketched out the idea of a general strike.[29]

Maréchal was a militant atheist, who argued vigorously that morality could be quite independent of religion: 'O Virtue, it is for your sake that I deny God'.[30] Politically he was closer to anarchism than either Babeuf or Buonarroti. As he put it: 'Anyone who is governed is to be pitied, every government is to be feared.'[31] He had little sympathy for the Jacobin leaders, being naturally hostile to any authoritarian regime, however radical its content. During the Terror his sympathies lay with Hébert. But his egalitarianism was not all-inclusive; as a disciple of Rousseau he was vigorously opposed to equality for women.[32]

Maréchal was one of the very few people other than Babeuf himself to write for the later numbers of the *Tribun du peuple*. In number 40 he contributed a sizeable unsigned article under the title 'The Opinion of a Man'. Much of this was devoted to praising Babeuf for his defence of equality and supporting his arguments. He quoted from the ancient Greek geographer-philosopher Strabo to show that societies based on equality had already existed; and he told a story of a man who went around proclaiming that 'The sun shines for everybody' (the refrain of a famous *babouviste* song).

But there were certain points at which his position diverged from Babeuf's. Like many later anarchists, he was a voluntarist. He argued that if the Revolution had been led in the right direction,

> the citizens . . . could within three days have organized that pure democracy, that perfect equality, the object of your concerns . . . Three days would have sufficed to avoid all the wars, all the crimes, all the calamities which followed a first movement which Paris was unable to take advantage of and which an evil genius rendered futile.

Babeuf may have been over-optimistic, but he understood that a transition would require more than three days and an act of will. The 'evil genius' in the passage above was presumably Robespierre. Maréchal also dissociated himself from the demand for the Constitution of 1793.

> But that of Hérault de Séchelles itself [the 1793 Constitution] was only a little more democratic than the charter of Boissy-d'Anglas [the 1795 Constitution] . . . Nature and your heart are surely worth more than all these rights of man and the citizen composed by hypocrites and ignoramuses.

This provoked Babeuf to add a long footnote defending Robespierre. He conceded that Maréchal was right in principle but considered he was wrong tactically: 'But perhaps this is too strong a diet at the present time to be easily digested by many people. Democrats do not like to hear the Constitution of 1793 spoken of in a derogatory tone . . . '.

Babeuf was much more guarded than Buonarroti about the 1793 Constitution; he accepted that it was not perfect, that it 'neither established nor guaranteed the highest degree of social happiness, but it must be admitted that it was an important step towards it.'

Maréchal also adopted a moralizing tone rather different from that used by Babeuf: 'It is not only bread that men need. Real equality is their first need, and they are no better than beasts if they agree to do without it.'[33] Babeuf, on the other hand, grasped that it was through the struggle for bread that human beings would come to understand the need for equality. Maréchal was a principled revolutionary and an able propagandist, but unlike Babeuf, he never really grappled with the problem of the transition to the equal society. If Buonarroti stood to the right of Babeuf, Maréchal stood to his left.

Joseph Bodson was seen by Daniel Guérin as a more consistent revolutionary than Babeuf. The truth is somewhat more complex. He had been a follower of Hébert; jailed after Thermidor, he met Babeuf in prison. He remained profoundly hostile to Robespierre. In February 1796 Babeuf had an exchange of letters with Bodson, which revealed just how far he had moved on the question of Robespierre since his writings in the aftermath of Thermidor. Bodson had urged that Babeuf should not endorse Robespierre's politics. Babeuf replied that Robespierre and Saint-Just 'were worth more on their own than all the revolutionaries taken together, and their dictatorial government was devilishly well contrived'. He went on to make a rather injudicious defence of Robespierre's policies:

> I won't enter into the question of whether Hébert and Chaumette were innocent. Even if they were, I still justify Robespierre. For he could rightly claim to be the only person capable of driving the chariot of revolution to its *true destination* . . . I imagine he said: 'Let's snuff out these importunate hobgoblins and their good intentions.' My opinion is that he was right. The salvation of twenty-five million people cannot be balanced against the preservation of a few dubious individuals. A regenerator must see things on a large scale. He must mow down everything that gets in his way, everything that obstructs his route, everything that can prevent him arriving promptly at the end he has set for himself . . . It is true that these ideas could carry you and me away. But what would that matter if common happiness came as a result?[34]

Two hundred years later, after the Dreyfus case and the Moscow Trials, Babeuf's formulation certainly seems unfortunate. Revolutionary justice may have to be hasty and will inevitably make mistakes, but it cannot proclaim itself indifferent to guilt and innocence. But those who have seen the germs of Stalinism in Babeuf's utterance are exaggerating. Babeuf was making up for his post-Thermidor position by overstating his case. He was grappling with the whole question of revolutionary dictatorship, and the debate with Bodson helped him to clarify his position.

Another key conspirator was Charles Germain, born in 1770 to a Calvinist family in Narbonne. He joined the army at the age of seventeen, but found the time to read widely. He admired Diderot, Mably, Rousseau and especially Helvétius. His Protestant background also influenced him. He saw the Essenians as forerunners of egalitarianism,[35] and in his defence at Vendôme referred to the Anabaptists, criticizing them as anarchists.[36] At his trial Germain made fun of the stereotypes of the 'revolutionary extremist' that were current even then:

> Citizens, I am a Frenchman, and I like to laugh. Of course, this joviality is not common among conspirators. 'The chin sunk into the chest, eyes haggard, stem forehead, mouth hermetically sealed, sad at heart, that's the conspirator.' It's not under this description that I appear before you.[37]

Pierre-Antoine Antonelle, born in 1747, was rather older than most of Babeuf's grouping. In November 1795 Antonelle, who had been a Jacobin, published an article in the *Orateur plébéien* critical of Babeuf, who replied in number 37 of the *Tribun du peuple*. Antonelle had argued that while the abolition of property was desirable, it was something that could not be achieved in practice. Babeuf responded with a historical perspective, arguing that the present was the right time for the overthrow of inequality: 'the present age is precisely the most favourable . . . infinitely more so than a thousand years ago.' He drew encouragement from the progress of the Revolution to argue that change was possible as well as desirable: 'The French Revolution has given us proof after proof that because abuses are ancient, that does not mean that they are ineradicable.'[38]

Augustin Darthé, born 1769, and a law student in Paris at the outbreak of the Revolution, was an energetic political ally of Babeuf, and veered towards the more authoritarian side of the conspiratorial group, urging the need for dictatorship after the insurrection.[39] In a fragmentary sketch of his career prepared during the Vendôme trial, Darthé took pride in his role in the storming of the Bastille, and as a revolutionary activist in the Pas-de-Calais, but made no mention of any specifically socialist convictions.[40]

Babeuf's family also played a role in the conspiracy. His wife and son Emile, then aged only nine, had worked on the *Tribun du peuple* before Babeuf's imprisonment, helping with folding and distribution,[41] and his wife continued to assist with subscriptions in 1795–6, a demanding and dangerous job for what was effectively a semi-clandestine journal. On 4 February 1796 she was arrested and when she refused to disclose her husband's whereabouts, she was held for forty-eight hours without food.[42]

Babeuf attempted to establish links with a group of ex-Jacobins who were also organizing against the Directory. But he did not dissolve his organization into theirs, seeking rather to maintain the integrity of his own grouping, and to co-operate where possible. He used the slogan of the '1793 Constitution' as a means of winning popular support. This demand had been raised spontaneously during the risings of *germinal* and *prairial* 1795, mainly because people had eaten better in the days of Robespierre. Babeuf admitted that the 1793 Constitution was defective on the crucial question of property, but since it enshrined the principle of universal suffrage, it would serve as a bridge to those who desired a greater degree of equality.

In fact, Babeuf's relations with the ex-Jacobins were not particularly successful. A small group around André Amar, an ex-member of the Convention, Robert Lindet and others, had been formed late in 1795; some of its members (including Buonarroti and Darthé) later joined Babeuf; the remnants reconstituted a group in April 1796. (Amar had played a key role in closing the women's clubs in 1793 and later helped to organize the overthrow of Robespierre.) Formal negotiations took place between Babeuf's group and the Amar committee, but there was too much distrust for any successful unity to be established. Babeuf and his allies regarded the Amar committee with some contempt, since it had no press and little organized support, and they did not refer to it in their public press.[43]

Also involved in Babeuf's attempt to link up with ex-Jacobins was Jean-Baptiste Drouet, the provincial postmaster who, in 1791, had recognized the royal family attempting to flee the country and had them apprehended, thus becoming a revolutionary hero. He became a Jacobin, and was later taken prisoner by the Austrians. He reinforced his legendary status by attempting to escape from the Spielberg fortress with a home-made parachute, breaking both legs in the process. Returning to France, still an elected member of the Convention, he was highly critical of the Directory. But his politics took a somewhat bizarre turn. On 15 May 1796 he published a pamphlet in which he argued that to avoid violence all patriots should simply take up their possessions and leave the country *en masse*, settling on the land of France's enemies.[44] The *Tribun du peuple* made favourable references to 'Worthy Drouet'.[45] Babeuf hoped Drouet might act as a bridge to other ex-Jacobins. He drafted a speech for Drouet to deliver to the Convention; when the latter refused, he wrote a violent letter in which he condemned Drouet's caution, and declared that his tolerance and tacit approval made him 'an accomplice of the edifice of tyranny'.[46]

The 'secret directory' consisted of Antonelle, Babeuf, Debon, Buonarroti, Darthé, Félix Lepeletier and Maréchal.[47] It appointed agents and received reports from them. Copies of all this documentation were kept and were seized at Babeuf's arrest and subsequently published by the authorities in two large volumes. Though this made the defence more difficult, historians can hardly regret it, since it gives us a fascinating and extensive insight into how the conspiracy operated.[48]

After the secret directory itself the key figures in the conspiracy were the twelve agents, one for each of the twelve *arrondissements* (administrative districts) of Paris. These were supposed to remain ignorant of each other, and of the identities of the members of the secret directory – though since Babeuf's name appeared on the *Tribun du peuple* they can hardly have been unaware of his involvement. Communication between the agents and the centre was to be maintained by 'intermediary agents' who would carry letters to and fro. Babeuf had managed to weld together an organization which had *ex-hébertistes* such as Bodson and ex-Jacobins such as Didier working in co-operation.

The first circular to the agents in the various *arrondissements* reveals the tension between clandestinity and mass agitation which was to characterize the whole conspiracy. Agents were to encourage the holding of meetings wherever possible, but to minimize their own public role.[49] However, a subsequent communication warned that excessive clandestinity could prevent the spreading of revolutionary ideas:

As far as possible you should pass on publications in a direct manner. You have to show a bit of boldness to inspire boldness in others: clandestine methods arouse distrust amongst the uneducated crowd. 'You smuggle your doctrine in; therefore it must be reprehensible.' Many people stick to that line of reasoning. Show great confidence in the rightness of your cause, and your air of confidence will easily make many recruits.[50]

To communicate the political aims of the conspiracy the *babouvistes* used a wide range of forms of publicity and propaganda. Firstly there were the newspapers, the *Tribun du peuple* and *L'Eclaireur*. Only the last three numbers of the *Tribun du peuple* belong to the actual period of the conspiracy; after a gap of over a month, these three issues – numbers 41 to 43 – appeared within a period of less than four weeks. They were in a rather different style to the earlier issues; they were shorter – around twelve pages each – and had a much larger typeface which must have been easier to read. Their style was that of a direct appeal to patriots and soldiers rather than the more philosophical discussion that had characterized earlier issues.

The circulation of the *Tribun du peuple* is generally reckoned to have been around 2000. This was small by comparison with the big sellers of the period. Loustalot's *Les révolutions de Paris*, published in the early years of the Revolution, sold 200 000 copies. But Babeuf's audience was undoubtedly much higher than 2000. Inn-keepers and wine and lemonade sellers often allowed public readings from newspapers on their premises. Indeed the style was deliberately declamatory, written for public performance rather than private perusal.[51] Babeuf's taste for inventing new words and phrases fitted well with this public, oratorical style.

A letter from Babeuf's son Emile, aged at the time ten-and-a-half, gives a graphic picture of the distribution of number 41 of the *Tribun du peuple*. He visited the local cobbler and various male and female citizens; in each case they took six or a dozen papers, paid for their own and one for a friend, and promised to pass on the rest to soldiers.[52]

Babeuf had set out his aims as a journalist in the 'Prospectus' for the new series of the *Tribun du peuple*. He pointed to the role of the paper as an organizer of political action:

> The people is apathetic and cowardly, say its detractors; therefore, they add, its inevitable fate is to be suppressed. Silence, imbecile rulers! Silence too, tame slaves! The people will prove to you that it is not irresponsible;

it will show you once and for all what it can do, when its enlighteners have shown it the value of revolution . . . when it has been told what is necessary so that this revolution should be for the people, in the last analysis, despite all the opposition of the enemies of *common happiness*.[53]

Alongside the *Tribun du peuple* Babeuf decided the time was ripe for a more popular paper. With Maréchal and Simon Duplay, Babeuf produced *L'Eclaireur du peuple ou le Défenseur de 24 millions d'opprimés* (The people's scout, or the defender of twenty-four million oppressed: the word *éclaireur* could mean either a military scout or a political agitator or 'enlightener'), under the name S. Lalande. Seven issues appeared between March and April 1795, each containing eight to twelve pages and consisting of a single long article; the circulation was 2000–3000, though as with the *Tribun du peuple*, copies were doubtless circulated and read collectively.[54]

The *Eclaireur* contained little discussion of long-term aims, and concentrated on attacking the day-to-day policies of the Directory. Soldiers were particularly targeted, and advised that if an officer forbade them to read revolutionary papers, they should reply: 'I've been on guard, I've done my duty; as a soldier I've obeyed you during my military service; as a free citizen I shall exercise my rights and will never submit to the authority of an individual.'[55] The seized papers contained a letter from Germain to Babeuf promising the appearance of a 'daily sheet' which would be sold at one *livre* ten *sous* and given free to 'true *sans-culottes*' who could not afford this sum.[56] But this project did not come to fruition.

There was also a need to reach out to a much wider audience which included many who did not buy newspapers or simply could not read – while most artisans could read, illiteracy levels were high among unskilled workers and the indigent poor.

Fly-posting – a form of propaganda which was developed in the pre-Revolutionary period and proliferated after 1789 – was central to the activity of the conspiracy. The posters made a considerable impact; the agent Moroy reported that posters of the *Analysis of Babeuf's Doctrine* had had a great effect in his area; though many had been torn down, people sought out the intact ones to read them, and in one case someone tearing down the posters received a smack in the face and a kick in the arse. In the seventh *arrondissement* the agent claimed – perhaps exaggerating somewhat – that 2000 people queued up to read a poster addressed to soldiers.[57]

THE SPECTRE OF BABEUF   69

Another way of spreading ideas among the illiterate was the use of songs; political songs had been highly popular ever since 1789. The centre of this activity was the Chinese Baths, a café where the main attraction was the singing of Sophie Lapierre, one of a number of women who played a significant role in the conspiracy. One of the songs that Lapierre sang was Maréchal's 'New song for the city districts':

> Mourant de faim, mourant de froid,
> Peuple dépouillé de tout droit,
>   Tout bas tu te désoles:
> Cependant le riche effronté,
> Qu'épargna jadis ta bonté,
>   Tout haut, il se console.
> (*Dying of cold, dying of hunger, people stripped of all rights, you grieve down below; meanwhile the shameless rich man, whom formerly you spared in your kindness, takes comfort up above.*)[58]

The agents were required to report regularly on the situation and mood in their area – to take note of the 'thermometer' of opinion. They were also asked to compile lists of known counter-revolutionaries in their districts, and to draw up contact lists of people who would be of use in various circumstances. The notes on contacts were often brutally frank, for example: 'Manque *fils*, doorkeeper at the *Egalité* stables . . . Aged 18, without talent; but vigorous, determined, and fit for exterminating scoundrels.'[59]

Propaganda material was produced which set out the aims of the conspiracy. In particular the *Analysis of Babeuf's Doctrine*, which was widely distributed (see Appendix), set out the aims of the movement. When a poster was made of the *Analysis*, it was reported from the fifth *arrondissement* that the *sans-culottes* believed it would be a more effective means of motivating the people than the Constitution of 1793.[60] Thus there is no basis for claiming that the objectives of the conspiracy were concealed; the aims of abolishing private property and establishing true equality were proudly proclaimed.

Rose, claiming that most of the rank-and-file supporters were looking to a revival of the golden age of 1793 rather than to a socialist future, alleged that the *Analysis* was 'carefully ambiguous' and contained 'nothing to which the most orthodox Jacobin could take exception'.[61] He was on shakier ground when he quoted the evidence of Jean-Baptiste

Goulard at the Vendôme trial, who defined 'common happiness' merely as 'a reduction in the price of all commodities necessary for the survival of the poor, and the recognition of paper money'. He used this to support his conclusion that 'the prevailing winds were Jacobin rather than communist'. (Rose's 'quotation' was in fact a second-hand summary of a rather more complex statement by Goulard.) But the defence of the conspirators at Vendôme was precisely to deny the existence of a conspiracy and play down the originality of the movement's aims. Goulard's statement was part of this strategy.[62] Goulard was a long-standing revolutionary, who had served fourteen months in jail, where he met the main *babouviste* leaders in 1795. He was no political virgin, and Rose was distinctly unwise to take his words at face value.[63]

In fact it seems unlikely that many of Babeuf's followers were unaware that the conspiracy aimed, not simply at restoring the Constitution of 1793, but establishing a socialist order (the word socialist was not yet in use; the term used by the conspirators was *bonheur commun* – common happiness). For example, J. Goulliart in Béthune promptly broke off relations with Babeuf when he recognized from the publications he received that Babeuf was going far beyond a return to Jacobin values.[64] In a letter to the secret directory, Juste Moroy described how he had to explain to his 'uneducated brothers' that Babeuf was not advocating the 'agrarian law' and that the property that would be confiscated was not an individual's home or patch of land but 'any sort of industry'.[65] The *babouviste* vision of 'common happiness' may have been unsophisticated and not fully elaborated, but the conspirators seem to have behaved with complete honesty to their audience.

Buonarroti stated that while planning the overthrow of the tyranny, 'the committee never stopped concerning itself with the definitive legislation for equality, and with the legislation whereby they intended to gradually arrive at it'. The papers dealing with the plans for the future society were not seized at the time of the arrest, and were destroyed; but Buonarroti attempted to reconstruct the outlines of the society being contemplated by the secret directory. The basic principles were the abolition of private property, the sharing of work among all, and the equal distribution of wealth. Measures for welfare, education and democratic assemblies were considered in detail, and plans were made for festivals and for the role of religion in society.[66] That the committee spent so much time on long-term aims during the hectic month-and-a-half in which the insurrection was being planned is testimony enough to the socialist character of the conspiracy. Arguably, it also shows that Babeuf, more deeply committed to the specifically socialist content of the conspiracy than many of his associates, was anxious to thrash out a perspective and develop a small nucleus of people committed to 'true equality' so that something would survive even if the immediate venture proved unsuccessful.

There were important political divergences between the various members of the secret directory. Maréchal was effectively an anarchist, while Darthé – who favoured the establishment of a one-man dictatorship – was closer to Jacobin authoritarianism than to Babeuf's brand of communism. Yet the committee seems to have functioned reasonably well during its brief existence, though if it had taken power the divergences might well have emerged more strongly. It would quite wrong to impose on the conspiracy a model of monolithic leadership derived from modern Stalinist parties. The equals had a healthy respect for the confrontation of differing standpoints within a united enterprise.

One important source of disagreement was Maréchal's *Manifesto of the Equals* (see Appendix), which was rejected by the secret directory.[67] This *Manifesto* contained the famous sentence, looking forward to socialist revolutions of the future: 'The French Revolution is only the forerunner of another revolution, which will be greater and more impressive, and which will be the last.' According to Buonarroti, the *Manifesto* was rejected because of two sentences which the committee found unacceptable. In one we see a clear expression of Maréchal's anarchism: 'It is time for you to disappear, sickening distinctions between rich and poor, between great and small, between masters and servants, between *rulers and ruled*.' It was the last phrase which provoked the objection of those who insisted on the importance of a revolutionary dictatorship in the transitional period. But it probably also outraged those of the 'equals' who had not thought through the inextricable connection between equality and democracy. Since Babeuf obviously had thought that one through, he may well not have objected so strongly.

The other sentence that caused outrage was: 'May all the arts perish, if necessary, providing true equality remains.' (The term arts (*les arts*) should be understood to mean not only art but all forms of craft and technology.) Doubtless Maréchal's comrades felt that this suggested some reversion to a Rousseauesque state of nature, with an abandonment of all the gains of progress and civilization. This Babeuf and his allies emphatically did not want. But Maréchal's draft did not actually advocate such a reversion; it merely stated that equality was the prime consideration, and all else must be sacrificed to it. (He was being quite consistent, since he had already published a virtually identical statement in 1792.)[68]

The *Manifesto* also contained an expression of the extreme voluntarism that characterized Maréchal's politics: 'The very day after this true revolution, they will say in astonishment: So! Common happiness was so easy to achieve? We only had to wish it. Oh! why did we not wish it sooner?' This evaded all the questions of the objective conditions necessary for social change, precisely the questions with which Babeuf was grappling. Maréchal's *Manifesto* was a fine piece of propaganda, powerfully written, but it was open to misinterpretation and the underlying political analysis was weak. Doubtless that was why the conspirators rejected it completely rather than simply amending it to remove the offending phrases.

The point of all this activity was to organize the insurrection to overthrow the Directory. Babeuf and his comrades were embarking on this task with tiny resources and no historical experience to draw on. The wonder is not that they made some mistakes, but that they got as far as they did.

Documents from the secret directory repeatedly recognized the importance of timing. A premature or mistimed rising could be a disaster. A circular of 18 April told agents that while the 'effervescence of the multitude' was welcome proof that the people were not apathetic, it was still necessary to 'inflame the mind of the soldier to the same degree as that of our fellow-citizens', since co-operation between army and *sans-culottes* was vital.[69] The *babouviste* leaders decisively rejected individual terrorism and short-cuts. In his testimony at Vendôme the traitor Grisel told how he had suggested setting fire to castles outside Paris in order to divert troops from Paris during the insurrection; Darthé had welcomed the suggestion, but Babeuf had opposed it. Since Grisel was aiming to discredit the conspiracy as far as possible, his evidence on this point seems reliable. Likewise Babeuf rejected an offer from a captain in the Police Legion to assassinate the five Directors, saying this on its own would achieve nothing.[70]

The insurrection was intended for the very near future, and careful plans were made. The committee drew up a 'Declaration of Insurrection' (*acte insurrecteur*) which set out the practical measures to be taken immediately on the seizure of power. This laid down quite ruthlessly that 'opponents will be exterminated'. It also promised to kill known royalists, anyone who issued a call to arms to resist and any foreigners found on the streets. This last measure has often been cited as proof of the bloodthirsty nature of the conspiracy. But the exiled monarchy were known to be conspiring to overthrow the Republic; a number of foreign agents were rumoured to have arrived in Paris. The clause was simply a warning to all foreigners to stay off the streets.[71]

Many detailed arrangements were made. There were to be snipers to fire on any deputies who might try to influence the people against the insurrection.[72] There were also to be banners with slogans reading 'people's army'; 'down with tyrants'; 'people's vengeance',[73] and agents were instructed to manufacture pennants.[74] All food stores in private hands were to be requisitioned; the 'telegraphs' (semaphore signalling devices) were to be seized;[75] the National Treasury was to be captured (whereas in the Paris Commune in 1871 the Bank of France was never taken over);[76] property in the pawnshops would be restored to its owners – undoubtedly a move that would win support among the poor.[77]

Buonarroti claimed that there were 17 000 men in Paris ready to take the initiative for an insurrection.[78] It is difficult to confirm or challenge this figure; certainly the documentation suggests that the secret directory evaluated the balance of forces honestly and did not delude themselves with fantasies. But equally 17 000 would not have been enough for a seizure of power unless popular support could be won over.

Much of Babeuf's support came from *sans-culottes* who had played an active role in the 1793–4 period. This was suggested by Soboul's analysis (see Chapter 8) of the subscribers to *Le Tribun du peuple*[79] and has been confirmed by more recent research by Raymonde Monnier.[80] Nearly all the agents had been active militants in the Paris sections in 1793–4. However, the case should not be overstated. The price and style of *Le Tribun* selected a certain sort of subscriber, and its message reached a wider audience through public readings. If some aspects of the conspiracy looked back to 1793, others looked forward to the working-class struggles of the nineteenth century.

For there was a working class in Paris (see Chapter 11) and the conspiracy made efforts to relate to it and win its support; the existence of this layer of support was connected to the fact that the *babouvistes* had a more radical programme than any current within Jacobinism. In particular, Moroy in the twelfth *arrondissement* did have some success in identifying workplaces with more than a handful of workers.[81] He noted that while many merchants were rotten with royalism, the 'class employed by them is sound and good'. He noted that at the Gobelins tapestry works there were over a hundred workers, but they would back any government that would support their trade. (This was often true of workers in luxury trades, who had opposed the Revolution because it robbed them of their customers.) He found a dye-works at which the *sans-culottes* were enlightened though the bosses were not worth much; he found similarly good attitudes in another dye-works employing some thirty workers and about twenty tanneries employing between fifteen and fifty workers each, though the employers were all royalists. He also noted the good state of mind among the market porters (whose practical support for Babeuf we have already mentioned) and the dock-workers (Paris at this time was a major port). In the eighth *arrondissement* the agent reported on a potential industrial dispute, where an employer had raised wages because of the falling value of the *assignat* (paper money) but had not given an adequate increase so that in fact he was robbing his employees.[82]

The *babouvistes* knew that to succeed they must win over a section of the armed forces. They took careful note of changes in consciousness within the army. A report by a serving soldier, Captain Grisel, later a traitor to the conspiracy, noted that the army had changed radically since 1789; since officers were now almost all former common soldiers who had no income but their army pay, they ate from the same mess bowl as the ranks, and there was consequently a much greater familiarity and trust between common soldiers and officers. Grisel claimed that the ardent defenders of the fatherland in 1792–3 were mostly dead; urban youth had generally managed to evade the army, so most soldiers were of peasant stock; only one in ten could read and write. Most of them would 'happily trade the Republic for a cake from their own village'.[83]

Obviously this posed problems for revolutionary agitation, but it also suggested the army was not wholly committed to the government. Demoralization had produced a high rate of desertion. The secret directory devoted a lot of attention to discussing how to approach soldiers. A document circulated to the military agents started with the premise that 'it is a long recognized truth that men are only moved strongly by their own interests'. It argued that agitation must speak to the soldiers' real interests, to the fact that they were hungry, lacked shoes and could not afford to have their shirts laundered. It also noted that it was the most militant sections of the army that were being given extra rations of wine and brandy in an attempt to buy them off.[84]

The conspiracy devoted a great deal of attention to propaganda directed at soldiers. Virtually the whole of number 41 of the *Tribun du peuple* was an address to the army. Other material was written in a language more directly related to that of common soldiers, as in the letter of a soldier nicknamed 'Franc-libre' to his friend 'la Terreur' in the army of the Rhine, which begins: 'We're fucked, my poor friend la Terreur, yes we're fucked and flat broke if we swallow the pill they've shoved in our gobs.'[85] One draft leaflet told soldiers they were being treated like automatons, and that they were going to be sent to Turkey like a herd of cattle to pasture or the slaughter.[86] The famous poster *Soldier: stop and read* appealed: 'No! citizen soldiers! you will not shoot on your brothers, as you did in *germinal* and *prairial*.'[87]

A particular opportunity was offered by the Police Legion. Intended to provide security in the capital, it had been reorganized by Bonaparte in the autumn of 1795 and recruited its ranks from the popular classes in Paris. As a result, attitudes were very different from other regiments stationed in the capital. When the government decided to move the Legion out of Paris an agent reported that many soldiers said they would like to shove a bayonet in the Directory's guts before leaving.[88] A circular from the committee gave special advice on how to deal with the Police Legion, and in particular how to exploit the threat to transfer them out of Paris:

> Let anyone who has his habits, his mistress, his father, his relatives, his wife, his children, his friends here, be prepared to fight to stay close to them . . . Let us cherish them, promise them help and assistance, on condition that they reciprocate in favour of the people; we can await with confidence the results of this sort of concern.[89]

At the end of April the Police Legion did mutiny; but the *babouvistes* were not able to generalize the movement, and it was easily crushed, with seventeen militant soldiers being shot. This defeat revealed the weakness of the conspiracy.

Among methods to be used in winning over the army was the involvement of women. A circular to agents urged that use be made of 'the moving and persuasive eloquence of women', who should present 'civic crowns' to the soldiers urging them to join the people.[90] Other circulars stressed the importance of women because of the influence exercised by 'this interesting sex',[91] an indication of the importance attributed by the *babouvistes* to the role of women in the struggle.

The *babouvistes* did not imagine that they could establish socialism in one city, and they gave considerable attention to building links in the provinces. Schiappa has shown how they had an extensive network of contacts in the various *départements* of France, especially in Babeuf's old territory of Picardy and the Mediterranean South. Contacts and readers of the *Tribun du peuple* were to be found from Saint-Omer near Calais to Fréjus near the Italian border. Supporters of Babeuf in Marseilles produced a paper.[92] But the organization outside Paris was very much looser; only a handful of the papers seized at Babeuf's arrest deal with the provinces. In terms both of the state machine and the popular masses, Paris was the obvious centre, and the *babouvistes* were obviously right to concentrate their efforts there. But their inability to develop a coherent organization on a national scale was undoubtedly a sign of their weakness. In particular, they had no programme for the peasantry, who made up the bulk of the French population.

Despite its weaknesses, the conspiracy made a real impact and attracted a range of supporters. Rossignol, a former general in the French army, associated with the *babouviste* leaders in 1796. Rossignol had been one of the commanders of the French army in the Vendée, and in his book on the Vendée Babeuf had denounced him for reducing the French army to 'stumps and corpses'.[93]

In recent years various historians have attempted to show that the conspiracy was a futile effort doomed to disastrous failure. Two of the most significant of such efforts are those of Richard Andrews and Richard Cobb. Andrews argued that police surveillance and penetration meant that the conspiracy could never get off the ground; that in any case the potential audience was passive, and that Babeuf's socialist ideas were not communicated to his followers.[94] For Cobb the conspiracy was 'ridiculously overoptimistic' and Babeuf's contact lists merely made activists more vulnerable to police persecution.[95] The work done by both historians on police archives is valuable and helps to give us a more rounded picture of the reality of events. But both displayed a rather smug reliance on the virtues of hindsight, and both jeopardized their historical objectivity by personal vituperation: Andrews accused Babeuf of compiling lists merely as 'nourishment for his self-intoxication'. If the conspiracy was as futile as they claimed, then why did the prosecution have to struggle so hard to get convictions at Vendôme? If the police were so well informed, why did the prosecution case rely so heavily on the testimony of the single informer Grisel? (See Chapter 5.) Andrews saw the conspiracy as made by 'men [he ignored the women in the conspiracy] torn between a dead past and an imaginary future, men without present'. But the conspirators precisely had to fight in their own time; it is no use telling a starving man that his revolt is fifty years premature. Babeuf put his head on the line and paid the price; if his successors know a little more about what is and is not historically feasible, it is precisely because Babeuf and his colleagues were willing to risk everything to probe the limits of the possible.

Any movement will attract unwelcome attentions, and has the problem of how to deal with them. In Babeuf's conspiracy this problem was highlighted by the case of Georges Grisel.

Grisel was a serving captain in the army, and made contact with the conspiracy early in April 1796. In view of their concern to agitate among soldiers, the secret directory regarded him as an asset. He was fluent and confident, and well-informed about the state of mind of soldiers in Paris; he gave the conspirators some perceptive advice and wrote some agitational material that was probably better suited for soldiers than the rather overintellectual material written by Babeuf and Lepeletier. Not surprisingly, Grisel was welcomed into activities. On 30 April he was invited to attend a meeting of the secret directory, along with others like Rossignol and Germain who had special responsibility for military work. As Buonarroti pointed out, the secret directory broke its own rules in admitting him to this meeting.[96]

In retrospect it is easy to condemn this lax attitude to security. But a movement that takes no risks makes no progress. The ability to rapidly absorb able recruits like Grisel was a necessity for any movement that was to succeed. Perfect security is attainable only in complete isolation from activity. Doubtless with more time and more experience the secret directory could have found a way of integrating people like Grisel without allowing them to identify the entire leadership of the movement.

It is unclear whether Grisel joined the conspiracy intending to betray it, or whether he began as a sincere supporter who later decided he had a better future with the other side. But Grisel's information to the Directory brought the conspiracy to its catastrophic end.

5
The Trial

On 10 May 1796, following a tip-off from Grisel, and after one abortive attempt and considerable bungling, the police arrested Babeuf and Buonarroti and seized a large quantity of weapons and documents. Eventually a total of 65 people were charged with involvement in the conspiracy. The extent of the haul showed the limits of police information. According to Buonarroti (writing some thirty years later, when any need for deception was past) only 29 of the 65 had actually been involved in the conspiracy, and even that figure included members of the Amar committee, which had had only loose and spasmodic connections with the *babouvistes*.[1] Contrary to Cobb's claim that the government had 'caught the lot',[2] only three out of seven members of the secret directory were arrested in May; Antonelle was not arrested till the autumn, Lepeletier was tried *in absentia*, and Debon and Maréchal were never charged. Dommanget argued that Maréchal was not arrested because, having a stammer, he did not participate much in discussion and Grisel was unable to identify him (in addition he may have had friends in high places).[3] Doubtless the authorities were not too worried. Since the main aim was intimidation, it did not really matter who was in the dock.

Most accounts claim there was general indifference to the arrest of the conspirators, perhaps not surprisingly since many working people were demoralized by poverty and hunger. Even Buonarroti conceded that at the time of the arrests the people of Paris was a 'motionless spectator'.[4] But it would be wrong to allege total popular indifference. Police reports over the next few weeks noted that the arrests were widely discussed in cafés.[5] Late in May a group of men entered a workshop where several hundred women were making sacks and persuaded them to strike for the Constitution of 1793; armed force was needed to get them back to work.[6] On 22 May Julienne Guilhem and Madame Ficquet, wives of two of those arrested, attempted to incite workers in a flour store, telling them the insurrection had begun. They too were arrested.[7] At the end of August a report by the Police Minister Cochon (the conspirators were amused by the name, which in French means 'pig') alleged various provocations by 'anarchists' and claimed they were collaborating with royalists to undermine the government.[8] In September an attempt by a band of *sans-culottes* – encouraged by *agents provocateurs* – to subvert the army camp at Grenelle led to disaster; the troops did not fraternize, and some fifty patriots were killed or executed, while many others were arrested.[9] Soboul has claimed that the Grenelle rising was the work of Jacobins, not of *babouvistes*, pointing out that of the 131 arrested, *only* six were subscribers to the *Tribun du peuple*.[10] But *babouviste* influence extended well beyond subscribers to a journal, and six hard-core supporters of the type who were subscribers might have exercised considerable influence.

The government repression which intensified after the Grenelle rising prevented the opposition gaining momentum or coherence; but the care the regime took in preparing the trial is evidence enough that they did not consider that the threat had evaporated.

The arrests revealed some of the weaknesses of the conspiracy. The police were not particularly well-informed, so Grisel's treachery, which had been possible only as a result of the conspirators' own laxness, made all the difference. Even more seriously, the conspiracy had failed to take measures in case of arrest. No alternative leadership had been set up.[11] On 16 December Babeuf wrote a letter lamenting that those not arrested had failed to act; he argued that an issue of the *Tribun du peuple or L'Eclaireur* should have been produced within two or three days and signed 'the continuers of G Babeuf'.[12] It was a valid point, but Babeuf himself must take some responsibility as a member of the committee that had failed to plan for the eventuality of collective arrest. Jean-Marc Schiappa has recently discovered a pamphlet entitled *The French People's Cry of Indignation against the True Conspirators*, published in the weeks after the arrests, which he argued may well have been written by Maréchal.[13]

Both sides distorted the facts in their own political interests. At the trial the conspirators deliberately underplayed their achievements in order to minimize their guilt. Buonarroti declared that it was ludicrous to imagine that a couple of pamphlets could subvert eight or ten thousand soldiers.[14] On the other hand, the prosecution were anxious to claim that the conspiracy had nearly succeeded, in order to frighten the middle class and reflect credit on their own repressive measures. The chief prosecutor Viellart declared: 'Thanks be to the guardian angel of France, which turned away such a violent storm!'[15]

Hippolyte Carnot, in his memoirs of his father, a member of the Directory, claimed that the Directory would have inevitably fallen if Babeuf and his allies had not been arrested.[16] There was much truth in the analysis of the *babouvistes* that the Directory was engaging in a rather precarious balancing act between royalists and republicans. But neither they nor anyone else foresaw the actual outcome. They all saw the alternatives available as being either restoration of the monarchy or a return to Jacobinism – though Babeuf had some inkling of the danger of military dictatorship.[17]

Michelet argued that Babeuf had paved the way for Bonaparte.[18] If so, it was not entirely to the discredit of the conspirators. Bonaparte established a state structure which enshrined at least some of the gains of the Revolution, whereas a restored monarchy would have tried to dismantle the whole edifice.

After the arrest Babeuf himself seems to have panicked momentarily. On 12 May he wrote a bizarre letter to the Directory in which he offered to negotiate with them 'as one power to another'. He claimed that his organization was as strong as theirs, and that they needed his support as a counter-balance to the royalists. He urged them not to make the conspiracy public, but to negotiate with him.[19] Subsequent historians have almost unanimously dismissed this as folly, and it is hard to make a defence of Babeuf on this point. It was an unprincipled gambit which had no chance of success, and which was used to undermine the subsequent defence. The best that can be said is that it was a mistake by a man facing a difficult and unprecedented situation.

The authorities rejected the defendants' wish to be tried in Paris and decided that the case would be heard by the High Court, sitting at Vendôme, a small town some hundred miles to the southwest of Paris. The decision to stage the trial there was spurious. One of the 65 defendants was Drouet, although his role had been marginal, and in July he published a pamphlet dissociating himself completely from Babeuf, claiming to have met him only twice.[20] In mid-August Drouet escaped from jail and never in fact stood trial; it was widely rumoured that Barras, a member of the Directory, had facilitated his flight. But since Drouet was an elected member of the legislative assembly, it was argued that he could be tried only by the highest court in the land; since the others were accused of the same crimes, they must all be tried together.

Behind the legal formalism the motives seem to have been twofold. Firstly, Babeuf still had enough popular support to make a trial in Paris a considerable embarrassment. Secondly, the authorities were anxious to use the occasion as a show-trial before the most prestigious court in the country. Under the Terror the legal process had been speeded up, with short trials and rapid verdicts. The Directory were anxious to re-establish legal formalities, and to consolidate the use of juries, first introduced by laws of 1790 and 1791. Hence the slow and laborious procedures adopted by the court, and what appears to be the considerable degree of latitude granted to the defendants, which they exploited to the full. Babeuf got a fairer and more extensive trial than he would have had under either Louis XVI or Robespierre, though the verdict would probably have been the same.

At the end of August a group of prisoners were taken to Vendôme in specially constructed coaches with bars on the side, like cages.[21] Babeuf's wife, five months pregnant and with her ten-year-old son, walked all the way to Vendôme with the wives and partners of some of the other prisoners.[22] The unfailing support of his wife and son throughout his ordeal was one of the few consolations remaining to Babeuf amid the collapse of his hopes.

Babeuf was not a docile prisoner at Vendôme and the stress of the situation weighed heavily upon him. On one occasion he smashed his crockery and when food was brought round offered his chamber pot; the cook put the food in the pot, and Babeuf promptly threw it back at him.[23] Various escape attempts were planned; a rope and saws were smuggled into the prison. In another escape bid Babeuf wrote a complicated acrostic letter to his wife; the first and last words of each line spelled a message. When family visits were suspended, the prisoners' relatives walked on a nearby hill visible from the jail, where they could hear the prisoners singing.[24] Sometimes local republicans from Vendôme joined in the singing to communicate support to the prisoners.[25]

Babeuf sought to exploit the legal system, aiming to delay the trial for as long as possible, in the hope that the elections to be held in early 1797 would create a more favourable situation. This hope was to be dashed; the elections showed a swing to the royalists. Paradoxically, this might have pushed the Directory to seek support on the left as a counterbalance. But when the trial opened on 20 February 1797, it soon developed its own dynamic that took it beyond government manipulation.

Our understanding of the proceedings is greatly facilitated by the fact that we have a complete stenographic transcript of the fourteen-week trial. This was published in sixteen-page instalments, and the full record runs to well over 2000 pages. Babeuf's friend Hésine published an alternative report of the trial in his *Journal de la haute-cour de justice* which appeared roughly every two days throughout its duration.

The court was presided over by judge Gandon, assisted by four other judges. The prosecution was led by two national accusers, Viellart and Bailly. There were 47 prisoners in court; 18 other defendants were being tried in their absence, including Drouet, Bodson, Lepeletier and Rossignol. The accused had seven defence lawyers, most prominent of whom was Réal, who had a long history in revolutionary politics, but was now a convinced Thermidorian; he defended with vigour, but was unsympathetic to what seemed the more extreme aspects of the defendants' case. Babeuf requested formally but unsuccessfully that Hésine should act as his lawyer.[26]

In the months before the trial the defendants had had to attempt to thrash out a common defence strategy. As far as Babeuf was concerned there were two aims, not wholly compatible with each other. The show-trial set up by the Directory offered a wonderful opportunity to make propaganda to a large audience; but open avowal of the conspiracy's existence and its socialist aims would undoubtedly have brought down the severest penalties. Since Babeuf's eye was on the present as much as the future, he was concerned to preserve what he could of the nucleus that had been built up during the conspiracy. The Jacobins and those only marginally involved favoured a defence which denied the very existence of the conspiracy. In the end Babeuf, recognizing that unity in action was essential if anything was to be achieved, accepted the strategy of disowning the conspiracy. This meant denying that there had been any organization and denying his own role as leader; the documentation seized was explained away as being material for Babeuf's journalistic work, and correspondence among republicans alarmed at the royalist threat.[27] As Buonarroti quite rightly put it, the whole thing was a 'dutiful lie', and the defendants 'blushed at it in their hearts'.[28]

Some political compromises were inevitable. When the prosecution cited Maréchal's *Manifesto*, Buonarroti dismissed it as 'the incomprehensible production of an eccentric mind',[29] although later he was to reproduce it as an important document of the conspiracy. The front was not unanimous; Augustin Darthé, Sophie Lapierre and Adélaïde Lambert refused to recognize the legitimacy of the court, and took part in the proceedings except to make statements on their own terms.

Both sides saw the court as a means to address a wider public. Babeuf had an eye to posterity; in a text written before the failure of the conspiracy he had declared: 'we may as well sell our lives as dearly as possible to the tyrants and oppressors, and thus win, even in the event of failure, our right to the grateful and honourable remembrance of future generations.'[30] But it is not enough to talk of this in terms of a 'messianic streak'[31] in his character. Babeuf was no mystic and he knew that the survival of his ideas depended on the physical survival of at least some of his comrades. Before Babeuf's death Buonarroti had promised to publish the truth about the conspiracy;[32] if Buonarroti had gone to the guillotine too, then Babeuf would have forever remained a shadowy and unknown figure. There was no contradiction for Babeuf in accepting the agreed defence strategy.

Rose stressed the disagreements and conflicts of interest that existed between the various defendants.[33] Certainly real differences existed; but to a reader of the transcript the thing that comes over most strongly is how well the defendants preserved their unity on most if not all occasions; and above all, how courageously they fought. Babeuf and his main allies were like cornered animals; they never gave up their fight, taking every conceivable opportunity to challenge, obstruct and disrupt the proceedings of the court, and delay its verdict. They gave no inch of ground willingly, and the fact that the trial was stretched out to 97 days (as against only 41 that the conspiracy itself had lasted) was a tribute to their tenacity. It was a fight for the present as well as for the future – and one that was almost won.[34]

At the start the accused challenged the legitimacy of the prosecution witnesses, in particular Grisel, whose evidence would undoubtedly be decisive. When Grisel did appear on 12 March he was met with violent hostility. Every contradiction in his testimony was seized on in order to undermine his trustworthiness. Other witnesses managed to make their evidence implausible. When Pillé, the one conspirator who had turned informer, admitted that he believed in demons, his evidence too lost most of its credibility.[35]

One of the most telling pieces of evidence against the conspirators was a piece of paper found at the time of Babeuf's arrest. Written by Darthé, this contained a list of immediate tasks for the insurrection, the first of which was – allegedly – 'Kill the Five' (that is, the five members of the Directory).[36] During the preliminary investigations, Babeuf had been asked to initial the documents seized, and in this case, he had added a flourish which went right over the crucial words. He now claimed that the words had been crossed out as soon as written. For hour after hour the court and the two handwriting experts laboured over the question as to whether there was one crossing-out or two, and whether the words beneath were legible. All this could only help to sow doubt into the jury's minds.[37]

Every opportunity was taken to defy and obstruct the functioning of the court, and to assert the unity and confidence of the defendants. At the end of the day's session, the accused would join together to sing a revolutionary song, often led by Sophie Lapierre. Only at the very end of March did the court authorities forbid this demonstration of solidarity.[38]

The main burden of the defence fell on the most articulate of the conspirators, Babeuf, Buonarroti and Germain. As the trial progressed the strain on Babeuf, who was literally fighting for his life, became unbearable. But he was not finished yet. On 3 May he finally had the opportunity to sum up his defence. His speech extended over five days, and was interrupted by the judge who objected to his claim that the Directory was opening the door to the royalists.[39]

Much of the speech was a detailed and laborious reply to prosecution charges, repeating the arguments made in the course of the trial and insisting on the implausible claim that no conspiracy had ever existed. But Babeuf also succeeded in making the speech into a political testament in defence of the principles of socialism. He began with a roll of honour that included Socrates, Jesus – who had preached 'hatred of the rich' – and the Gracchi.[40] He went on to invoke some of the great names of eighteenth-century philosophy, writers revered as forerunners of the Revolution. He criticized ironically the monarchist government for not having suppressed the works of Mably, Helvétius, Diderot and Rousseau, which he called 'philosophical poisons'. Savagely, he added: 'Without them, I might have your morals and your virtues.'[41] In particular he cited

Diderot's (actually Morelly's) *Code of Nature* as calling for a society in which citizens would show 'such a perfect reciprocity of assistance that no-one should go short, not only of what is *necessary* and *useful*, but even of what is *agreeable*', and in which 'every citizen will contribute his share to the public authority, according to his strength, his talents and his age'.[42]

As his speech finally drew to a close, Babeuf once again invoked his ideal of 'general happiness', in a formulation of bitter irony. While on the face of it, it was a protestation that he did not conspire because he believed his aim to be unrealizable, the passage can in fact be read as a bitter indictment of those who had blocked the Revolution and prevented it from reaching its true goal:

> this doctrine, which I recognize very well cannot be put into practice amid so many cries, passions and prejudices, which form a barrier around the old institutions which can never be overcome, a barrier which ensures for all their supporters a tranquillity which is as unchangeable as that which was never shaken by the principles formerly proclaimed in great freedom, by those other levellers, Mably, Diderot, Rousseau, Helvétius . . .

Typically, Babeuf's last sentences were addressed to his children. He foresaw his own death and the restoration of the monarchy. His words could be seen as an acceptance of tragic destiny, but they are more plausibly understood as an appeal to unending struggle: 'I leave you as slaves, and this thought is the only one which will rend my soul in my last moments. In that case, I should give you advice on how to bear your chains more patiently, and I know that I am not capable of doing so.'[43]

This was not quite Babeuf's last word. On 18 May he spoke again for an hour and a half, and in concluding said: 'I welcome death if, without it, I am condemned soon to see this Republic for which I have sacrificed everything disappearing under waves of blood in the shadow of Louis XVIII's flags.'[44]

The prosecution had not had it all their own way. Dufort de Cheverny, an aristocrat sympathetic to the prosecution, noted that the judges seemed to be paralysed and fearful that the outcome would not be as they hoped.[45]

In his summing-up the chief judge, Gandon, accepted that many of those charged should be acquitted, including all the women and most of those from the alleged provincial organization. The government had recognized the need to cut its losses, but was determined to get the main ringleaders. On 24 May the jury were presented with the five questions they had to answer. In a very dubious legal move, two extra charges had been added in a desperate bid to ensure conviction.[46]

How justified this desperation was is shown by the jury's verdicts. On the original three points the jury considered that, despite the volumes of documentation, there was no proof that a conspiracy had actually existed. However, on points four and five, they did accept that there had been oral and written provocation to restore the 1793 Constitution, a capital offence. The jury acquitted the vast majority of the defendants. Seven men (Buonarroti, Germain, Moroy, Cazin, Blondeau, Bouin and Menessier) were found guilty with 'extenuating circumstances' (never defined) and sentenced to jail and deportation. In the cases of Babeuf, who despite his denials was obviously the central leader, and of Darthé, who had systematically insulted the court and who had probably written 'Kill the Five', they found no extenuating circumstances.[47]

The French jury system worked by a system of majority verdict, requiring at least thirteen out of sixteen to support conviction. There is no record of the jury vote, but according to Buonarroti and the *Mémoires* of Dufort de Cheverny it appears that there were three jurors solidly supportive of Babeuf and his allies; twelve equally solid in favour of the prosecution; and one waverer. All the decisions therefore hung on the decision of that solitary juror. Moreover, both Hésine and Dufort de Cheverny reported there had been intimidation in the jury room.[48]

A last attempt was made to claim that the law of 16 April 1796 was now obsolete, but the court rejected it. Buonarroti appealed to the spectators, but troops drew their bayonets to prevent any action by the crowd in the court. After attempting suicide, Babeuf and Darthé were taken to the guillotine. On 27 May 1797 one of the most remarkable figures of the revolutionary era was at last silenced.

It had been a very close thing. But the Directory had got what it wanted. When the Italian Communist Gramsci was tried in 1928, the state prosecutor said: 'We must stop this brain from functioning for twenty years.'[49] Mussolini only imprisoned Gramsci; the Directory made no mistake with Babeuf.

On the night before the sentence Babeuf wrote a final letter to his wife and children. As always he linked his personal affections to his politics, and made a modest assessment of his achievement:

> My friends, I hope you will all remember me and that you will often speak of me. I hope you will believe I loved you all a great deal. I couldn't imagine any other way of making you happy except through common happiness. I have failed; I have sacrificed myself; it's also for you that I am dying.[50]

Babeuf's defence strategy, however reluctant he himself may have been to adopt it, proved to be a highly realistic one. Grisel's damaging evidence was neutralized to such an extent that the jury refused to convict for conspiracy; if the fourth juror had not succumbed to pressure, all 65 might have been acquitted. Didier, commended by Buonarroti for his zeal, energy, skill and discretion as the sole link between the secret directory and the district agents,[51] walked from the court a free man (the prosecutor Bailly had pointed out that conviction rested on Grisel's evidence).[52] The fact that Buonarroti escaped the guillotine meant that Babeuf's ideas would live to inspire a new generation of militants. Of the seven members of the secret directory, two were never charged and two more (Lepeletier, Antonelle) were acquitted. Of the five military agents, three were charged (one of the others was the traitor Grisel), but only Germain was found guilty. From the twelve *arrondissement* agents, eight were charged and four found guilty (Moroy, Cazin, Menessier, Bouin – the two latter were tried in their absence and were not caught). The only other activist to be found guilty was Blondeau.[53] One report claimed that after the sentences Germain boasted publicly that the jury had been fooled.[54]

The trial gave the *babouvistes* and their ideas far more publicity than they had achieved through their own propaganda.[55] Those who criticize Babeuf's defence see him purely as a utopian speaking to the future. Babeuf was a practical revolutionary, whose aim was to preserve as much as he could of the organization and the cadre that had been built up.

A final irony of a conspiracy for equality was that the authorities tried to divide the prisoners on class lines. In his summing up Bailly had noted Buonarroti's 'propriety and courtesy', and expressed regret at seeing him involved in the conspiracy.[56] After conviction the 'educated' prisoners Buonarroti and Germain were given privileged conditions of imprisonment denied to lower-class prisoners such as Moroy. Buonarroti was allowed to share quarters with his wife, Teresa Poggi.[57] If the authorities thought they could buy him off, they were much mistaken; he was to prove the toughest and the most faithful of them all.

Many of those sentenced and acquitted reappeared as political activists in later years; a new paper called *Le Tribun du peuple* appeared in the autumn of 1797.[58] But there was little continuity with the socialist politics that had inspired Babeuf and those closest to him. The slide towards Bonapartism made republican defence seem paramount; more long-term objectives were largely abandoned. The short time-span over which Babeuf operated had prevented his developing a politically coherent cadre that could have regrouped and continued in the political direction he had tried to follow.

In 1799 came a new wave of oppositional activity, and the Club du Manège (Riding School Club, called after the premises where it met) was established. It was presided over by Drouet, and former *babouvistes* Didier, Bodson and Lepeletier were among its members. It was a purely republican venture; the socialist content of *babouvisme* had disappeared. But if few *babouvistes* remained socialists, equally few capitulated to Bonapartism (though Antonelle, after many years of opposition to Napoleon, ended his life a royalist). Some individuals continued to be politically active for many years; Baudement, agent of the second *arrondissement*, remained closely linked to Buonarroti during and after the Empire.[59]

Babeuf's son, Emile, remained politically active; he was involved with various publications, and suffered imprisonment, though his politics were somewhat erratic; he had Bonapartist sympathies. He intended to publish highly unreliable *Memoirs* of his father, but Buonarroti dissuaded him. His mother became a small trader in Paris, selling old clothes, jewellery and fabrics, until at least 1840.[60]

Was the whole thing a marginal and futile episode? Certainly on the face of it the conspiracy achieved neither its long-term nor its short-term aims, nor did it leave any lasting organization behind. But it should not be dismissed too easily. As Lukács argued, defeat is 'the necessary prelude to victory';[61] the experience of struggle always provides lessons for the next wave. Moreover, as a general rule the oppressed are treated worse when they don't fight back than when they do. If the Paris *sans-culottes* had remained dormant in 1796, they would have had less respect from the Directory and from Bonaparte, and their sufferings would probably have been worse.

As for Babeuf himself, he was undoubtedly one of the most remarkable minds of the French Revolution. He died at the age of thirty-six, younger than Marx when he began to write *Capital*. If he had survived to spend thirty years exile in the British Museum, who knows how far he might have taken his thinking. Babeuf in 1789 had nothing behind him but some unsystematic reading. He had to invent his own theory as well as his strategy and tactics. He deserves neither the neglect nor the condescension of historians.

PART 11

The Condescension of Posterity

6
First Opinions

Babeuf was dead, but the problem did not go away. Was the Revolution completed, or was it just the forerunner of a final revolution to come, as Maréchal had predicted? Over the next two centuries the Revolution's children – parliamentary democracy and the market economy – showed their strengths and their limitations. Through the struggles of 1848 and 1871 the working-class movement emerged as a major political force. The patriotism of 1793 gave way to the nationalism of 1914. The Russian Revolution of 1917 aroused and then dashed hopes that it was to be the successor that Maréchal had looked to.

All these events were reflected in the tortuous history of the way the French Revolution has been understood and appropriated over the last two centuries. Babeuf's place in the competing discourses of the history of the Revolution – often marginal and sometimes a complete absence – may help to illuminate the ideological conflicts at stake.

François Furet has written that for the generation succeeding the Revolution there were basically three choices: to unmake the Revolution, to make it complete, or to remake it (*défaire, parfaire*, or *refaire*).[1] Furet identified these three options with the counter-revolution, the July monarchy and the heritage of Babeuf. More generally, they can be seen as the three traditions of interpreting the French Revolution: conservative, liberal and socialist.

Conservatism and liberalism differ in their approach to their socialist opponents. Conservatives seek to exclude, to vilify, to demonize; liberals seek to incorporate and render anodyne. For conservative historians Babeuf is a bogey-man, an example of the dangers that await the most well-intentioned moderate who embarks on the slippery slope of revolution. For liberals Babeuf is one of them, somewhat extreme in his language, but fundamentally on the right side, and not so different from his more moderate associates.

The debate is of more than antiquarian interest; these strategies are used towards the living as well as the dead. For two hundred years the essence of the conservative case against Babeuf has been that he was a fanatical believer in violence, and that he was an ascetic – that is, he didn't want people to enjoy themselves. The arguments are still central to the case against socialism.

The first source of conservative criticism of the French Revolution lies in the work of Edmund Burke. It would be no exaggeration to say that all conservative histories of the Revolution have embroidered on themes first stated by Burke. Burke died in July 1797, only a few weeks after Babeuf was executed. He may never have heard of Babeuf – I have found no reference to him in Burke's writings. His main text – *Reflections on the Revolution in France* – was written as early as 1790. But the principles which Burke enunciated were to provide the basis for many subsequent critiques of Babeuf.

Firstly, Burke attacked the whole tradition of the Enlightenment, the belief that reason could provide a basis for the reordering and improvement of human society:

> The science of constructing a commonwealth, or renovating it, or reforming it, is, like every other experimental science, not to be taught *à priori* ... Political reason is a computing principle; adding, subtracting, multiplying, and dividing, morally and not metaphysically, or mathematically, true moral denominations.

Babeuf's computation was purely and blatantly mathematical; the equal right of every human being to food, clothing, shelter and a decent life. Burke would undoubtedly have responded with the same scornful hatred as to the 'epidemical fanaticism' of the Anabaptists.

Secondly – and here Burke showed his greatest prescience – he detected even in the relatively moderate developments of 1789–90 a dynamic progression which would lead to the worst consequences. The revolt of the middle classes against the aristocracy could only inspire the revolt of the lower classes against their exploiters. 'As the colonists rise on you, the negroes rise on them.' Soldiers informed of the rights of man would no longer obey their officers. Peasants who had seen the old feudal rights denied would no longer want to pay rent to any owner.

Behind the limited reforms of 1789 Burke saw the spectre of the 'swinish multitude'.[2] This notion that a revolution, even if made in the name of apparently reasonable and moderate principles, will spill over into an upsurge by the poorest and most oppressed, was to become a major weapon in the armoury of conservative thought. With a little licence it could be described as the right-wing obverse face of the theory of permanent revolution.

Yet Burke's two themes contradicted each other. If abstract reasoning is fanatical, contrary to the principles of common sense and natural experience that hold society together, then the frenzied dreamers who pursue it are doomed to remain marginal to society, exercising little or no influence. Yet Burke stressed that the threat from below was all too tangible. His successors have not hesitated to deploy both arguments, arguing that Babeuf was both an irrelevance and a fearsome threat – sometimes on the selfsame page.

Babeuf's contemporary opponents in France added little to the arguments developed by Burke. The royalist Mallet du Pan left France in 1792, but kept himself well-informed of developments in Paris. Writing from Berne at the time of Babeuf's arrest, he described him as a 'wretched revolutionary plagiarist, a gutter hack-writer'. In general Mallet was so hostile to Jacobinism – and he considered the Thermidorians and the Directory to be essentially Jacobins – that he failed to distinguish any specific contribution made by Babeuf. Thus, commenting on the Vendôme trial, he claimed that the jury had been bribed by the Directory itself to ensure acquittals. He was originally confirmed in his prejudices by a false report that Babeuf had been sentenced to only two years in jail; when he found out the truth his indignation was still primarily directed at the fact that over fifty of the accused had been acquitted.[3]

Perhaps the most perceptive conservative thinker of the early nineteenth century was the novelist Balzac. There are only two references to Babeuf in the novels of the *Comédie humaine* cycle; both come in *Une ténébreuse affaire*, and cite participation in Babeuf's conspiracy merely as a token of republican integrity.[4] André Wurmser, however, quoted a remark allegedly made by Balzac, which summed up the Burkean analysis neatly: 'I would gladly accept the Republic; what I don't accept are its social consequences. Babeuf is the inevitable successor of Danton and Robespierre.'[5] (Unfortunately Wurmser did not provide a satisfactory source for this quotation. He attributed it to Alexandre Weil, but it is not in Weil's *Mémoires*. But if Balzac didn't say it, he ought to have done.)

In Britain the name of Babeuf returned to haunt the heirs of Burke. The poet and essayist Robert Southey devoted two substantial articles to the critique of Babeuf. After a brief period of radicalism, Southey had become disillusioned with the French Revolution and with all attempts to improve the human condition; yet he retained some sympathy with the ideas of Owen, and was aware of the dangers posed to the social order by the advance of industrialization.

Southey's first article was an unsigned review of a translation of the French book *Biographie moderne*.[6] Southey focused his attention on Babeuf, who, as he pointed out, was virtually unknown in Britain. The text reviewed was based on the documentation published for the trial, and gave a rounded account of Babeuf, though the picture of the actual trial was confused.

Southey wrote out of general hostility to the Revolution; he believed all such revolutions must end in 'military despotism'; he spared no venom for the *hébertistes* – 'the party of the vilest and most loathsome wretches that disgraced the revolution'. But he gave a certain credit, at least for sincerity, to the *babouvistes:*

> Perhaps the most disinterested and least culpable of all the revolutionists are to be found among the adherents to the constitution of 1793, who were proscribed by the Directory. They employed no artifices to hurry on the overthrow of the monarchy, and they adhered to republicanism when it was a sinking cause. They lived through the worst times of the revolution, because, as they never thrust themselves forward, they never excited the jealousy of any party: but when the reaction had begun, the tendency of which they perceived to be not merely towards monarchy, but towards despotism, sincerity then became in them a sufficient crime, and they suffered as unjustly as the royalists, in whose condemnation they had joined.[7]

Southey recognized the political uniqueness of Babeuf's conspiracy, with its focus on equality; he quoted at length from Maréchal's *Manifesto of the Equals*, attributing it to Babeuf. He gave a hostile and tendentious, but not wholly inaccurate, account of how Babeuf sought to link means and ends: 'he deliberately organized a plan for establishing the maximum of virtue and justice, by turning the poor loose upon the rich, and literally delivering up all France to pillage!' He concluded by drawing a parallel between France and Britain, referring to 'our Héberts and Marats and Chaumettes, who go on inflaming the passions of the ignorant and ferocious part of the community . . . '[8]

Southey returned to the topic of Babeuf nineteen years later, with another unsigned review, this time based on Buonarroti's *History* and the documents seized at the time of Babeuf's arrest.[9] The article was considerably better informed than the previous one and while highly critical gave credit where Southey believed it was due. He commended Buonarroti for his 'disinterestedness', in that he never sought riches for himself, although among a 'host of harpies'.

Southey understood the aims of the conspirators, recognizing clearly that they advocated the 1793 Constitution only 'as a step towards something further'. But he had little patience with their orientation to the most deprived in society:

Of the whole rabble they were sure; that unhappy class, the reproach of society, even more than the disgrace and the nuisance, may be looked upon as ready for any mischief anywhere, wherever the established order of society shall be shaken.[10]

Southey stressed that Babeuf saw private property as the main source of evil in society, and added that 'no government . . . can allow that doctrine to be preached to the mob'. He claimed that

it was only by means of perfect tyranny that perfect freedom could be obtained; and terror and blood were the indispensable means by which the friends of humanity were to make the love of virtue general, and reform the manners of the nation!

Like Burke, he saw that the inherent logic of the Revolution was to arouse a challenge to property amongst the lowest strata of society:

What have the populace, who are the tools by which the agitators seek to bring about their own purposes, whether selfish or vindictive, – what have they to gain by the destruction of royalty, by the overthrow of an established church, by the abolition of primogeniture and the peerage, and of all distinctions in society, if the distinctions of property remain? Is any man fool enough to suppose they are such fools as not to know and to feel that this is the only inequality by which human happiness is affected?[11]

In a passage where he commended Babeuf's character while deploring his ideas, Southey commented that 'Mrs Wollstonecraft said of him, that she had never seen any person who possessed greater abilities, or equal strength of character'. Mary Wollstonecraft had died in 1797, when Southey was 23 years old; this recollection from 34 years later must obviously be subject to doubt, but it is the only basis for the claim that Babeuf and Wollstonecraft met during the latter's time in France; there is no corroboration in the papers of either individual of what would have been a fascinating encounter between nascent socialism and incipient feminism.[12] (Bronterre O'Brien claimed that Wollstonecraft 'knew Babeuf well' but followed the claim with the exact words used by Southey, so it is probable that Southey was his source too, though O'Brien may have known other people who knew Wollstonecraft.)[13]

The liberal interpretation of the French Revolution was first elaborated in the early years of the nineteenth century by French historians who counted among their number some prominent statesmen of the age: Guizot, Thiers, Lamartine. Their aim was to defend the gains of the Revolution, which had given birth to the society they were now striving to make their way within, but to dissociate themselves from any extremism which might evoke emulation. They detested Robespierre and the Jacobins; Babeuf was such an embarrassment that he scarcely got a mention; often they preferred to suspend their narrative at Thermidor. Guizot regurgitated a few facts from Buonarroti and concluded that 'perhaps corrupted or deceived, the Directory had nonetheless protected the peace of a trembling society from the criminal madness of Babeuf.'[14]

Thiers called Babeuf a 'crazy Jacobin' who wanted to repeat the September massacres on a wider scale.[15] Lamartine's influential *Histoire des Girondins* (1847) ended at Thermidor and made no mention of Babeuf.

The one really insightful history of the Revolution produced by the liberal tradition came from Jules Michelet. Michelet's monumental history was based on massive archival research; if at times he gave his imagination too free a rein, it was the necessary price for his intense identification with the revolutionary process, an identification that enabled him to grasp its dynamic in a vivid and concrete manner. Michelet was the first liberal to understand the profound originality and importance of Babeuf.

Michelet's understanding of Babeuf was illuminated by the links he made with the history of the nineteenth century, and in his last years with the experience of the Paris Commune. He wrote of himself: 'Born under the Terror of Babeuf, I see before my death that of the International.'[16]

Quoting Desmoulins, Michelet used a striking image to render the new currents that emerged in 1793: 'Beyond Marat . . . we must say what the old geographers put on their maps for lands that had not been visited: *terra incognita* [unknown land]. It is this *terra incognita* which begins to appear.' Michelet identified this unknown territory with the revolutionary mysticism of Chalier in Lyons, with Jacques Roux and the *enragés* . . . and with Babeuf. He even placed the spectre of Babeuf in the mind of Danton, citing a speech in which he contrasted equality of rights and happiness with 'the impossible equality of possessions'.[17]

Michelet was often inaccurate about Babeuf's life, and knew nothing of his intellectual development; he denied the very existence of the conspiracy, believing it to be pure fantasy on Babeuf's part.[18] But, more clearly than any of his contemporaries, Michelet seemed aware that Babeuf had a powerful and distinctive presence in the revolutionary process.

Michelet's intuitive grasp of historical processes was strengthened by the way that he saw himself as personally engaged in the course of events. His passionate awareness of Babeuf derived partly from circumstances related in his autobiography. Before Michelet's birth, when Babeuf was in prison awaiting trial at Vendôme, a supporter of Babeuf brought his father, a printer, a seditious document to print. One morning a policeman visited the Michelet household; the *babouviste* document was on the table. But Michelet *père* led him into the printshop, while his pregnant wife, white with terror, threw the incriminating document onto the fire. Michelet attributed to this episode the fact that his elder brother was stillborn. Behind the reasoning and the documentation Michelet saw Babeuf as the man who killed his big brother.[19]

To trace the place of Babeuf in the socialist tradition it is necessary to begin with his old comrade-in-arms Buonarroti, whose *Babeuf's Conspiracy for Equality* was first published in 1828. Buonarroti was the one leader of the conspiracy who had remained totally committed to the aims of the movement. Imprisoned at Cherbourg, he was then sent to the island of Oléron near La Rochelle. There he was freed under police supervision, and worked as a school-teacher. Later he went to southeast

France, then Geneva, earning his living as a music teacher. He returned to Paris after the 1830 revolution. All the time he maintained political links, being involved in various republican organizations, often working within the framework of freemasonry. In his last years he knew many of the new generation of the left: Cabet, Blanqui, Mazzini and Blanc. He was involved in the Society for the Rights of Man in the early 1830s, alongside Albert Laponneraye, author of a Robespierrist history of the French Revolution, and J.-R.-T.-G. Kersausie, who organized the street-fighting in the working-class rising in Paris in June 1848.[20]

Buonarroti initially opposed the Lyons rising of 1834, one of the first major upsurges of the French working class, but he participated in the defence of those victimized after it.[21] He died in 1837. Gioacchino Prati, who knew him as an old man, described him as: 'a man of seventy, with silver hair floating over his most prepossessing countenance, with a Prometheus-like energy, bidding defiance to the powers of the earth, arousing all far and near to break the chains of despotism.'[22] In his later years he extended his political horizons, showing sympathy for Robert Owen and ideas for progressive taxation, but he always remained true to his basic communist commitment.[23]

Buonarroti thus acted as an important means of continuity between the *babouvistes* and the emerging socialism of the early nineteenth century. He always took the conspiracy as a reference point for his values. In a letter to Emile Babeuf in 1828 he wrote: 'Already your illustrious father had seen the true cause of the ills of society and had the good fortune to live at a time when it was still possible to apply promptly a radical cure . . . '[24] thus implying that in some sense 1828 was further from the desired goal than 1796 had been. In the preface to *Babeuf's Conspiracy*, Buonarroti stated that, after long consideration, he was convinced that 'this equality which they cherished is the only institution capable of reconciling all true needs, of guiding useful passions and controlling dangerous passions, and of giving society a free, happy, peaceful and lasting form.'[25]

Buonarroti's work was not just an account of the conspiracy; in many ways it initiated some of the themes that were to be central to the left-wing historiography of the Revolution over the following century. He stressed the role of the popular masses, gave Robespierre his rightful place as a key figure of the Revolution, and showed the Thermidorian reaction as a major victory for the forces of bourgeois conservatism. It helped to shape the whole radical perception of the Revolution.

Having left writing his history for thirty years after the defeat of the conspiracy, Buonarroti felt able to tell most of the truth. Many of those who had been involved were dead; the pretence that there had been no conspiracy could be dropped. Buonarroti concealed the names of surviving conspirators behind rather transparent anagrams which would give little trouble to the average crossword-puzzle *aficionado;* doubtless he did not have too much respect for the intelligence of police agents. He said little about the conspiracy's finances, or the reasons for the non-arrest of Debon and Maréchal.[26] Buonarroti had a number of differences from Babeuf; he did not share Babeuf's atheism, nor his belief in the equality of women, and these positions may be reflected in the account he gave of the conspirators' views. His own long experience of activity in secret societies – forced by the conditions of repression under Napoleon and the Restoration – may have led him to stress the clandestine aspects of the conspiracy, and underplay its public agitation.

None the less, Buonarroti gave a remarkable account of the conspiracy, setting out both its organizational practice and its socialist aims. His account (like Trotsky's *History of the Russian Revolution*) was simultaneously a personal memoir and a carefully documented history, the overall accuracy of which is unimpeachable.[27] It was and remains the starting-point for any serious study of Babeuf.

It also provided the foundation for certain confusions which have bedevilled the history of *babouvisme* ever since. No-one can doubt Buonarroti's dedication to the memory of Babeuf, but his true hero was Robespierre. Bronterre O'Brien, who knew Buonarroti as an old man, recalled:

> I have seen that brave and venerable old man at the advanced age of 78 shed tears like a child at the very mention of Robespierre's name; and the slightest aspersion thrown on his memory would fire the old man with an indignation such as no possible injury to himself could make him feel.[28]

Buonarroti wrote a short biographical sketch of Robespierre (first published in 1837) comparing him to Moses, Jesus and Mahomet as one of the rare men whose genius changes the state of the world.[29] Babeuf's attitude to Robespierre was far more complex (see Chapters 3 and 4), and though his admiration was genuine enough, it is scarcely possible to imagine him coming out with such statements.

Buonarroti made no attempt to conceal the socialist aims of the conspiracy; he gave a vivid account of the secret directory's plans for a future society based on equality. But in dealing with Robespierre he fudged the question of private property. He made it quite clear that the conspirators did not regard the 1793 Constitution as perfect, and that its 'positive defect' lay in the defence of the right of property. But in attempting to preserve Robespierre's reputation, he insisted on the *Declaration of the Rights of Man and the Citizen* (see Chapter 4). To a careful reader it is clear that there was a difference between Robespierre and Babeuf on the question of property, but Buonarroti contrived to suggest that the divergence was only a secondary one.

Thus Buonarroti restored Babeuf to his rightful place in the history of the French Revolution. But Buonarroti's own attachment to Robespierre meant that he failed to draw a clear line between Jacobinism and socialism (although by the 1840s it became more common to make a dissociation of Robespierre and Babeuf).[30] This was not simply a historical question. In February 1848 the leaders of the Paris working class accepted alliance with the radical wing of the bourgeoisie. In June 1848 the Paris working class paid the price for that trust in massacre and deportation. This is not to say that if Buonarroti had written a different book the defeat could have been avoided. It was a lesson to be learnt in practice. Only after that defeat could Babeuf's true originality begin to become apparent.

Buonarroti had put Babeuf on the map, yet his influence on the French socialist left before 1848 was relatively slight. The reason for this must be found in the weakness of the socialist tradition. Although the working class itself was steadily growing stronger, the radical current had taken such a hammering from the repression of Napoleon and the restored Bourbons that there had been a retreat from the politics of the 1790s. The strength of Babeuf was his concern for the unity of theory and practice, for the linking of immediate struggle and long-term objectives. In that sense he had already gone beyond utopianism; French socialism between 1815 and 1848 was characterized by a retreat to utopianism.

The central weakness of socialists in this period was the question of agency. They were experts at depicting the socialist goal, but had little notion of how to get there. Blanqui believed small groups of dedicated men could act on behalf of the working class; Fourier advertised for a millionaire to finance his socialist plans and waited twenty years in vain for him. (The story may be apocryphal, but it symbolizes Fourier's politics perfectly.) The two are opposite faces of the same coin.

The French Revolution was an important reference point for the socialists of the utopian period, and several of them made important contributions to the historiography of the Revolution. In general Babeuf got little attention from them. One reason for this may be the way in which Buonarroti had conflated Babeuf with Robespierre. For the pro-Jacobins Babeuf was seen as a disciple of Robespierre with little original significance; for the anti-Jacobins his socialism was contaminated with complicity with Robespierre.

Cabet vehemently denied Babeuf's originality and stressed the weak base and recklessness of the conspiracy; above all, he insisted that socialism could not be established by minority violence but only by 'the power of public opinion' (though conceding that Babeuf himself had recognized this).[31] It has been claimed that his motivation was personal jealousy,[32] but he was obviously also concerned to establish the distinctiveness of his own school of socialism.

Buchez and Roux, representatives of Christian socialism, made an enormous contribution to revolutionary historiography with their 40-volume collection of documents, used as a source book by most nineteenth-century historians of the Revolution. But their account of Babeuf added little to the understanding of his place in history; it was almost completely derivative of Buonarroti, and while not unsympathetic, presented Babeuf as a follower of Hébert, though it made it clear that the aim of the conspirators was a society based on the 'community of goods and work'.[33]

Louis Blanc was a convinced pro-Jacobin and admirer of Robespierre. His twelve-volume *History of the French Revolution* (1847–62) ended in 1795, making no mention of Babeuf. Proudhon conceded that Babeuf was brave and honest, but denied any value to his ideas, saying that they were merely a hypothesis and not a system.[34]

Auguste Blanqui is often seen as a direct disciple of Babeuf and Buonarroti. The question is in fact rather more complex. Blanqui probably had some contact with Buonarroti, but he scarcely mentioned Babeuf in his writings.[35] The Blanquists had little sympathy with Robespierre and saw themselves rather as the heirs of Hébert;[36] in an interview with

The Times Blanqui explicitly rejected the idea that he was a disciple of Babeuf.[37] Rather than being a disciple of *babouvisme*, Blanqui developed methods that were in many ways a regression from it. Babeuf's attempted mass agitation contrasted with Blanqui's attempted insurrection of 1839, made with a few hundred men not properly informed in advance.

Among the workers of Paris the memory of Babeuf remained. Heinrich Heine, visiting in 1840 workrooms in the Faubourg Saint-Marceau (Juste Moroy's old territory),

> there discovered what works were read among the workmen who are the most vigorous portion of the lower class. There I found, for instance, several new editions of the speeches of old Robespierre, also Marat's pamphlets in two-sous form, the 'History of the Revolution' by Cabet, the venomous libels of Cormenin, Baboeuf's Teachings, and Conspiracy of Buonarroti – writings which smell of blood . . . [38]

Heine's observations support Georges Duveau's claim that for Paris workers in the 1840s, Robespierre and Babeuf 'reappeared in the republican pantheon as demigods of fraternity'; the differences between them were unknown or ignored.[39]

It was not only in France that Babeuf was to be remembered with the slow rise of the working-class movement. The first account of the conspiracy in English after Southey's first article came in Maria Aletta Hulshoff's *Peace-Republicans' Manual*, published in New York in 1817. The author was a Dutch woman who had fled from Napoleon; as her title suggests, her politics were republican and pacifist, and she had little inkling of anything distinctively socialist about the conspiracy, described as 'this great enterprise to restore the French People to the enjoyment of their rights.'[40] But she did make some of the documents of the conspiracy available in English.

With the rise of Chartism, Babeuf again appeared on the scene in Britain. In 1836 Bronterre O'Brien, a leading Chartist, translated Buonarroti's *History of Babeuf's Conspiracy for Equality*. It had a rapid success, with some fifty thousand copies being sold. But O'Brien was far from being an uncritical supporter of Babeuf's doctrine. His real hero was Robespierre. His two books on Robespierre both effusively praised their subject;[41] neither mentioned Babeuf, apart from a few passing references to Buonarroti's book. In his translation of Buonarroti, O'Brien added

THE SPECTRE OF BABEUF 105

footnotes to clarify his own position in relation to Babeuf. He insisted that Robespierre had represented the class interests of the workers:

> Under Robespierre the workpeople had power. The Government was in the hands of their friends, and the Conventional Decrees were, in a greater or lesser decree [*sic*], all favourable to them; but when the Usurers and Aristocrats accomplished the destruction of Robespierre, the Government, as a matter of course (for this was the object sought), passed into the hands of the Bourgeoisie, or middle classes.[42]

O'Brien went much further than Buonarroti in aligning himself with Robespierre and against Babeuf. He defended the position on property expressed in the 1793 Constitution, and saw Robespierre's *Declaration* (with some justice) as a defence of property rather than an attack on it:

> The National Convention had no right to say to Frenchmen – you must all club your means and resources, you must live in community, and work and enjoy on equal terms. That would be to subject the whole to the opinions of a sect; and hence do I differ from Babeuf and Buonarroti, in preferring Robespierre's Declaration in favour of private property to their proscription of the institution. If people choose to renounce private property, and live in community, they have a right to do so; but they have no right to compel others to the same course. The system of community must, as I observed before, be the spontaneous growth of wisdom.[43]

On O'Brien's plan, the rich could choose to keep their property while the poor could choose to share their poverty between them. O'Brien can scarcely be seen as a follower of Babeuf; to agree with Babeuf except about property is like agreeing with Newton – except about gravitation. Mathiez's claim that English and French socialism both derived from *babouvisme*, the English tradition via O'Brien, was untenable.[44]

The ideas of Babeuf, as presented by O'Brien, became assimilated into the Chartist movement. At the Festival of Nations held in London in 1845, George Julian Harney spoke in praise of Robespierre, before invoking Babeuf as one of his successors who had advocated 'a veritable republic . . . in which, private property and money, the foundation and root of all wrong and evil, should cease to be'. He was greeted with 'great cheering'.[45]

In the long term, the discussion of Babeuf in Germany was to prove more influential. The Vendôme trial was reported in Germany in the

Hamburg journal *Minerva*,[46] and interest in the French Revolution and French socialism grew among the post-Hegelian German left in the 1830s and 1840s. But as Heinrich Heine, who did much to make Germans aware of French social and intellectual life, pointed out, since Germany was far more backward than France in social development, his compatriots tended to translate concrete French experiences into intellectual abstractions.[47]

The first German writer to attempt a serious critique of Babeuf was Lorenz von Stein, a conservative hostile to the very idea of socialism. Stein saw Babeuf as in the tradition of Münzer and the Anabaptists, and called him a 'fanatical priest of a blind emotional life'. However, Stein saw clearly the distinction between Babeuf's egalitarianism and Jacobinism, and indeed criticized the *babouvistes* for using the 1793 Constitution as a 'pretext'.[48]

Wilhelm Weitling, a leading figure in the League of the Just (forerunner of the Communist League for which Marx and Engels wrote the *Manifesto*) had been influenced by Buonarroti. But the first German socialist to attempt an extended examination of the ideas of Babeuf was Moses Hess, who converted Engels to communism in 1842 and was later to be associated with the 'true socialists' criticized by Marx and Engels in the *Communist Manifesto*. In collaboration with Marx and Engels, Hess had planned to translate Buonarroti's *History* into German. This plan fell through, but Hess set out to refute Stein in an essay called 'Socialism and Communism'.

Hess was prone to the Germanic fault of translating French socialism into the language of German idealism; he was fond of establishing rather implausible parallels, such as Hegel and Fourier. In this essay he tried to make such a parallel between Fichte, the founder of German atheism and Babeuf, the founder of French communism. (Fichte's abstruse philosophy was an extreme idealism; politically he advocated a closed authoritarian state; it is hard to imagine what Babeuf would have made of the comparison.) His aim was to establish the link between atheism and communism (the Polish philosopher Edward Dembowski made a similar parallel in 1845).[49] Hess examined Babeuf's stress on equality, and made the important point that freedom and equality were not antitheses but parts of a higher unity.

But Hess went on to argue that Babeuf's socialism was essentially ascetic, a false accusation (see Chapter 10) with a long history: 'The equality which Babeuf had in mind was therefore a *sans-culotte* equality, an equality of poverty. Wealth, luxury, arts and sciences were to be abolished, the cities to be destroyed; Rousseau's state of nature was the ghost that then haunted their minds.'[50]

It was in this intellectual context that Marx confronted Babeuf. There are a handful of passing references to Babeuf in the works of Marx and Engels – future research might have been better served if there had been none, for the tendency of later Marxists to regard them as scripture led to their being invested with far more importance than they deserve.

In Section I of the *Communist Manifesto* Marx and Engels set out a dialectical account of the historical role of the bourgeoisie that they had developed over the previous few years. The bourgeoisie was seen as simultaneously a force for liberation and the agent of a new oppression. This framework allowed the French Revolution to be seen (as Cabet had seen it)[51] as a bourgeois revolution, a necessary stage in the emancipation of humanity, but one which left the bourgeoisie firmly in power. Hence the task for socialists was not to imitate the French Revolution (as Bronterre O'Brien believed) or to push it to its conclusion (as the French Jacobin Socialists believed). Rather, Marx took up the insight that Maréchal had glimpsed; the French Revolution must be followed by another, greater revolution which would be the last.

Having made the theoretical separation of bourgeois and proletarian revolutions, Marx was faced with the problem of how they were articulated in practice, perceiving that in most bourgeois revolutions there was the emergence of an embryonic proletarian revolution. It was in this context that Marx and Engels made their few passing references to Babeuf. It should be remembered that much of the relevant material was not easily available; it is doubtful if Marx and Engels ever knew more of Babeuf than was contained in Buonarroti's history and the limited coverage in Buchez and Roux.

In *The Holy Family* (1844) Marx and Engels challenged the notion that ideas alone could achieve any change in the world; but they accepted that the French Revolution produced ideas that pointed beyond itself:

> The revolutionary movement which began in 1789 in the *Cercle social*, which in the middle of its course had as its chief representatives *Leclerc* and *Roux* and which finally with *Babeuf*'s conspiracy was temporarily defeated, gave rise to the *communist* idea which *Babeuf*'s friend *Buonarroti*

re-introduced in France after the Revolution of 1830. This idea, consistently developed, is *the idea of the new world order*.[52]

This established a clear line of communist thought, quite independent
of Jacobinism, running from the *enragés* to Babeuf, and made this the
source of modern communism.

The argument was taken a stage further in the *Communist Manifesto*.
Babeuf was named in the section on the utopian socialists, but it was
made clear that he did not belong to this category: 'We do not here refer
to that literature which, in every great modern revolution, has always
given voice to the demands of the proletariat, such as the writings of
Babeuf and others.'[53] Marx's critique of the Utopians was based on the
question of agency; they did not identify the social force that would
turn their visions into reality. Babeuf was exempted from this charge,
since he was seen as the voice of the proletariat (though in Marx's first
draft Babeuf was listed as a utopian after Fourier and Saint-Simon).[54]
Marx and Engels added that the first attempted risings of the proletariat
necessarily failed because of objective conditions, and that therefore:
'the revolutionary literature that accompanied these first movements
of the proletariat had necessarily a reactionary character. It inculcated
universal asceticism and social levelling in its crudest form (*eine rohe
Gleichmacherei*).'[55] 'Reactionary' here seems to mean 'backward-looking'
rather than 'counter-revolutionary'. In this and the charge of asceticism
Marx and Engels were following the position adopted by Hess; the only
explanation can be ignorance of the key texts.

Many years later, in *Anti-Dühring*, Engels took up the same argument about the embryonic proletarian revolution:

> From its origin the bourgeoisie was saddled with its antithesis: capital-
> ists cannot exist without wage-workers . . . in every great bourgeois
> movement there were independent outbursts of that class which was the
> forerunner, more or less developed, of the modern proletariat.[56]

The Anabaptists, the Levellers and Babeuf were cited as the prime examples. In one of the preliminary notes to *Anti-Dühring* not included in
the final text, Engels referred in passing to Babeuf's 'insane . . . attempt
to jump from the Directorate immediately into communism'.[57] This was
wholly consistent with the Marxist position that history has an objective
pattern of development which cannot be overcome by pure acts of will.

THE SPECTRE OF BABEUF   109

'Insane', however, was a little uncharitable. Even if Babeuf's attempt was doomed to failure, it none the less, on Engels' own testimony, contributed to the movement which produced modern communism.

One of the most authoritative accounts of Marx's thought is Hal Draper's *Karl Marx's Theory of Revolution*. But on the question of Babeuf, Draper is less than reliable. He repeatedly linked Babeuf to the Blanquist tradition, and referred to 'the Babouvist-Jacobin tradition, newly represented by the Blanquists, later by Bakunin'.[58] Draper's central concern was to rescue Marx from Stalinist misinterpretation and to attack the whole tradition of 'socialism-from-above', as he did in his magnificent pamphlet 'The Two Souls of Socialism'.[59] But his undoubted erudition with respect to Marx did not extend to Babeuf, of whom he adopted a second-hand evaluation, and whose theory of organization he quite unfairly lumped together with that of Blanqui and Bakunin, failing to see that in many ways Babeuf was very much a part of the 'socialism-from-below' tradition (see Chapter 11).

7

1848 and After

The revolution of 1848 redrew the map of French politics. The working class, first incorporated, then betrayed and massacred by its republican bourgeois allies, took its first steps towards political and organizational independence. At the same time it put socialism at the centre of the fears of the French bourgeoisie. (In 1851 Paris shops were selling engravings of Vernet's popular *Two Scourges of the Nineteenth century, Socialism and Cholera*.)[1] Over the succeeding fifty years the heritage of Babeuf was to be repeatedly reassessed.

The first historian to take up the question was Edouard Fleury, brother of Champfleury, the pioneer of the realist novel. In his *Baboeuf and Socialism in 1796*,[2] a book widely promoted by the conservative press,[3] Fleury stressed the parallels between the communists of 1796 and those of 1848: both advocated plunder and violence, both were hypocrites. Fleury exploited the well-worn rhetoric of counter-revolution; the *babouvistes* were 'wild beasts enticed by the smell of blood', while the *babouviste* women wished to imitate the 'shrews of Versailles' and the *tricoteuses*.[4]

But in this first book-length study of Babeuf since Buonarroti, Fleury did add some useful insights. As a local historian he drew on valuable archive material. He saw Babeuf's originality in the fact that he had moved beyond the utopianism of Thomas More and Rousseau and brought the 'ethereal heights of speculation' down to the level of action and struggle. He also drew out the 'apparently incredible' fact that Babeuf had been 'constantly at war with the Jacobins', though arguing that the antagonism between Robespierre and Babeuf expressed a battle for power rather than one of principle. While accusing Babeuf of manipulation, he recognized the influence exercised by the *babouviste* fly-posting campaign. He was the first to point to the significance of

Babeuf's activity in 1793, and while accusing Babeuf of fanaticism, conceded that he had died with 'great courage'.[5]

The events of 1848 also provoked a brief encounter between Babeuf and Alexis de Tocqueville, undoubtedly one of the most acute conservative minds of his age. He observed the apparently irresistible trend towards democracy and equality with regret, since he believed in the 'perennial incompetence of the masses'.[6] He echoed Babeuf from the other side of the barricade in seeing the question of property as central; 'the great battle-field will be property', he wrote in 1847.[7] His pathological hatred of socialism was revealed in a passage where he described his first sight of Blanqui: 'sick, evil, unclean appearance . . . he looked as if he had lived in a sewer and had just emerged from it'.[8]

Tocqueville's major study, *The Ancien Regime and the Revolution* (1856), was concerned with the origins of the Revolution, and did not refer to Babeuf. But in 1848 he was elected to the National Assembly, and in September intervened in a heated five-day debate about the right to work. Ledru-Rollin, a moderate socialist who advocated co-operatives, farmers' loan banks and the nationalization of the railways, supported with some of his associates an amendment to the draft constitution to include the principle of the right to work – something that had been a major demand of the Paris workers and unemployed in the course of the year. Tocqueville spoke against the amendment, which was defeated. Tocqueville was very much a capitalist conservative; in his speech he argued that the *ancien régime* had believed in what modern conservatives would call a 'nanny-state' – it had considered its subjects to be 'feeble beings who must always be held by the hand lest they fall or hurt themselves'. The Revolution of 1789, he claimed, had defended the principle of individual property and hence the free market; thus the socialists who argued that the state had a responsibility towards the unemployed were actually reactionaries who defended the values of the *ancien régime*.

In order to discredit socialism, he evoked the memory of 'Baboeuf, that grand-father of all modern socialists', quoting from Buonarroti to the effect that 'the abolition of individual property and the establishment of the great national community was the final aim of all his activities'. It was a neat debating point, but it did not impress the deputies overmuch; one heckled him, shouting out 'there are no *babovistes [sic]* here'. In seeing Babeuf not so much as the continuation of the Revolution of 1789 but rather as its negation, Tocqueville had grasped the specificity and originality of Babeuf's socialism.[9]

Subsequent conservative thinkers added little to Fleury and Tocqueville, and it would be tedious to follow them in any detail; Hippolyte Taine will serve as a typical representative. Taine was a distinguished philosopher and literary critic whose materialist sympathies had made him enemies on the left; but he was so horrified by the Paris Commune of 1871 that he abandoned his other work and devoted his last two decades to a massive study of the Revolution, *The Origins of Contemporary France*. Following Burke, Taine saw the roots of the Revolution in what he called the 'classical spirit', an abstract reason attempting to mould the world in accordance with its principles. He saw the Revolution as embarking on a slippery slope that would lead to socialism – and as result he tended to use the term 'socialist' in indiscriminate fashion, applying it to many individuals and tendencies in the Revolution.

Taine's knowledge of Babeuf was mainly second-hand – he was greatly indebted to Fleury – and he was not even consistent in the spelling of his name. His main aim was to discredit Babeuf's character, hence he made much of Babeuf's conviction for forgery, describing him as:

> carrying along the pavements of Paris his frustrated ambitions and his empty pockets, in company with fallen rogues who, if they do not climb back on to the throne by means of a new massacre, will forever drag their worn shoes in the streets . . . selling a snuff-box, their last asset, to buy their morning drink of spirits.

While at times Taine tried to distinguish between moderate and radical currents in the Revolution, his hatred of the Revolution was so strong that it often made him incapable of distinguishing different tendencies within it. He could not see any clear distinction between Babeuf and the Directory – they were all Jacobins – and he was at a loss to understand why the repression was exercised against them. Following Mallet du Pan, he argued that the Directory saw the *babouvistes* as its 'lost children' which it might need at some point, and hence alleged that great leniency was shown to Babeuf and his associates; for Taine, two executions were not enough.[10]

A major step forward in the understanding of Babeuf was taken in 1884 with the publication of Victor Advielle's *History of Gracchus Babeuf and Babouvism.* Advielle was an unlikely contributor to Babeuf studies. He was not a professional historian; he served as a public official under the Second Empire and the Third Republic, and between 1874 and his retirement in 1896 worked in the Finance Ministry. He published a number of carefully documented studies of various French regions and towns. His main interest seems to have been local history, and as a native of Arras he may have been attracted to the study of Babeuf because of his connections with northeastern France. Advielle had no political involvement, and no particular knowledge of the history of socialism – obviously a barrier to his understanding of Babeuf's significance. His book was published at his own expense, and only a few hundred copies were printed.

Such a work might seem destined for total obscurity; but it remains a major point of reference in the history of Babeuf scholarship. In the first volume Advielle made an honest and thorough attempt to establish Babeuf's biography; in the second he published, for the first time, Babeuf's final speech at the Vendôme trial and an incomplete version of the correspondence with Dubois de Fosseux. At last the life and ideas of Babeuf before 1789 were rescued from the realm of myth and given a sound factual basis.

In working on his study, Advielle was able to consult and quote extensively from the collection of documents made by a wealthy collector, Pochet-Deroche. This collection was sold by auction in 1883 and later dispersed, many documents subsequently being acquired by the Marx-Engels Institute in Russia. Until the publication of Dommanget's *Pages choisies* in 1935 it remained the most important collection of Babeuf's writings.

Unfortunately, Advielle's analysis was not up to the standards of his scholarship. He insisted that his work was 'neither an apology nor a defence', though he did express anger at the picture of Babeuf given by Taine, and called his book a 'crushing refutation' of Taine's 'atrocious lines'.[11] But despite his good intentions, Advielle's account reduced Babeuf's socialism to an anodyne moralism. He claimed that Babeuf's ideas could be summed up by the essentially Christian teachings 'Love one another' and 'Do not do unto others what you would not wish them to do unto you'.[12]

Advielle agreed with Babeuf's prophecy of the incompleteness of the revolutionary process: 'The Revolution will not have benefited the true people, the people of the working-class districts and the people of the countryside.'[13] While accepting that Babeuf's central theme was equality, Advielle claimed to give the 'true meaning' to the word, and thus catastrophically diluted the revolutionary content of Babeuf's ideas:

> This word *Equality*, which frightens so many people, is in reality no more than a cry of the human conscience, instinctive and implacable, rising, like a cry of distress, from the lower layers of society, where everything is lacking, to the upper layers, where everything is in abundance . . . With Babeuf, we simply ask that there should be work and bread for all, that everyone should live decently, and that we should see fewer scandalous fortunes above, and fewer rags below.[14]

He insisted that absolute equality was 'absolutely impossible' and identified Babeuf's politics with better welfare provision for the old, sick and unemployed.[15] He had provided a foundation on which others could build, but to rescue Babeuf from this humanitarian co-option would need historians more closely related to the class struggle.

Yet to rescue the originality of Babeuf meant challenging not only the humanitarianism of an Advielle, but the whole republican tradition which stressed the unity of the revolutionary heritage, and which was to be an important influence on the historiography of the Revolution. This was encapsulated in a famous phrase of Clemenceau's. In 1891 a play by Victorien Sardou entitled *Thermidor* was staged at the Comédie Française. It depicted Robespierre as a villain and saw the Thermidorian reaction as a happy liberation from terror and bloodshed. Following disturbances in the theatre, the Minister of the Interior banned the play. In a heated parliamentary debate on the question, Clemenceau defended the ban, proclaiming 'The French Revolution is a *bloc*,' that is, there could be no separating out of more and less acceptable elements within it.[16] No-one could better symbolize this indivisibility of the Revolution than Clemenceau, who began his political career admiring Blanqui and ended it smashing a miners' strike and serving as prime minister in World War I. The myth of the Revolution as a *bloc* functioned as an encouragement to class collaboration; it also served to suppress the examination of the specific and unique role of Babeuf.

The rise of Marxism and the growth of the French working-class movement naturally led to deeper interest in Babeuf. During the Commune, Victor Simond and Prosper-Olivier Lissagaray revived the name of Babeuf's *Tribun du peuple*. But the most important advance came at the turn of the century with the publication of Jean Jaurès' *Socialist History* (1900–8). This was an innovative venture in both form and content. Constructed as an attempt to re-tell the history of France since 1789 in a way relevant to the modern labour movement, it was based on collective work, with representatives of various currents of French socialism being involved. The eclectic approach was symbolized by the cover of Volume One, which was decorated with the faces of Babeuf, Saint-Simon, Fourier, Marx, Blanc, Proudhon and Blanqui. Jaurès was not a professional historian, but an active socialist politician, and is said to have written parts of his work in the National Assembly during parliamentary debates[17] (presumably hoping to avoid intellectual distractions).

Jaurès stood on the right wing of pre-1914 French socialism (which would put him right off the left of the spectrum of any modern social-democratic party). As against the more rigorous (though often dogmatic and sectarian) Marxism of Jules Guesde and Marx's son-in-law Paul Lafargue, Jaurès insisted that socialism should not be counterposed to the republican tradition, but rather seen as flowing out of it (thus providing a left version of Clemenceau's *bloc*). In a speech in 1890 he declared:

> The French Revolution contains the whole of socialism . . . there is in France, despite appearances to the contrary, an immense socialist party, which is the party of the Revolution, and since socialism was contained from the outset within the republican idea, the most unconditional socialists work against themselves when they isolate themselves from the great republican party.[18]

In keeping with this attempt to reconcile socialism and republicanism, Jaurès claimed that his interpretation of history was 'both materialist with Marx and mystical with Michelet'.[19] While Jaurès examined the emergence of a working class during the French Revolution – what he called 'a revolution within the Revolution'[20] – he argued that the workers could have had no separate class interest in this period:

> even if they had had a clear class consciousness, even if they had formed a working-class Third Estate quite distinct from the bourgeois Third Estate, the proletarians would, in their own interest, have marched with the revolutionary bourgeoisie.[21]

Although he had no specialized knowledge of Babeuf, Jaurès was naturally drawn to him as a figure who represented the emergence of socialism in the Revolution. But while Jaurès greatly admired Babeuf and presented a very positive picture of him, he was at pains to play down the originality of *babouvisme:* 'The communism of Babeuf and his few disciples was only a sublime convulsion, the last spasm of the revolutionary crisis before the calm of the Consulate and the first Empire.'[22] When he commended Babeuf's politics, Jaurès often slanted them towards his own political views. Jaurès quoted with great approval Babeuf's letter to his wife from Paris in 1789, but all Jaurès' emphasis went on Babeuf's hatred of violence, transforming him virtually into a pacifist, rather than bringing out his clear grasp of the roots of violence in oppression.[23] Discussing Babeuf's tactics in 1791, Jaurès praised his 'admirable opportunism' for recognizing that communism could not yet be openly advocated: 'Through him communism, still too weak to take over the Revolution, to provoke and defy the wrath of the bourgeoisie, tries to slide within democracy in motion.'[24] Behind these words undoubtedly lay a defence of his own political practice against the more principled Guesde.

Jaurès did not himself write the volume dealing with Babeuf's conspiracy; he entrusted this to Gabriel Deville. Deville in his earlier years had been a supporter of Blanqui, then of Guesde, and had suffered imprisonment for illegal activity. But he became a supporter of Jaurès before leaving the Socialist Party to become a professional diplomat. He had already published a short book on Babeuf, in which he stressed the premature nature of the conspiracy (it was translated into German by Eduard Bernstein, the founder of revisionist socialism, who added a postface in which he used Babeuf's support for the 1793 Constitution as an argument to defend socialist use of bourgeois democracy).[25] When Deville dealt with Babeuf in the context of the post-Thermidorian regime, he drew political lessons that fitted his own rightward evolution.

Thus he commended Babeuf's defence of the 1793 Constitution in Number 34 of the *Tribun du peuple*, and argued that its political spirit could serve as a model since it proved that in France 'defence of the republican form is the true socialist tradition'. He gave great importance to the (in fact very limited) collaboration with Amar and friends, saying that Babeuf had 'agreed to collaborate with the ideas and men of bourgeois democracy'.[26]

It was not only socialists who were looking with interest at Babeuf. One of the most important histories of the Revolution in this period came from the Russian anarchist Kropotkin. Kropotkin was one of the first to stress the role of the common people in the Revolution; indeed, he was a pioneer of what has now become known as 'history from below'. And he had great influence on a whole generation of socialists. Despite their political differences, Lenin praised Kropotkin's history: 'He really understood and demonstrated the role of the people in that bourgeois revolution', while Trotsky is said to have preferred Kropotkin's history to Jaurès'.[27]

Kropotkin was an active revolutionary whose research was disrupted by the fact that he was liable to arrest on French soil. What Jaurès had seen as Babeuf's strengths, Kropotkin saw as his failures. He used the word 'opportunism' as an indictment, not a compliment, and picked up critically Jaurès' remark that Babeuf 'sought to shuffle communism into democracy'. (The quotation was not exact in the French.)[28] In fact, Kropotkin, by greatly overstating the conspiratorial theme in Babeuf and understating everything else, sought to make Babeuf the source of the most authoritarian trends in modern socialism:

> Altogether Babeuf's conception of communism was so narrow, so unreal, that he thought it possible to reach communism by the action of a few individuals who were to get the Government into their hands by means of the conspiracy of a secret society. He went so far as to be ready to put his faith in one single person, provided this person had a will strong enough to introduce communism, and thus save the world! A sad illusion, which paved the way for Bonaparte and, continuing to be cherished by a great number of socialists during the whole of the nineteenth century, gave us Caesarism – the faith in a Napoleon or a Disraeli – the faith in a saviour which still persists even to this day.[29]

Kropotkin, while not denying Babeuf's significance, was far more sympathetic to the *enragés*. The *enragés* had some pertinent criticisms of Robespierre, but they had neither programme nor coherent organization; Kropotkin recognized their affinity with the anarchist tradition.

Guesde and his ally Lafargue also rejected Jaurès' use of the French Revolution, claiming, rather excessively, that the Revolution had been a purely bourgeois affair and little more than a swindle for the working class. Yet Guesde, too, saw Babeuf as a point of reference; in the

National Assembly in 1896 a conservative declared that modern socialists were the heirs of Babeuf; Guesde responded with pride: 'We accept
his patronage.'[30] Indeed the whole Socialist Party honoured the name
of Babeuf; when the Party Congress was held at his birth-place, Saint-
Quentin, in 1911, there was a special tribute to the great revolutionary;
a demonstration of over a thousand people attended a rally chaired by
Jaurès and addressed by Albert Thomas.[31]

The only problem was that different people drew quite different lessons. Thomas, a Socialist minister during World War I and later a key
bureaucrat in the International Labour Organization, had begun his
career by editing a book of selected writings by Babeuf. Thomas's typically reformist approach diluted the content of Babeuf's work; in his
preface he claimed that Babeuf's specific ideas were irrelevant to an
industrialized society, but that his ideas on natural right – basically that
human beings are born equal – still had 'real force'.[32] But the reformist co-option of Babeuf did not go unchallenged. Victor Méric, on the
extreme left of the Socialist Party, also wrote a study of Babeuf in which
he showed him as an uncompromising revolutionary who had seen that
the Revolution had been blocked while still incomplete by a privileged
bourgeoisie; he drew out Babeuf's criticisms of representative democracy
and compared his views to those of contemporary anarchists.[33]

The debate on Babeuf also had some impact in Britain. In 1911 there
appeared the first full-length book on Babeuf in English since O'Brien's
translation of Buonarroti, This was *The Last Episode of the French
Revolution – being a History of Gracchus Babeuf and the Conspiracy of the
Equals*, by Ernest Belfort Bax, one of the pioneers of British Marxism
and a close associate of William Morris.[34] In fact the book was written
at the request of William Morris, who had died in 1896, and who was
presumably interested in the particular position Babeuf held between
utopian and scientific socialism. Morris gave Bax a copy of Advielle's
book 'on condition that the said Bax writes a clear account of the Babeuf
episode'.

Bax clearly benefited from his reading of Advielle, though he added
little to what was known of Babeuf at the time. Bax was strongly hostile
to Robespierre, whom he had described in an earlier work as 'a petit-
bourgeois, a Philistine to the backbone . . . pedantic Rousseauite prig'.[35]
He recognized clearly that Babeuf could not be seen as 'a mere follower
of Robespierre', but he lumped Babeuf together with the Utopians who

had produced 'a scheme of social reconstruction'. However, he stressed the originality of Babeuf, in relation to Mably and Morelly from whom he had taken his 'communistic idea', in that he had aimed at the unity of theory and practice:

> What was original in Babeuf was his attempt to place it as the immediate goal of the society of his time, to be directly realised by political methods. Babeuf was the first to conceive of Communism in any shape as a politically realisable ideal in the immediate or near future.[36]

8
The Shadow of October

Since Advieile and Jaurès, several generations of historians have enhanced our knowledge of Babeuf. They worked in a violent century which saw the rise and fall of fascism and Stalinism, and their work could not fail to be influenced by the world around them. For those who saw Stalinist Russia as the consummation of Marxist communism, Babeuf took his place as a pioneer of that tradition. Equally important, in the context of the struggle against fascism, was the idea of the 'Popular Front'. In France especially, Popular Frontism inherited from nineteenth-century republicanism, from Clemenceau and Jaurès, a view of the relation between socialism and the republican tradition which exerted enormous influence during the twentieth century, and lay behind the Popular Front policies of alliance between the 'progressive' bourgeoisie and the working class. Popular Frontism is sometimes seen as an invention of the Communist International, but its roots in French politics lay far deeper. Hence the Communist Party's Popular Front policy flourished in France while achieving nothing in Britain. Popular Frontism had enormous influence on the appropriation and interpretation of the French Revolution.

The events of 1848 were the first major spur to the increased appreciation of Babeuf; the Russian Revolution of 1917 was the second. However, there is no evidence of any significant influence of Babeuf on the Bolshevik leaders; there are only a couple of passing references to Babeuf in Lenin's writings.[1]

In the first years after the Revolution, research into the pioneers of socialism was encouraged and Riazanov acquired many valuable Babeuf manuscripts; in 1927 the Marx-Engels Institute staged an exhibition dedicated to Babeuf.[2]

In the late 1920s the spectre of Babeuf began to acquire more than antiquarian significance. As the Stalinist bureaucracy consolidated its grip, the Left Opposition began to discuss the question of a Soviet Thermidor, that is, a rolling-back of the course of the Revolution. The implication of the debate was clear; if the turning-point of Thermidor had been reached, then the mantle of Babeuf would fall on the Left Opposition. They would have to organize their own conspiracy of the equals.[3] The Left Oppositionist Victor Serge said in 1927: 'We are *babouvistes* who still have our heads on our shoulders.'[4]

The fact that Thermidor was so often invoked shows how important the memory of 1793–7 was for the Russian revolutionaries, but the Thermidor parallel was not a very helpful one. At Thermidor a radical faction of the bourgeoisie had been overthrown and replaced by the rule of the bourgeois mainstream; in Russia the danger was that the rule of the working class would be replaced by that of a bureaucracy.

The debate encouraged one of Trotsky's associates, Christian Rakovsky, to look closely at the experience of Babeuf. In an essay called 'The "Professional Dangers" of Power', written from deportation in Astrakhan, he examined the material causes which led to the decline of militancy among the Parisian *sans-culottes*:

> Babeuf, after his emergence from the prison at Abbaye [in fact the Abbaye prison in Paris – not actually the prison Babeuf emerged from], looking about him, began by asking himself what had happened to the people of Paris, the workers of the Faubourgs St Antoine and St Marceau, those who on 14 July 1789 had taken the Bastille, on 10 August 1792 the Tuileries, who had laid siege to the Convention on 30 May 1793, not to speak of numerous other armed interventions. In one single phrase, in which can be felt the bitterness of the revolutionary, he gave his observation: 'It is more difficult to re-educate the people in the love of liberty than to conquer it.'
>
> We have seen why the people of Paris forgot the attraction of liberty. Famine, unemployment, the liquidation of revolutionary cadres (numbers of these had been guillotined), the elimination of the masses from the leadership of the country, all this brought about such an overwhelming moral and physical weariness of the masses that the people of Paris and the rest of France needed thirty-seven years' rest before starting a new revolution.[5]

It was an important insight and Trotsky quoted it with approval in *The Revolution Betrayed*.[6] But in a sense Rakovsky had learnt the wrong lesson. He had grasped a sense of the long-term rhythm of events, saw that it might be a generation or more before the Russian working class rose again. But if the Opposition's only hopes were to be placed in the remote future,[7] was it worth the persecution and the sacrifice? In 1934 Rakovsky abandoned the Opposition. It was Trotsky, though he showed only a passing interest in Babeuf,[8] who learnt the lesson of *babouvisme*. The time is always right for the unity of theory and practice, and that means organization, however bleak the objective conditions. If Babeuf had retired to write books for the generation of 1830, his name would not have been remembered by the revolutionaries of 1919. (In his biography of Trotsky, Tony Cliff argued that Trotsky's failure to oppose Stalin openly in 1923 may have resulted from a memory of Babeuf's mistakes after Thermidor, but he gave no source for this interpretation.)[9]

Another work which evoked Babeuf in the context of the debate about Thermidor was Ilya Ehrenburg's novel *The Conspiracy of the Equals*[10] (first published in Russian in 1928 and translated into French in 1933). Ehrenburg was initially very critical of the Russian Revolution, but in the early 1930s made his peace with Stalin. The book on Babeuf, written while Ehrenburg was living in Paris,[11] represented an important turning-point in his career in both aesthetic and political terms. With it he turned his back on satirical works like *Julio Jurenito* to produce a novel more in keeping with current trends in post-revolutionary Russian literature. The aim was to produce something on the boundaries of fact and fiction.[12] His book was a fairly straightforward account of Babeuf's life, with some genuine quotations worked into the invented dialogue.

Throughout there were parallels between the French and Russian Revolutions. Behind the plot the theme of Thermidor was ever-present; a circle of Thermidorian characters, with the vain, unprincipled Barras at their centre, was constantly contrasted to the *babouvistes*. In the background he showed the emergent working class, and vividly depicted the silence of Paris after Babeuf's arrest.[13] (He might have been thinking of the public indifference as Trotsky was deported from Moscow in January 1928.)

Ehrenburg depicted the political debates among the conspirators, showing Maréchal's anarchism, and noting how Babeuf defended women's rights against his comrades (though his portrayal of Babeuf's wife, devoted but understanding 'nothing of politics', was offensive and patronizing).[14] He speculated on Babeuf's changing attitude to revolutionary terror, clearly projecting onto Babeuf the dilemmas which would lead to his own decision to line up with Stalin:

> How did Babeuf, who had disavowed Robespierre because of the Terror, himself come to Terror? Perhaps he had simply got used to the Revolution; until then had he not always been in prison? and the Revolution, as we know, was generous in everything: in ideas, in paper money and in blood . . . He was preparing himself for a high destiny: to transform Humanity. He knew that what was necessary for that was sunshine, fraternity, and the bitterest of all – time. Like a crazy doctor, he had recourse to the time-tested cure: blood-letting.[15]

In the first half of the twentieth century the academic study of the Revolution was dominated by three men: Alphonse Aulard, Albert Mathiez and Georges Lefebvre. All were profoundly influenced by Jaurès and the new perspectives he had introduced; all were deeply affected by the evolution of the Russian Revolution. Their contribution to the interpretation of the Revolution was immense and covered many aspects; what follows attempts merely to see what they added to the understanding of Babeuf.

Alphonse Aulard stood within the tradition of French radicalism, but argued for reconciliation between socialism and republicanism. In 1902 he wrote:

> The *Marseillaise* glorifies our great historic memories, our heroic revolutionary origins, it is still our illustrious national song. The *Internationale* glorifies our great and bold hopes for the future, for the advent of total democracy; it is the song of vanguard Republicans. These two songs are not enemies, they must not quarrel . . . [16]

While having some sympathies for the Russian Revolution, he stood as an election candidate in 1919 under the slogan 'Neither Bolshevism nor Reaction'. Aulard's means of reconciling socialism and republicanism consisted quite simply in watering down the concept of socialism. He argued that the 'social question' in the eighteenth century had been the destruction of feudal property, and that the national appropriation of Church property was thus equivalent to a modern 'socialist' policy such as the nationalization of the railways. He saw as socialist anyone who wished to diminish inequality and defined socialism as 'tending to equality by the solidarity of men and interests'.[17]

In studying the socialism of Babeuf, Aulard tended to stress the continuity with earlier periods of the Revolution, thus denying him any particular originality. He cited a letter from Laplanche of Bourges, arguing simply for redistributive taxation to help the poor, and commented 'Is not Laplanche here speaking as Babeuf will speak?' When he cited Babeuf's 'socialist ideal' as expressed in the *Tribun du peuple* of the Year IV, he asked:

> Is this dream of the future anything other than a memory of the past, a memory of the collectivist community which had been seen in outline in France two years earlier, and whose organs and functioning Babeuf does not so much imagine as describe, according to a recent reality.[18]

It is not surprising that Aulard could call Babeuf's conspiracy 'the equivalent of the Radical Party'.[19]

On the face of it, Albert Mathiez was well to the left of Aulard. He joined the French Communist Party (PCF) at its foundation, and for two years wrote regularly for its paper, *L'Humanité*; typically, he left in 1923 when Party membership became incompatible with freemasonry.[20] While Aulard's hero had been Danton, Mathiez's was Robespierre; one of his major contributions as a historian was to force a reassessment of Robespierre. Mathiez went much further than Aulard in recognizing socialist tendencies in the Revolution; he argued quite forthrightly that Robespierre was a socialist, and indeed, was superior to later socialists.[21]

Mathiez followed Buonarroti in establishing a continuity between Robespierre and Babeuf, but was far less scrupulous in ironing out or wishing away any contradictions or discontinuities that might emerge. He could not entirely write out of history Babeuf's Thermidorian phase, but he did his best to minimize its significance: 'Doubtless since he was a journalist, and had to reckon with public opinion, Babeuf was obliged, in the paper which he founded on 17 *fructidor*, Year II, to disown Robespierre, and dissociate himself from a compromising name.'[22] Here and elsewhere Mathiez demonstrated a method based on intuition rather than respect for the texts; when Babeuf praised Robespierre, it was proof of a true identity; but when he criticized him, the statement was somehow not an expression of Babeuf's true feelings. Since socialism had apparently already been fully developed by Robespierre,

Mathiez denied any theoretical originality to Babeuf: 'Communism for him is something purely secondary which has not much to do with his true politics . . . a hasty construction, a sort of improvised mosaic, a decorative addition to a building in a completely different style.'[23]

Mathiez gave an impulse to Babeuf studies by commissioning Dommanget to edit a selection of Babeuf's writings, which made the total figure much more accessible. Babeuf haunted him to his last day. On 25 February 1932 in Mathiez's Sorbonne seminar, a student was presenting a paper on Thermidor. When he reached Babeuf's conspiracy, Mathiez interrupted him to ask: 'Say a few words about it.' A moment later, he dropped dead.[24]

Georges Lefebvre was the greatest of the three as a historian. But though he drew more explicitly on Marxism than either Aulard or Mathiez, he remained caught within the logic of Popular Frontism. Lefebvre was a member of the Socialist Party (SFIO) from 1905 to 1940; after the war he was sympathetic to the PCF, but retained his intellectual independence. He assisted with the making of Jean Renoir's movie *La Marseillaise* (1937), and supported the Resistance (his brother was executed by the Nazis). At the Liberation he wrote a short article on the importance of the heritage of the Revolution. Its very title, 'About Her' (*D'Elle*), was reminiscent of Michelet in its personification of the Revolution. (The French pronoun *elle* can refer to any feminine noun, such as *révolution*. But as the well-known magazine title shows, *Elle* on its own translates as *She*.) Here the normally austere historian described how young men had come straight from the barricades to ask him to speak about the Revolution. He concluded: 'And in this sense, from one end of France to the other, all those who, risking their lives, fought against the enemy and the counter-revolution, its accomplice, are barricade fighters and the eldest sons of the Republic.'[25] Lefebvre repeatedly used the image of the Popular Front as a key to the Revolution and considered an alliance of the Third and Fourth Estates still valid in the second half of the twentieth century.[26]

Lefebvre, grandson of a peasant who had gone to work in a factory, identified with the frugal values and ascetic way of life of the Jacobin *petit bourgeois*. But he was far more rigorous with his categories than Aulard and Mathiez. Socialism for him was the collective ownership of the means of production, while Robespierre's 'social ideal' was a 'society of small producers'. Lefebvre was unwilling to identify

Babeuf with modern communism, since he did not (allegedly) advocate collective exploitation of the means of production (something that
Lefebvre identified with Russian collective farms). Lefebvre's main
contribution was to insist that Babeuf's communism had its roots in
the pre-Revolutionary collective practices of the Picardy peasantry. To
this he added the claim that Babeuf's communism was a communism
of consumption and distribution, not of production.[27] Hence he saw
Babeuf's socialism as essentially backward-looking, rather than as the
starting-point of modern socialism, while conceding that he was neither ascetic nor moralistic.[28]

There is no doubt that Lefebvre made an important contribution
to the understanding of the formation of Babeuf's mentality. But his
account left a number of problems. By identifying modern socialism
with the Russian model, Lefebvre underestimated the important libertarian elements in Babeuf's thinking. And in stressing the peasant roots
of Babeuf's socialism, he failed to explain why Babeuf chose Paris, and
not the countryside of Picardy, as the base for his conspiracy. Popular
Frontism leads inevitably to an underestimation of the independent role
of the working class in both present and past; and in Lefebvre's case it
also led him to underestimate the originality of Babeuf.

However Lefebvre played a key role in stimulating research, including work that was to challenge some of his own positions. Together with
Soboul he encouraged an international grouping of scholars concerned
with popular movements in the French Revolution. This included Victor
Dalin, as well as the Italian scholars Galante Garrone and Armando
Saitta. The latter made a particular contribution with their work on
Buonarroti's role in the conspiracy. They thus helped to draw out the distinctive contributions of Babeuf and Buonarroti and Buonarroti's work
in ensuring the continuity of the *babouviste* tradition, and confirmed the
overall accuracy of Buonarroti's history as a historical source. They also
helped to show that *babouvisme* had both roots in the eighteenth century
and profoundly original features.[29]

If the Russian Revolution awakened a new interest in Babeuf, the rise
of Stalinism inevitably had a distorting effect. Many of the historians
who worked on Babeuf from the 1930s to the 1970s were Communists
or close allies; while this in itself did not affect the value of their research,
it did affect the political perspectives underlying their work.

As far as the role of Babeuf is concerned, a number of themes can be identified which had a distorting effect. In the first place, there was a distrust of the study of 'precursors' of Marxism. Marxism was dressed up as a 'science' – in fact something akin to a revealed religion – and hence it was necessary to deny any continuity between the Marxist 'classics' and their predecessors; that would have revealed Marxism to be a human product, open to criticism and in a process of continuing evolution. Roger Garaudy wrote that 'Marx and Engels . . . discovered the scientific method for history, as Descartes did for physics, Lavoisier for chemistry and Claude Bernard for medicine'.[30] Logically the study of precursors could be of solely antiquarian interest, and meant measuring their achievement against a subsequently discovered 'truth'. (In this respect, as in others, Louis Althusser was a very unoriginal Stalinist.) The PCF journal *La Nouvelle critique* once published a formal apology for referring to Hobson as a 'precursor of Lenin', describing the statement as a 'dangerous mistake'.[31] A letter to Maurice Dommanget from the historian J. Zilberfard described the intellectual climate in Russia:

> This was the common fate of studies of pre-Marxist socialism in our country for some time. After the remarkable achievements of Soviet historians in the twenties and thirties, then the necessary interruption during the last world war, there was a dark period. Although the history of socialism was not condemned like genetics, cybernetics, pedagogy and psychotechnology as being 'bourgeois pseudoscience', it nonetheless became *non grata*. There were a few words in Stalin about 'the desert of utopian socialism' and a statement that 'Marx was the enemy of the Utopians', so they drew the conclusion . . . They ignored all that Marx, Engels and Lenin said about the contribution of the great precursors. That is why our researches in this branch of historical science were frozen for many years.[32]

Secondly, there was a tendency to underplay divergences and contradictions within the Revolution. The tradition of Clemenceau's *bloc* and the Popular Frontism of Mathiez and Lefebvre (highly regarded in the PCF) were reinforced by the Stalinist cult of monolithic unity. Maurice Thorez, for many years PCF leader, was reputedly deeply distressed to learn that the 'giants of the Revolution' were not all in agreement.[33] It is quite true that Babeuf entered into alliances with Jacobins and other middle-class elements; in the historical situation, he had little alternative. But he also fought unceasingly for his own, explicitly social-ist, programme. A 'Popular Frontist' reading overstates the alliances and what Babeuf had in common with the Jacobins at the expense of playing down his distinct historical originality.

Thirdly, there was the problem that pre-Marxist socialists like Babeuf offered a basis for a left critique of aspects of Russian 'socialism'. The concern of Stalinist theoreticians to distinguish between 'socialism' and 'egalitarianism' was undoubtedly motivated by the large inequalities of wealth and power that existed in Russia. When Jean Dautry compared Babeuf unfavourably to Saint-Simon because he did not recognize the potential of technological progress (see Chapter 10), he revealed the mentality of a whole generation of Stalinists. Socialism for them was essentially rapid industrialization (electrification without *soviets*) rather than social justice or human liberation.

The leading PCF historian in the Stalinist period was Albert Soboul. Soboul's family background steeped him in the republican tradition, and he was first drawn to the PCF in the 1930s. Arrested for organizing an anti-German demonstration in Montpellier on 14 July 1942, he worked with the Resistance until the Liberation. His work on the Parisian *sansculottes* was a major historical contribution, though his thesis was to stress that the *sans-culottes* were predominantly artisans and shop-keepers, not proletarians, and ideologically backward-looking.[34] None the less he incurred the disfavour of the PCF bureaucracy by claim-ing that there was a popular movement to the left of Robespierre; he was formally rebuked by Jean Poperen, and made a self-criticism.[35] He remained ready to endorse the PCF line; in an adulatory review of a volume of Thorez's works from 1932, he gave unqualified praise for the exposition of the sectarian Third Period line (social democrats are no different from fascists).[36]

One of Soboul's main contributions to the study of Babeuf was his essay 'Sectional personnel and Babouvist personnel'.[37] Here Soboul attempted to show that most of Babeuf's supporters were artisans and shopkeepers, attached to a belief in small property, and hence in contra-diction with the aims of the conspiracy. Soboul had a valid point here; *babouvisme* was not predominantly a proletarian movement. But Soboul's Popular Frontism led him to overstate his thesis, invoking some dubi-ous evidence in its support. Thus he used the list of subscribers to the *Tribun du peuple* in an uncritical manner. We know from Babeuf's trial that many activists obtained the journal but were unwilling to let their names go on the subscription list, while others, because of the price, participated in group subscriptions.[38] The *Tribun du peuple* was not only expensive, but written in a fairly heavy theoretical style. To judge the class nature of the conspiracy from the readers of the *Tribun* is rather like deducing the class nature of the Labour Party from the readership of *Fabian Essays*. Moreover, as Michio Shibata has pointed out, police records tend to overstate the continuity, as long-standing *sans-culotte* militants were the prime target of surveillance, whereas the *babouvistes* were looking for new people.[39]

The contribution of other historians in the PCF orbit was less impressive. Gérard Walter was a fellow-traveller who in 1948 published a hagiographic history of the PCF. His 1937 book on Babeuf was a light-weight contribution which gave no sources for its assertions, and deliberately set out to debunk the conspiracy, dismissed as an 'imperfect and abortive first draft' with no working-class support.[40] When G. & C. Willard published selected writings of Babeuf with a PCF publishing house in 1950, they underestimated his originality, saying that Babeuf had not gone beyond Rousseau in making a purely moral critique of private property. In keeping with the sectarianism of the time their volume at no point acknowledged the existence of Maurice Dommanget's work, though he had produced the most comprehensive selection of Babeuf's writings to date.[41]

The PCF's main contribution since Soboul has been made by Claude Mazauric. Unlike Soboul, Mazauric combined his academic career with active political involvement in the French Communist Party. At the 1979 PCF Congress he spoke on ideological struggle, alleging that the bourgeoisie were attacking a whole range of targets from Descartes and Rousseau via Babeuf to the PCF.[42] Clearly he saw his two books[43] on Babeuf as part of this ideological war.

Mazauric has been anxious to draw Popular Frontist lessons from Babeuf. He argued (following Georges Lefebvre) that the 'necessities of action' led the *babouvistes* to form a 'popular front' with former *montagnards* and even left Thermidorians.[44] He saw as a 'negative aspect' of the *babouviste* heritage that it encouraged a 'libertarian, anti-parliamentary and egalitarian tradition' which took shape in revolutionary syndicalism.[45] (He did not add that revolutionary syndicalism provided the early PCF with its best cadres.) He found such sentences as 'Rulers make revolutions only in order to carry on ruling' distinctly embarrassing, and tried to use the suppression of Maréchal's *Manifesto* to show that the *babouvistes* were resisting such 'anarchist' sentiments.[46] In keeping with the 'peaceful road' line of the latter-day PCF, Mazauric stressed Babeuf's 'horror of violence and bloodshed',[47] despite the evidence for Babeuf's recognition of the necessity for revolutionary violence, and claimed that 'we can deny absolutely that *babouvisme* expressed the first version of a proletarian revolutionary movement of the modern type'.[48] On the other hand, he stressed Babeuf's 'republicanism', claiming that the 'unsurpassable universal values' of the 'republican and humanist ideal' motivated Babeuf's letter to the Directory after his arrest and his defence at Vendôme.[49]

In fact Mazauric omitted some of the most radical themes in Babeuf's work. Thus when he reproduced Babeuf's letter to Coupé of 20 August 1791, some of the key passages that had appeared in Dommanget's *Pages choisies* were missing, in particular those dealing with the development of democratic institutions, notably Babeuf's proposal to establish 'curators of liberty' and his assertion that 'the possibility of withdrawing the representatives' mandate is a useful and indispensable threat'[50] (see Chapters 3 and 10). The right of recall, essential to the Paris Commune and the early Russian *soviets*, was not widely practised in the post-Lenin USSR.

Some of the most important contributions to the understanding of Babeuf have come from socialists in an oppositional relation to mainstream Communism. Maurice Dommanget was an active socialist before the First World War, and organized one of the first teachers' strikes in France. He could have had a successful university career, but he was strongly influenced by the revolutionary syndicalist idea of the 'refus de parvenir' (the refusal to be a success) – namely that a socialist militant had a moral obligation not to pursue success, wealth or fame. (Dommanget claimed to find this idea in Babeuf's letter to Coupé of 20 August 1791, where he argued that revolutionaries should renounce personal ambition.[51]) He remained a primary schoolteacher and an active trade unionist throughout his working life.

Dommanget was a founder-member of the PCF, but soon became dissatisfied with the Party leadership. In 1924, when the former syndicalists Rosmer and Monatte were sacked from *L'Humanité*, he was offered a job in their place, but refused. His first book on Babeuf was published in Russian translation in 1925. He left the PCF in 1930. When Trotsky was exiled in France, Dommanget had political discussions with him. Trotsky praised his *Pages choisies* of Babeuf, but was less happy with his refusal to join the Socialist Party;[52] Dommanget's political sympathies lay with revolutionary syndicalism.[53] In a letter to Victor Serge in 1936 Trotsky argued that the only political contribution Dommanget was capable of would be writing occasional articles on Babeuf for the Trotskyist press.[54]

Dommanget wrote prolifically on the French Revolution, Blanqui and working-class traditions. His work was scrupulously documented, sometimes to the point of pedantry, but he always wrote as a committed socialist, concerned to be truthful about the past but equally concerned to mobilize the past in the service of the present. Dommanget produced three volumes on Babeuf: a short outline of Babeuf's life and ideas;[55] an annotated collection of Babeuf's writings; and a volume of essays on various aspects of Babeuf.

One of his most interesting contributions was an essay written in 1922 called 'Structure and Methods of the Conspiracy of Equals'.[56] Dommanget intended the experience of Babeuf to help arm the PCF for insurrectionary struggle. He noted that modern Communist Parties confined themselves to public propaganda; as a result 'when the revolutionary storm rages, they prove incapable of adapting themselves to the new conditions of struggle and leading the most heroic proletariat to victory.'[57] Dommanget used the documents from Babeuf's trial to present a detailed picture of how the conspiracy operated: the role of the agents, the use of the press, pamphlets, fly-posting and songs. He critically examined the conspiracy's finances and its failure to take security seriously enough, concluding that the conspiracy was the source of the 'modern proletarian movement'. Dommanget, who in the 1920s was involved in campaigns for women's rights and birth control,[58] was one of the first to point to the important role played by women in the conspiracy, especially the use of women to subvert the armed forces with 'a propaganda that was all the easier because it was accompanied by caresses'.[59] (Such tactics were very much a matter of contemporary relevance; at just this time Victor Serge was observing young women in Germany flirting at the barracks gates and saying: 'You'll bring out some grenades, won't you, dear?')[60]

Much of Dommanget's other work on Babeuf developed themes related to his political concerns. He was constantly aware of the importance in Babeuf of the key themes of revolutionary syndicalism, which he summed up as follows:

> federalism, direct action, antistatism, antiparliamentarism, antipatri-
> otism, general strike, boycott, sabotage, value of active minorities, dis-
> trust of political parties claiming to represent the proletariat, distrust of
> reforms, myth of the revolution.[61]

Dommanget felt particular affinity with Maréchal, to whom he devoted a whole book, and in whose call for an end to the distinction between rulers and ruled he found an anticipation of the struggle against bureau-cracy.[62] He also stressed Babeuf's contribution to the Marxist tradition, seeing the proposals for a 'provisional authority' as an anticipation of the dictatorship of the proletariat.[63] He even rather unwisely claimed that Babeuf was 'already a Marxist'.[64]

Dommanget – in most things as a disciple of Mathiez – firmly rejected Mathiez's view of Babeuf's relation to Robespierre, stressing the 'unquestionable and highly coloured communist aspect of the con-spiracy'.[65] For Dommanget the conspiracy must be related to both past and future, 'the last breath of the *sans-culotte* Revolution and the first breath of the proletarian Revolution'.[66] To him, Babeuf's advocacy of the 1793 Constitution was a secondary tactical question: 'Like Maréchal, Babeuf loved communism a thousand times more than all the constitu-tions in the world.' Dommanget's explanation of the tactic was that the conspiracy had two goals: 'an immediate goal, the establishment of the 1793 Constitution; a distant goal, the establishment of communism'.[67] In making this distinction, he was drawing on the experience of the pre-1914 social-democratic parties which had minimum and maximum programmes (see Chapter 11).

Although Dommanget stressed that the conspiracy could not have succeeded in its socialist aims, his study of the *babouviste* organization convinced him that there was a significant proletariat in Paris by 1796 which the conspiracy had failed to relate to:

> Instead of standing aloof from these economic movements, the Equals
> should have helped and co-ordinated them, and adapted themselves to
> the immediate demands of the proletarians, in short, entered into the
> thick of the struggle in order, if possible, to enlarge it into a class battle.[68]

This theme was taken up in Daniel Guérin's 1946 book *The Class Struggle under the First Republic*,[69] written during the Nazi occupation of France while Guérin was co-operating with the clandestine Trotskyists. He attempted to project Trotsky's theory of permanent revolution back to 1789, in order to show an embryonic proletarian revolution inside the bourgeois revolution, thus providing a framework for understanding the historical role of Babeuf. Contrary to Mathiez, who was embarrassed by Babeuf's post-Thermidorian critique of Robespierre, Guérin claimed that Babeuf was too uncritical of Robespierre during the conspiracy. 'He defended Robespierre posthumously; he didn't dare to openly display his communist flag.'[70] He claimed: 'If the Equals had been consistent, they would all have linked up with the handful of vanguard militants who, under Robespierre and against him, strove to push the Revolution further. They would have proclaimed themselves the continuers of Jacques Roux and Leclerc . . . '[71] Contrary to the claim that his account was voluntaristic and anachronistic, Guérin stated that 'the objective conditions of the time could not allow the insurrection of the Equals to triumph . . . the objective conditions for socialism did not yet exist'.[72]

Georges Lefebvre, while noting a number of disagreements, welcomed Guérin's book as a valuable contribution to the debate on the Revolution.[73] But Guérin's PCF critics confined themselves to vilification, citing Guérin's Trotskyist links to justify their animosity. Soboul and Rudé, whose own empirical work often brought them close to some of Guérin's positions, were obliged to demarcate themselves by polemic.[74]

Guérin's strength lay in the way in which he attempted to put working-class democracy at the centre of the picture. None the less he did lay himself open to charges of anachronism when he discovered '*soviets*' in 1793 (and indeed claimed that *soviets* were natural to human society and could be traced back to ancient Greece).[75] He was unwise to build up Joseph Bodson as a counterweight to Babeuf, citing Bodson's continuing hostility to Robespierre. Bodson was not necessarily to the left of Babeuf; at the Vendôme trial, the prosecutor Bailly quoted a letter from Bodson to Babeuf in which he stated 'under the revolutionary government the people . . . was stripped of all its sovereignty'; Bailly praised the 'author of this fine passage' and said that his ideas were 'both right and honourable for the people'.[76] How far this tribute contributed to his acquittal it is hard to say, but it seems difficult to claim that he was a more intransigent revolutionary than Babeuf.

Guérin claimed that while Babeuf could not have triumphed, he could have used his trial to bequeath to posterity the communist doctrine he had developed, but 'instead of unfurling his flag, he dissembled and quibbled',[77] This reduced the importance of Babeuf to propagandism, whereas his significance was precisely that he attempted to transcend propagandism towards organization. Thus Guérin tended to see Babeuf as less open and audacious than the *enragés*,[78] while the greatness of Babeuf was that he attempted to unite theory and practice, confronting questions of tactics which the *enragés*, forerunners of the anarchists with whom Guérin identified in his later years, serenely ignored. Guérin's work was conceived out of a profoundly justified hostility to Stalinist Popular Frontism, and helped clarify the context in which Babeuf was working, but ultimately it failed to appreciate the complexity of Babeuf's achievement.

The political itinerary of Victor Dalin went right back to the Russian Revolution; the details have become clear only after his death with the publication of an article by the grandson of the Hungarian Communist, Bela Kun. Dalin became a revolutionary in 1917 at the age of fifteen; at the age of eighteen he became a member of the Central Committee of the Komsomol (Communist Youth Organization). In 1923 he drew up a statement in support of Trotsky signed by eight Youth leaders.[79] He embarked on an academic career studying French history; though he seems to have repudiated his oppositional politics, that did not save him from two periods of imprisonment totalling 17 years. In the late 1940s he edited a translation of Buonarroti's *History*. By the time it was published he was again in a labour camp, and was not allowed to have a copy of the book – because it had the word 'conspiracy' in the title.[80] In 1963 he published his major study, *Gracchus Babeuf before and during the French Revolution 1785–1794*.

Dalin's main concern was with the formation of Babeuf's ideas before the conspiracy. His book, running to over 600 pages, scrupulously collected unpublished manuscripts in order to establish how Babeuf developed his view of communism, challenging Lefebvre's view of the formation of Babeuf's ideas. He rejected the importance given by Lefebvre to the communal traditions of land ownership in Picardy, and argued that Babeuf's roots were in the rural proletariat:

> If the Jacobins were linked to the intermediate and more prosperous social strata in the countryside, Babeuf... was linked to the neediest, the most proletarianized and semi-proletarianized elements of the French peasantry, whose interests he tried to defend.[81]

Basing himself on letters in which Babeuf argued for the creation of 'collective farms', Dalin claimed that Lefebvre was wrong to claim that the communism of the Equals went only as far as distribution, and did not envisage socialized production.[82]

Dalin's writings betrayed occasional accommodations to Stalinism. In writing about a figure whom he saw as an important precursor of Marx, he tended to take a 'teleological' attitude, that is, he assumed that there was a historical target defined and given once and for all, and that precursors were to be evaluated according to the extent of their anticipation of that target.

Dalin described Babeuf's attempt to exercise the right of recall as 'a very curious attempt'[83] – an odd description for a right which had been at the very heart of *soviet* democracy in the first years of the Russian Revolution. Likewise, in discussing a document in which Babeuf argued that officers in the National Guard should be elected, he referred to 'his egalitarian exaggerations'.[84] None the less Dalin's work represented a fundamental contribution to a reassessment of Babeuf's socialism.

While Communists, orthodox or dissident, have shown great interest in Babeuf, the social-democratic tradition has shown much less. One reason is the retreat from equality that has marked social-democratic politics in the twentieth century, so that even such mild and ineffective measures as redistributive taxation have been seen as excessively egalitarian. Social-democratic historians are much happier to see the origins of their politics in Robert Owen or Christian socialism.[85] In general social democrats have given Babeuf passing and inaccurate mentions (though the veteran Spanish Socialist Tierno Galván published the first book on Babeuf in the Spanish language).[86]

In 1930 a short study of *The Socialist Tradition in the French Revolution*[87] by Harold Laski was published by the Fabian Society. In this Laski gave a definition of socialism which helped to place him politically: 'I understand by socialism the deliberate intervention of the State in the process of production and distribution in order to secure an access to their benefits upon a consistently wider scale.' In terms of this definition – which totally omits any reference to proletarian democracy or

THE SPECTRE OF BABEUF   137

self-activity – Laski accepted that Babeuf represented the first appearance in the Revolution of 'socialism in a serious and effective form'. But Laski's elitist and statist method meant that while he appreciated Babeuf's importance, he missed the complexities of the issues. We are told as a fact that 'all revolutions are the act of a minority' and that Robespierre had a 'coherent doctrine which has clearly socialist affinities'.[88] Such confusions contributed little to an understanding.

G.D.H. Cole did recognize that the question of property distinguished Babeuf from virtually all his contemporaries. But he dismissed the conspiracy as 'in relation to the main development of the French Revolution, never more than a side issue'.[89]

9

Cold War and After

The revolutions of the twentieth century also stimulated new responses on the conservative side. One of the most important discussions of Babeuf in the Cold War period came from an Israeli scholar, Jacob Talmon, in *The Origins of Totalitarian Democracy* (1952).[1] The political motivation for Talmon's trilogy, of which this was the first volume, was quite explicit; Talmon was studying the Jacobins at the time of the Moscow Trials, and the parallel of the two suggested 'the existence of some unfathomable and inescapable law which causes revolutionary Salvationist schemes to evolve into reigns of terror and the promise of a perfect direct democracy to assume in practice the form of totalitarian dictatorship.'[2] In 1957 Talmon addressed a Conservative Party Summer School, paying tribute to British Toryism and claiming 'as an Israeli . . . to be part of a conservative tradition of immemorial antiquity'.[3]

Talmon's critique of the French Revolution was cobbled together from a number of sources. He acknowledged a debt to Tocqueville, and identified with Karl Popper's attack on Marxism. The attack on Rousseau and the Enlightenment which made up a major part of his book was scarcely new; the ground had been covered by many from Taine to Carl Becker. What was new in Talmon was the prominent place assigned to Babeuf; he identified three major stages whereby Enlightenment ideals become totalitarian democracy; 'the eighteenth-century postulate, the Jacobin improvisation, and the Babouvist crystallization'.[4] Babeuf was seen as a disciple of Robespierre, but also as an original figure in his own right.

Talmon made a thorough study of the primary sources, and consulted such works as Dommanget's selection of writings. His basic theme was the attempt to distinguish liberalism, which saw politics pragmatically as a matter of trial and error, and 'political Messianism', which 'postulates a preordained, harmonious and perfect scheme of things, to which men are irresistibly driven, and at which they are bound to arrive'. Socialism belonged clearly in the latter category, and was defined according to an image of Stalinism, its essential features being 'ownership of all resources and the organization of all production by the State'.[5]

Talmon was sufficiently honest to let Babeuf speak in his own words, yet employed a strategy which stood the meaning on its head. He described in detail Babeuf's policies for democratization – recall of delegates, assemblies open to the public – but added:

> such plebiscitary, direct democracy is . . . the preliminary of dictatorship or dictatorship in disguise. It is an invitation to a totalitarian party in opposition to whip up agitation, to 'organize' the discontent or the will of the people, by engineering mass petitions, manifestations, and pressure from below; and an encouragement to a totalitarian party in power to engineer referenda and mass resolutions of support.[6]

Hence Babeuf – because he saw the need to combat ideas instilled into the masses by centuries of oppression – was accused of not trusting the people. It was the ultimate conservative Catch-22; anyone who campaigns to change the world is guilty of undemocratic distrust of those who, from habit, weariness or indoctrination, accept the *status quo*.

Talmon identified a 'living and unbroken tradition' running from Jacobinism and *babouvisme* to Marxism.[7] It was a Cold War commonplace to blame Lenin for Stalin, and Marx for Lenin. Talmon took the argument one step further by blaming Babeuf for Marx. He thus established a principle of political original sin: as soon as we so much as start thinking about equality, we are on the road to the *gulag*.

The rise of the extreme right in France since the 1970s has led to reconsiderations of the French Revolution. Traditionally, fascist thought identified itself with the counter-revolutionary view, seeing the Revolution as made by Jews and freemasons. But Le Pen's Front National has shown a much more ambiguous attitude to the Revolution; it has been anxious to appropriate the Revolution as part of the national heritage, especially during the bicentenary celebrations.

The rise of the Front National was prepared in the 1970s by a number of intellectual groupings. One of these was the *Club de l'horloge* (clock club), formed in 1975 and combining extreme right-wing politics with liberal economics. A key figure was Yvan Blot, later a member of the political bureau of the Front National.

In 1980 Blot published an article entitled 'Republic, Feudalities and Bureaucracy', in which he attempted to identify two different traditions emerging from the Revolution: one based on individual freedom, and the other on state-imposed egalitarianism. The latter was identified with the left, while the former should be appropriated by the right.[8] This view was echoed in 1981, the year of Mitterrand's presidential victory, in a collective volume published by the *Club de l'horloge* in which Blot participated. This followed up Blot's argument:

> Contemporary egalitarianism is not the legitimate child of the Revolution. At most it is its bastardized offspring, fruit of petty-bourgeois passions which did not fail to flourish in the course of this troubled period . . . Far from being the corollary of the French Revolution, the egalitarian movement applied to the social and economic field will constantly operate to wreck the gains of the Revolution.

Babeuf was given a significant part in the process, being seen as the advocate of equality, the suppression of private property and class struggle; the *babouvistes* were described as having no popular support, and being 'authoritarians who did not seek popular approval'. Why, if they were so lacking in popular support, they were able to become such a sinister threat, was not explained. Communist sources were quoted to establish that Babeuf was a forerunner of modern communism, and the fantasy ended with a critique of the policies of the PCF and the French Socialist Party in the 1970s under the bizarre sub-heading, 'New conspiracy of the "Equals"'.[9] Not a very prescient forecast of Mitterrand's fourteen-year presidency.

A rather different approach came from Pierre Chaunu, an old-fashioned right-wing Catholic, who feared that without a militant Church 'the convergence of the *crisis of meaning* and the contraceptive revolution will sweep away the society of the living'.[10] Chaunu did not identify with the Front National, but publicly supported the National Joan of Arc Circle, an FN front organization. Chaunu's position, for which he achieved considerable publicity around the time of the bicentenary commemoration in 1989, was one of total hostility to every aspect of the Revolution and everything it stood for.

A bizarre element in his strategy was the attempt to co-opt Babeuf for the far right on the basis of his 1794 book on the Vendée. Chaunu quoted Babeuf's term *populicide* (people-killing) to justify his argument that the war in the Vendée was an example of 'Franco-French genocide'. He added: 'you won't challenge it, Babeuf is recognized in Moscow as one of the Fathers of communism.'[11] Chaunu associated himself with the historians Secher and Brégeon who prepared the re-publication of Babeuf's text in 1987; in his introduction Reynald Secher went so far as to say: 'In fact, as Gracchus Babeuf and Edmund Burke observe, the Vendée is not the result of chance, but is very much the logical consequence of a way of thinking . . . ,'[12] The logic of such historians is clear. Firstly, they are labelling the Jacobins as responsible for all the ills of the twentieth century. Secondly, while not endorsing those who deny Hitler's holocaust, they give comfort to them by debasing the significance of the term genocide.

But while the far right have made little serious contribution to understanding, the last thirty years have seen an important renewal of the conservative view, as a number of so-called 'revisionist' historians have sought to undermine the Marxist, and more generally the republican, account of the French Revolution. The roots of this attack can be found in Alfred Cobban's *The Social Interpretation of the French Revolution*.[13] Here Cobban argued that the Revolution had been primarily political rather than social or economic, and that the revolutionary bourgeoisie was a myth. However Cobban undermined his assault on the Marxist view of class struggle by a cavalier use of class categories, claiming that the *sans-culotte* leaders were 'well-off, middle-class ruffians', and that 'when we come to the most advanced political and economic movement of the revolution, the Conspiracy of the Equals inspired by Babeuf, it proves to be one of the most thoroughly middle-class of the lot.'[14] Such an assertion simply ignored the huge quantity of evidence about the social base of the conspiracy.

The main figure in the revisionist attack has been François Furet. Furet was a PCF member from 1947 to 1956. He then joined the left social-democratic PSU, and contributed to the weekly *Nouvel Observateur*. More recently, he moved to the centre right of French politics, denouncing the 1986 student demonstrations as an attack on 'the necessary social profitability' of the universities.[15]

Furet's task in attacking Marxism was made easier by the republican tradition that had dominated the history of the Revolution for a century or more. Clemenceau's *bloc* was absorbed by the Popular Frontism that characterized the work of Aulard, Mathiez and Lefebvre, and was taken over by the PCF historians. Furet found it easy to show that the Revolution was more complex than this. As he pointed out, the post-Thermidorian regime had to fight off challenges from moderates on the right and Babeuf on the left, leaving a continuing problem: 'how to think of the Revolution as a *bloc* against the *ancien régime*? Or again, which comes down to the same thing, how to adopt both 1789 and 1793?'[16]

Furet's account found a major stumbling-block in Babeuf. He fell into the classic conservative trap of simultaneously trying to dismiss Babeuf as insignificant and seeing him as a major threat. Thus he denied Babeuf's originality, saying he was 'an heir before being a precursor', because his closest comrades were 'bourgeois democrats' who wanted to remake 1793. Among these close comrades Furet listed Drouet, whose links with Babeuf were, to say the least, tenuous. He enquired whether it was the 'intellectual Buonarroti' who introduced the 'autodidact Babeuf to Morelly and Mably. Whether or not it was, Dalin has shown that Babeuf had gone a long way to developing communist ideas before 1789.[17]

Furet described Babeuf's correspondence with Dubois de Fosseux as 'without originality, wrapped in the spirit of the age, steeped in reforming optimism'. (Clearly 'optimism' is a prime insult for a conservative, but one wonders whether Furet ever read Babeuf's 1786 letter on the oppression of women.) He claimed the secret directory included the 'rich banker' Félix Lepeletier; but as Robert Legrand has shown, Lepeletier was not rich at the time of the conspiracy.[18] He asserted that the *babouvistes* took as their 'flag and programme' merely the Constitution of 1793, while 'the rest was known only to the small circle of conspirators'. (The *Analysis of Babeuf's Doctrine*, which was distributed and fly-posted through Paris, stated clearly: 'In a true society, there must be neither rich nor poor . . . The aim of the Revolution is to destroy inequality and to re-establish common happiness.') His patronizing conclusion was that Babeuf 'is not a great mind . . . he is a naïve and sentimental autodidact'.[19] (Not, hopefully, as naïve as those taken in by Furet's arguments.)

Furet's attempt to dismiss Babeuf as an obscure ignoramus contradicted another project: to imitate Talmon in making Babeuf responsible for the *gulag*. Furet's particular twist on this old theme was to establish an opposition between Marx and Lenin; apparently Marx 'never had a theory of the state' and dismissed as an illusion 'the belief that revolutionary action can and should change society'.[20] (Despite his years in the PCF, Furet seems to have missed *The Civil War in France* and the eleventh thesis on Feuerbach.)

> In this context Babeuf's alleged voluntarism falls neatly into place: it is the highest peak of the revolutionary belief that political will can do everything. The last wave of Jacobin extremism – and doubtless the only intellectual synthesis of the egalitarian passion of those times – elaborates here the theory of the revolutionary putsch, essential for the understanding of the nineteenth and twentieth centuries. The history of secret societies in Europe after the Treaty of Vienna has its origin here, as well as the Russian revolutionary tradition from populism to Bolshevism.[21]

Each of Furet's two hypotheses about Babeuf was fairly shaky in isolation; when the two were combined they led to further incoherence. Thus Furet stated:

> If the *babouviste* plot bequeaths some ideas and some passions to the future, at present it is only the last outburst of Jacobinism, liquidated in the indifference of the masses. In reality, everything had been settled the previous year, in *prairial*. The rest is judicial history. Because of Drouet, who was a deputy . . . Babeuf and his friends had to appear before the High Court, which sat at Vendôme, for fear of the response in Paris.[22]

So, in the selfsame paragraph we learn that Babeuf had no popular support and that the Directory were afraid to try him in Paris; Furet had deconstructed his own argument.

Furet entitled one of his most influential essays 'The French Revolution is Over',[23] a slogan much repeated at the time of the bicentenary. The phrase reflected a kind of wish-fulfilment; if it were true it would not be necessary to say it – nobody is writing best-sellers to announce that the Thirty Years' War is over. The claim that the Revolution was 'over' was adopted during the Revolution by those who felt things had gone far enough – for example, by Le Chapelier when moving his law to ban workers' organizations;[24] it was much used in the post-Thermidor period. The best response came in a phrase quoted with approval by Babeuf from a contemporary paper: 'They dare to claim shamelessly that they want to finish the Revolution. What am I saying? they dare to publish that it is over. Well, for my part, I shall say . . . that if the Revolution were over . . . *the poor would be able to live*.'[25] It is as true today as it was in 1795.

With the collapse of Eastern-bloc Communism there is now the possibility of a historiography of the French Revolution free from Stalinist
deformations and Cold War clichés. A number of recent works on
Babeuf suggest that this promise may be fulfilled.

Robert Legrand's *Babeuf and his fellow-travellers (Babeuf et ses compagnons de route*, 1981) was an example of how patient scholarship
could stand aside from political pressures. Legrand drew on the work
of Soboul and Mazauric, but made no reference to their political implications. After over four hundred pages he allowed himself a personal
comment merely to note that Babeuf was a 'passionate man' who had
'pettinesses and greatness'.[26] In its painstaking collection of documents
and biographical detail, Legrand's work was in the spirit of Dommanget,
but without the commitment to revolutionary politics that informed
every line Dommanget wrote. Thus Legrand produced an invaluable
biographical source, but added little to the debate about interpretation.

Jean-Marc Schiappa's *Gracchus Babeuf and the Equals (Gracchus Babeuf
avec les Égaux*, 1991) was written within the framework of a commitment to the politics of Trotskyism. He gave a solid narrative account
of Babeuf's life and ideas, and broke sharply with the Popular Frontist
myths that have distorted so much writing on Babeuf. He rejected 'direct
descent, either ideological or human, from Jacobinism to *babouvisme*',
seeing profound differences between the two, essentially on the question of private property. Against Furet he insisted that 'the aim of the
conspiracy was not a putsch, but was indeed a revolution'. He rejected
Lefebvre's claim that Babeuf's communism had exclusively rural roots,
pointing out that he put the products of industry on a level with those
of the land. And he concluded with a consideration of the importance
of Babeuf for Lenin and Trotsky, perhaps putting too much weight on
passing mentions.[27] It was a vigorous defence of the claim that Babeuf
was indeed a revolutionary socialist.

Philippe Riviale's *The Conspiracy (La conjuration*, 1994) rejected the
orthodoxies of both left and right, claiming his book 'belongs to no
school and will not found a school'. His rather eclectic list of intellectual
reference points included Karl Popper, Hayek, Nietzsche and the erst-
while Trotskyist and eventual post-modernist Castoriadis.[28]

The core of Riviale's argument was about historical choice. He
summed up the debate between left and right about Babeuf as follows:

> We have one party of historians who affirm that Babeuf, in communion
> with the democratic struggles of his time, but in advance of them, theo-
> rized the inevitable socialism which was to come; we have an opposing
> party who affirm the inanity of a conspiracy born of nostalgic brains and
> rubbish left behind by the ebb of the Revolution.[29]

Riviale rejected the determinism underlying both these positions. On a
philosophical level his exploration of historical choice risked ending up
in a post-modernist void. But in terms of the concrete understanding
of Babeuf, he added a valuable corrective. If Babeuf's conspiracy was
doomed to failure because it was retrogressive, premature or lacking in
popular support, then the details simply did not matter. It didn't matter
if the fly-posting was not done; didn't matter if the traitor Grisel was
allowed too easy access to the leadership; didn't matter if the wrong
defence tactic was adopted at Vendôme – everything was doomed to
failure anyway. It may be true, but it leads to rotten historical writing.

Riviale's framework allowed for a recreation of the conspiracy
in which it was an affair of real human beings making real historical
choices, choices on which their lives might depend but whose result was
unpredictable. Once Riviale had finished with a rather tortuous disquisi-
tion on historical inevitability, he produced one of the finest accounts of
the conspiracy, making copious use of the documents seized at Babeuf's
arrest in order to draw a picture of the organization as a lived reality.

The fact that three such significant books could be written in the
space of fifteen years, nearly two centuries after Babeuf's death, showed
that the questions bequeathed by Babeuf are still very much alive.

ADDITIONAL NOTE
The previous chapters have traced Babeuf through the main stages of the
historiography of the Revolution over the last two centuries. Babeuf also
cropped up in some unexpected places on the intellectual map, of which
three are worth noting.

a) A Structuralist Babeuf
In 1926 Claude Lévi-Strauss published a slim pamphlet entitled
Gracchus Babeuf and Communism.[30] Lévi-Strauss was aged only seventeen when he wrote it and was still at school; it was done at the request
of a friend who had recruited him to the Parti ouvrier belge (Belgian

Workers Party) and who had introduced him to Marx. The booklet was produced by the POB publishing-house L'Églantine.

As a contribution to Babeuf scholarship, the pamphlet is not worth mentioning; it contained many errors and was highly derivative of the work of André Lichtenberger.[31] Lévi-Strauss has said he 'prefers to forget its existence',[32] and it is missing from most bibliographies of his work.[33] But it may not be wholly insignificant in the genesis of Lévi-Strauss's thought, and thereby in the formation of modern structural anthropology. He stressed the originality of Babeuf as a socialist thinker and in particular examined his account of the transition from the 'state of nature' to civilization. Lévi-Strauss was deeply influenced by both Rousseau and Marx, and Babeuf was a link in the chain between them. Lévi-Strauss claimed that Babeuf saw education as the key to social evolution, stating that this notion was 'related to the most modern theories, inspired by the reaction against the Marxist school, which aim to substitute psychology for the economic factor as the basis of sociology.'[34]

b) A Green Babeuf

A novel perspective on Babeuf was developed in the 1970s by Wolfgang Harich, a long-standing East German dissident Marxist. Strongly influenced by contemporary ideas on ecology and the limits of growth, he sought to integrate these into Marxism. In his book *Communism without Growth: Babeuf and the 'Club of Rome'* (1975), he argued that Marx was closer to Rousseau and Babeuf than to the tradition emanating from Voltaire and Saint-Simon, which looked to abundance produced by unlimited technological progress. He argued that a planned economy like East Germany's could adopt a policy of total rationing, and that to do so would be the 'negation of the negation'. Harich wrote from no great knowledge of Babeuf, and seemed to accept the mistaken view that Babeuf was an ascetic. But Babeuf recurred as a point of reference throughout the argument.[35]

c) Babeuf in Alexandrines

One interesting literary representation of Babeuf was Henri Bassis' play *Gracchus Babeuf* (first performed in 1954).[36] Bassis, poet, Communist and educationalist, had previously written plays on the Paris Commune and the life of Maurice Thorez.[37] Bassis chose to give the work the form of a classical tragedy, written in alexandrines, possibly to emphasize Communist attachment to the great tradition of French literature. Bassis gave more attention to political exposition than to dramatic action; much of the first three acts was devoted to rather static debate, followed by two more animated acts dealing with the arrest and trial.

Much of the text was versified politics; in Act II Babeuf was shown writing an article for Le *Tribun du peuple* and reciting it aloud in verse. Maréchal was set up as the stereotypical 'ultra-left' whose arguments were neatly crushed by Babeuf. Babeuf's defence of alliance with Amar and Drouet (vigorously opposed by Maréchal) had clear echoes of the PCF's own alliance strategy:

> Pour eux, comme pour nous, l'ennemi est le même.
> Donc, ils sont nos alliés.[38]
> (*For them, as for us, the enemy is the same. Therefore they are our allies.*)

Bassis took some liberties with historical fact; Maréchal was put on trial at Vendôme while Sophie Lapierre was in the audience, not the dock. Bassis' rather wooden verse and his concern for political orthodoxy seem to have prevented him from exploiting the enormous dramatic possibilities inherent in the subject.

PART III

Babeuf's Socialism

10

Common Happiness

Babeuf was a revolutionary socialist, who differed from the most radical Jacobins in both theory and practice. This is not to deny that Babeuf owed much to those who preceded him. His thought was both a continuation and a negation of the previous course of the Revolution.

It has been argued that the *babouvistes* were backward-looking, resisting the modernization imposed by economic development. But the making of any working class involves the tearing away of workers from their previous patterns of ownership and production; their resistance forges their consciousness as a new class.

Babeuf, amid the conflicts of the Revolution, was the first to grapple with the problem of relating day-to-day political practice to the goal of a recognizably socialist society. Some of the questions of agency, organization and tactics that have preoccupied socialists for the last two hundred years were first confronted by Babeuf. His writings cover some of the most basic questions for socialists. How do we define socialism; what is the relation of equality to freedom? How do we unite theory and practice; what means can achieve the socialist end? How do we resolve the problem of ideology; how can the oppressed liberate themselves from the ideas of the oppressors? How has the concept of socialism itself evolved in struggle? Babeuf did not have neat solutions to these questions; what is interesting is how he he grappled with them.

Babeuf did not have the vocabulary of modern socialism – the word 'socialism' itself was not yet in currency. (In fact the earliest uses of the terms 'communism' and 'socialism' can be traced to Restif de la Bretonne and Drouet respectively, both of whom had links with Babeuf.)[1] The term Babeuf most commonly favoured to describe the society he aspired to was 'common happiness' (*bonheur commun*). In a passage in *L'Eclaireur*

– doubtless read aloud to hundreds of illiterate soldiers and workers –
Babeuf explained what was meant by the term:

> a Republic where the immense majority is in command and is sovereign;
> where every citizen enjoys the same rights; where we don't see unbridled
> luxury insulting the most terrible poverty; from which penury and cor-
> ruption are banished; where every member of society can rely on subsist-
> ence, independently of the whims of fortune or of any individual; where
> virtue is honoured and crime punished; where in short true equality
> reigns, that is, common happiness.[2]

The term 'common happiness' may seem vague (it was taken from the
first article of the 1793 Constitution). But in using the term Babeuf was
aligning himself with that strand of revolutionary thought which saw
happiness as the ultimate goal of politics. At Vendôme he cited Saint-
Just's declaration that 'happiness is a new idea in Europe'[3] (in Europe
because the American Declaration of Independence had already legiti-
mized 'the pursuit of Happiness').

The assertion of the right to happiness has profound revolutionary implications. It is intimately linked to the question of democracy.
Human beings may be deluded about systems and policies, but they can
scarcely be deluded about their own happiness. Only the people themselves can determine whether a society is delivering the happiness which
they believe they have a right to. Georges Lefebvre argued that the term
bonheur was equivalent to the modern *bien-être* (welfare).[4] This desic-
cates a concept rich in subjectivity and human fulfilment into a narrow
set of social policies. Likewise, Belfort Bax's translation of the term as
'universal well-being' or 'common welfare' rather missed the point.[5]

In 1794 Babeuf wrote to his son, then aged eight:

> Don't do to others what you would not like to be done to you. That is the
> finest maxim of all. If men followed it closely, they would all be happy
> . . . My friend, this equality which is so precious, the sublime principle
> of which has impressed you, it's my morality, it's your father's religion, it's
> his constitution, his law . . . [6]

Equality was the central theme of Babeuf's socialism, and as here,
it was often treated as a moral principle. Forty years before Proudhon,
Babeuf proclaimed that property was theft; the poverty of some 'derives
only from the fact that others have robbed them. Robbed legitimately,

if you like; that is, with the aid of brigand laws, which, under recent regimes as under older ones, have permitted all thefts.'[7] But it would be wrong to see equality in Babeuf as no more than moralism; it was the basis of his whole political philosophy. The idea of equality had been widespread in the Enlightenment, but in general the concept was carefully qualified; a good example is Jaucourt's article on 'Natural Equality' in Diderot's *Encyclopaedia:*

> No-one should make the mistake of imagining that out of some spirit of fanaticism, I would in any state approve of the fantasy of *absolute equality*, which even an ideal republic could scarcely give birth to; I am here referring only to the *natural equality* of men: I know only too well the necessity of different conditions, of grades, of honours, of distinctions, of prerogatives, of subordinations which must be maintained in all regimes, and I would go so far as to add that *natural* or *moral equality* is not opposed to such things.[8]

What distinguished Babeuf from most of his contemporaries is that he did not want to qualify equality in any way, but to push it as far as it would go. It was a matter for mathematical precision; as he wrote to Coupé in 1791: 'One should not be able to equivocate on questions of equality any more than on questions of figures. Everything can be reduced to weights and measures.'[9]

Babeuf challenged the view that some forms of work required more skill and intelligence than others; why, he asked, should a day's work by a watchmaker be worth twenty times as much as a ploughman's – the watchmaker was expropriating the ploughman. He explained this by saying that the intelligent had established the conventions. If those with physical strength laid down the rules, then physical effort would be better rewarded than brain-power.[10] He gave some ground to those critics who accused him of wanting to level down by arguing that

> even the man who would prove, by the effect of his natural strength alone, that he is capable of doing as much as four men, and who, as a result, would demand the remuneration of four men, would none the less be a conspirator against society, because he would upset the balance by this means alone, and thus destroy precious equality.
>   . . . wisdom imperiously orders all his fellows to repress such a man, to pursue him as a social scourge, to reduce him at least to being able to

do no more than one man's job, so that he cannot demand more than one man's remuneration.[11]

There is nothing particularly socialist about this; it reflects a common attitude among journeymen: the refusal to undercut one's fellow-workers and the development of working practices that imposed a maximum on the amount of work to be done in a week in order to safeguard employment.[12]

The *babouvistes* did not identify perfect equality with the state of nature, but rather saw it as something to be defended by society; according to the *Analysis of Babeuf's Doctrine*, in the state of nature equality was often attacked by the strong and wicked.[13] Equality for Babeuf was not just a long-term aim; it was relevant to all current issues. In 1791 he urged that in the army officers be elected and all ranks receive the same pay; this would produce 'fraternity beneath the flags'.[14] His sense of equality extended across national and racial boundaries; he denounced anti-Semitism and welcomed measures to end slavery, hailing 'this benevolent decree which has broken the odious chains of our brothers the blacks'.[15]

Some of Babeuf's formulations were crude; but his notion of quantitative equality provided a measurable criterion – and thus bears comparison with the notions of 'ethical socialism' fashionable two centuries later. Yet such a concept of equality still lay within the framework of individualism. It sought to equalize the contributions and rewards of individuals, rather than seeing society as a collective in which each person makes a different contribution, and all participate in the diversity of achievement. However, if a collectivist society were to exist without a high degree of social and economic equality, it would have little to do with socialism, and would have to justify its inequalities by some organic ideology.

The appeal of *babouviste* equality was obvious in circumstances of extreme poverty. In a situation of scarcity it matters a great deal that everyone gets one loaf of bread; in a situation of abundance it isn't very important that you have three chocolate éclairs and I have only two. Saint-Just's proposal that all citizens should wear the same uniforms[16] may not have much appeal to the fashion-conscious 1990s, but it made sense to those who had nothing to wear but rags.[17] The attempt to campaign for the ideas of equality obviously produced problems in a society

THE SPECTRE OF BABEUF   155

where many were still small producers. In the last issue of the *Tribun du peuple* Babeuf responded to the accusation that he wanted to see 'the looting of the smallest shop and the simplest household'. As he pointed out, the present regime was already making small proprietors suffer at the hands of speculators and 'gilded rogues', so that there was nothing left to loot.[18]

Babeuf's concept of equality was, of necessity, shaped by his own age; but it has stood the test of time well. His 'crude' criteria would have cut through a great deal of the rhetoric about the so-called 'socialist countries' of the Eastern bloc, where 'true equality' patently did not exist. (Hence the hostility of Stalinist ideologists to 'egalitarianism'; it was Stalin himself who insisted that socialism was not about equality but about 'correct economic relations'.)[19] But though modern-day social-democrats recoil from the mildest redistributive taxation, the idea of equality has not lost its resonance. Opposition to discrimination on the basis of race, gender, age and so on enjoys considerable popularity. A campaign for 'true equality' might find unexpected support.

Georges Lefebvre claimed that Babeuf's communism was merely a 'communism of distribution'; individual producers would put their products into a common store which would then be distributed equally.[20] In fact Babeuf's thinking went much further than this. By 1795 he categorically rejected the agrarian law (division of land), recognizing that 'the day after it was established, inequality would reappear'. He saw the necessity of 'institutions capable of ensuring and maintaining a permanent condition of true equality'.[21]

Many eighteenth-century thinkers saw 'commerce' as a liberating force in society; for Babeuf the market held no such promise. In his letter to Germain of July 1795 (see Chapter 4) he argued that competition led to wasteful overproduction of poor quality goods.[22] In support of his claim that a planned economy could work, he cited his own experience of working on food distribution for the army in 1793; what had been possible for 1 200 000 soldiers would be possible for the whole republic.[23]

In the course of the conspiracy the secret directory drew up a number of plans for the future society. In the commentary which Buonarroti printed with the *Analysis of Babeuf's Doctrine* he explained how labour would be organized:

> What do we mean by community of labour? Do we want all citizens to be tied to the same occupations? No; but we want the various tasks to be divided so as to leave not a single able-bodied person idle; we want the increase in the number of workers to guarantee public abundance, while diminishing individual effort; in return we want everyone to receive from the nation enough to satisfy their natural needs and the small number of artificial needs that all can satisfy.[24]

Beyond this a whole host of measures were considered by the *babouviste* leaders; a summary was set out in Buonarroti's history.[25] A study of these leaves no doubt that Babeuf's thinking had gone beyond a communism of distribution to the notion of a socialist planned economy. In particular, the *Draft Economic Decree* (see Appendix) probably written by Buonarroti makes it clear that production as well as consumption was to be communally organized. Babeuf's vision had little in common with a Stalinist model of centralized planning, which is probably why Lefebvre and others denied that was a 'communism of production'. It had rather more in common with Marx's notion of 'an association, in which the free development of each is the condition for the free development of all'.[26]

In the two centuries since the Revolution the relation between equality and democracy has been much debated. Babeuf insisted that the two were inseparable. Before 1789 France had been an absolutist monarchy; democracy was a matter for theorists like Rousseau and memories of ancient Greece. The eight years that followed were years of intense democratic experimentation, and Babeuf learned quickly from the struggles around him; he was remarkably perceptive about the workings of democracy. While the French Revolution can be seen as ushering in the epoch of representative democracy, the practice of the *sans-culottes* often went beyond parliamentarism and anticipated the more radical forms of democracy to be practised in the Paris Commune and the Russian *soviets*. Classic representative democracy – already criticized by Rousseau – allows voters to elect a delegate, after which he or she is free for a period of years to obey the dictates of conscience or the party whips. The *sans-culottes*, with their insistence on the right to petition and, if necessary, recall delegates, wanted a much higher level of accountability.

From the beginning Babeuf's sympathies were with direct rather than representative democracy. In the *Eclaireur* Babeuf recalled his memories of the early days of the Revolution, and the participatory democracy that had flourished then:

The slightest question to be debated in the National Assembly aroused all minds; people gathered in crowds around the sanctuary of the laws; the People itself discussed the question; everyone waited impatiently for the result, convinced in advance which policy would be the most beneficial. I have even seen patriotic deputies leave the Assembly and visit the numerous groups which had formed in the surroundings, deriving precious ideas from the citizens' discussions.[27]

This is a long way from the 'expectation of unanimity' which Talmon claimed characterized Revolutionary democracy.[28]

For Babeuf the struggle to extend democratic rights at every level, and the struggle between rich and poor were simply two aspects of the same thing. Democracy could not exist unless all had rights of citizenship; he opposed any property restriction on the right to vote. At the assembly of citizens at Roye in August 1792, Babeuf moved an amendment to the Declaration of the Rights of Man to the effect that: 'The law may not establish any distinction of rights between one man and another, whatever difference in wealth there may be.' At the *départemental* electoral assembly, he developed the point far beyond civil rights: 'The association must guarantee work to all members, and determine wages in proportion to the prices of all goods, so that these wages shall suffice for the acquisition of subsistence and all the other needs of each family.'[29]

Democracy could only be guaranteed if the people participated actively in the running of the state. In his letter to Coupé of August 1791 Babeuf insisted:

The people's *veto* is essential. Without this *veto*, an assembly of representatives of the people can produce nothing but decrees contrary to popular wishes and interests. The assembly must not take any decision or pass any law which cannot be annulled by the people.[30]

In 1794 he argued that elected representatives must be subordinated to those who elected them:

Our political education over five years taught us very well that the essential feature of the sovereignty of the people was the right to elect all our agents; that if the rulers are made by and for the ruled, then the former must be under the control of the latter, so that they never lose sight of where they come from, so that this brake may hold them back and prevent them becoming the oppressors of those who appointed them.[31]

With only a few years experience of elective institutions, Babeuf realized the danger that representatives might get out of the control of their electors: 'the basis of a free government is not blind *trust*, but perpetual *distrust*.'[32] But Babeuf's distrust was directed at the professed representatives of the people, not at the people themselves. Among the documents quoted by the prosecution at the Vendôme trial was an instruction from the secret directory to the agents; this contained the phrase: 'when the people are free and can be consulted, we cannot presume that others can judge better than they what is good and advantageous for them.'[33]

The *babouvistes* – echoing earlier radicals like the British Levellers – were prescient about the dangers of parliamentary practice. The considerations of the secret directory about political institutions contained a prophetic warning of the dangers of parliamentarism:

> if a class were formed in society which was exclusively acquainted with the art of running society, with laws and administration, it would rapidly discover in the superiority of its intelligence, and above all in the ignorance of its compatriots, the secret of how to create distinctions and privileges for itself; exaggerating the importance of its services, it would easily succeed in getting itself considered as the necessary protector of the fatherland; and disguising its impudent undertakings with the pretext of the public good, it would continue to speak of liberty and equality to its unperceptive fellow-citizens, already victims of a servitude which would be all the harsher for seeming to be legal and voluntary.[34]

In particular, Babeuf was anxious to assert the right of recall as the ultimate means of establishing the accountability of elected representatives. He tried to exercise this himself in his campaign against the deputy Prévost (see Chapter 3), and in a letter to Coupé he set out a plan for the establishment of *curators of liberty*. Seven of these would be elected in each *canton* at the same time as the deputies; they must be over twenty-five and live from their own work in the exercise of an independent profession. They would meet every three months to consider whether the elected representative was faithfully carrying out his mandate, and if necessary revoke him and call a fresh election.[35] While falling short of the full principle of the right of recall, it was an interesting attempt to introduce 'distrust' and ensure the accountability of elected representatives.

It is often alleged that the society proposed by the Equals would have been totalitarian and undemocratic. But the secret directory's plans laid down a complex structure of highly democratic institutions with safeguards to be implemented once the transitional period was over.[36] They stressed that a free press was 'the best bulwark against the usurpation of the sovereignty of the people'; the only writings to be banned would be those directly contrary to the principles of equality and popular sovereignty, and those relating to revealed religion. On the other hand, an assembly of citizens could demand that any text about the form of government and administration should be sent to all libraries in the republic. Buonarroti noted that in a regime where all labour was rationally planned and shared, the working day need only be three or four hours, thus increasing greatly the degree of concrete freedom available to the citizens.[37]

Babeuf was perceptive, not simply about the formal structures of democracy, but about how these functioned in practice. In one of his post-Thermidorian pamphlets, he denounced Robespierre for manipulating formally democratic structures in order to control public opinion: 'The surest way to make tyranny invincible is public opinion; and the whole policy of a tyrant consists in the means of capturing it.'[38]

An insight into Babeuf's ideas is given by a document he wrote in 1794, making proposals for the organization of the Electoral Club (see Chapter 4). Babeuf attacked the formalism of the club, in which only those with a membership document could speak:

> I call a true popular society one where all the people can go, take their places and make their voices heard, without being subject to a thousand and one formalities of corporations imitating those of fanaticism and royalty . . . I call a true popular society the one where the people without money are not below those who have money.[39]

He argued against aping national assemblies. Much of the procedure was unnecessary and made the society remote from the common people; there was no need for elected chairs and secretaries, minutes and records: 'If perhaps a petition has to be drawn up, let anybody or the person who proposed it act as secretary; likewise, anybody, at each session, can be appointed chair.'[40] It is interesting that in his account of the Panthéon Society Buonarroti identified as weaknesses precisely those qualities which Babeuf saw as valuable: absence of minutes, no regular chair, and so on.[41] This shows the divergences between the two men in temperament and in approach to organization.

Babeuf perceived how easily political meetings were dominated by the articulate, and urged that those who were not accustomed to speaking should be encouraged:

> Moreover, citizens ! The shy man, the man who says nothing, give him courage, don't try to impress him with the display of all your erudition, have the patience to let him develop; perhaps it is from his mouth that the best truths, the best accounts of the general interest, will emerge.[42]

Babeuf advocated that women should have full rights in political meetings. Admittedly he based his appeal on the role of women as mothers, but this should not detract from the fact that he represented a minority current in his defence of women's rights at a time when women's clubs had been closed down:

> And do not impose silence on that sex which does not deserve to be despised. On the contrary, raise the dignity of the finest portion of yourselves. Let your womenfolk participate in the interest of the fatherland; they can do more than you think for its prosperity. How do you expect them to rear men as heroes, if you crush them? . . . If, in your Republic, you count women for nothing, you will make them into hangers-on of the monarchy, and they will restore it for you.[43]

The last sentence was especially perceptive. Having been excluded from playing a role in the revolutionary process, women after Thermidor played a key role in the religious and royalist revival.[44] Subsequently, right up to 1945, a significant part of the French left was opposed to female suffrage because it believed that women were under the influence of priests and would vote for the forces of conservatism. Babeuf understood that women were not naturally reactionary, but that it was necessary to win them over to full participation in the revolutionary struggle. If he had been heeded, French history might have taken a different course.

In this concern for women's rights, Babeuf showed that the ideas he had developed in his 1786 letter to Dubois de Fosseux had remained with him. The *Draft Economic Decree* made it clear that all French people 'of either sex' would be full members of the national community,[45] that is, they would have full citizenship – a position most Jacobins would have rejected. In the *Manifesto of the Plebeians* (see Appendix) Babeuf rejected 'heredity by families' as a great 'horror' that 'makes each household into a little republic, which cannot fail to conspire against the greater republic'. But to abolish inheritance would mean abolishing the family as an economic unit, the very opposite of the Jacobin ideal, totally transforming the social position of women.

Many have argued that Babeuf's commitment to equality meant a levelling down, a destruction of culture in the name of ascetic moralism. William H. Sewell Jnr set out the case.

> This paper attempts to show that in spite of their surface similarities, the 'revolution of the equals' proposed by Babeuf in 1796 and the 'social revolution' proposed by Louis Blanc in 1840 belong to two utterly different discursive universes. They are not so much linked by a continuous filiation as divided by a profound epistemic rift.[46]

He claimed that 'Babeuf . . . had a classical hostility to luxury and opulence, which he saw as destructive of equality and virtue. In this respect he remains . . . light years away from the nineteenth-century socialists' celebration of universal abundance'. As a result Babeuf rarely saw labour as transformative or creative, and generally assimilated it to nature. Consequently, Blanc's socialism was qualitatively superior to Babeuf's: 'Rather than achieving equality by levelling down, by limiting all to an ascetic subsistence, Blanc's socialism promised to achieve it by levelling up to a universal abundance.' Sewell based his article mainly on one text, the *Manifesto of the Plebeians*, quoted from Dommanget's anthology, suggesting he had not studied the *babouviste* press at first hand. Louis Blanc, whom he preferred to Babeuf, believed in fair distribution between capitalists and workers and in 1848 he was the first socialist to enter a coalition government; hence he was a suitable figure to be enthroned as the pioneer of modern reformist socialism. More generally, Sewell reinforced the traditional claim that socialists are killjoys who want to stop you having a good time.

The argument was not unique to Sewell. Jean Dautry, a French Communist historian, wrote on the 'economic pessimism of Babeuf',[47] and Claude Mazauric has adopted a similar position, arguing that abundance seemed to be 'a dream' to Babeuf.[48] Mazauric saw Babeuf's view in 1795 as heralding 'Malthusian pessimism', a position which he saw as a realistic response to the severe economic crisis of 1795–6.[49] Other authorities on Babeuf, notably Schiappa, have denied that he was an economic pessimist.[50]

The actual position was complex, and 'light years away' from Sewell's caricature. Babeuf had a forthright approach to the enjoyment of life, scornfully dismissing

> the Christian paradise. If we want to enter it for eternity, we have to begin by being as wretched as possible here below. The Republican is not the man of eternity, he is the man of time; his paradise is this earth, he wants to enjoy freedom and happiness here, and to enjoy them while he is here, without waiting, or at least waiting as little as possible; all the time he spends not in this condition is wasted for him, he will never get it back.[51]

Scarcely the language of an ascetic! Babeuf at Vendôme quoted with approval Morelly's advocacy of a society in which no-one would ever lack 'not only the *necessary* and the *useful*, but even the *agreeable*'.[52] (Babeuf would have doubtless approved the demand for 'bread *and* roses'.)

Any reading of *babouviste* texts will show that certain words recur again and again: *jouissance* (enjoyment), *abondance* (plenty), *aisance* (comfort). Buonarroti, explaining why society would require all to work, said it was in order 'to provide in superabundance *[avec surabondance]* things which are necessary to all, and to provide them with objects of pleasure *[agrément]* which are not condemned by public morality.'[53] The 'New song for the city districts' (sung at the Chinese Baths and reprinted in *L'Eclaireur*), promised that 'equality will restore abundance'.[54] In the *Draft Economic Decree* it was decided that the new order would offer every citizen a guarantee of the following:

> Healthy, comfortable and decently furnished accommodation;
> Clothing for work and leisure, in wool or yam, in accordance with the national costume;
> Laundry, lighting and heating;
> A sufficient quantity of food – bread, meat, poultry, fish, eggs, butter or oil; wine and other drinks used in the different regions; vegetables, fruit, seasonings, and other objects, the combination of which constitutes a moderate and frugal comfort;
> Medical assistance.[55]

Two centuries later, many people, in Los Angeles and London as well as in Calcutta and Mogadishu, would be glad of such 'frugality'.

It is true that the *babouvistes* did denounce 'luxury'. But what was meant by the term? In the *Eclaireur* Babeuf thundered against the 'Asiatic luxury' of the Directory, spelling out that this meant 'great treasures, magnificent clothes, beautiful carriages, fine houses and handkerchiefs at 40 000 *livres* each, while 24 million French people were going short of bread.'[56] People still remembered Marie-Antoinette, who had notoriously had a new pair of shoes every day. By luxury Babeuf meant the conspicuous consumption of a ruling elite, designed to display privilege and far beyond anything needed for physical or intellectual satisfaction.

Engels in *The Peasant War in Germany* argued that the early stages of every proletarian movement were marked by asceticism, because it needed to strip itself 'of everything that could reconcile it with the existing social system'.[57] But Babeuf had moved beyond this stage and begun to sketch out the politics of mass agitation, in which asceticism would serve as a barrier between the revolutionaries and their potential supporters. (Many Parisian workers derived their livelihood from the luxury trades. The wigmakers had been driven into conservatism because aristocratic wigs had gone out of fashion. Only in the context of a planned economy giving work to all would it be possible to effectively attack unnecessary luxury.)

Although Buonarroti recounted the views of the conspirators as a collective, there were times when his own views – more ascetic than Babeuf's – crept through, for example when he wrote affectionately of the 'frugality, simplicity and modesty of the glorious days of Sparta'.[58] He had a Rousseauesque distaste for city life: 'The greater the population of a town, the more likely you are to encounter there servants, dissipated women, starving writers, poets, musicians, painters, wits, actors, dancers, priests, pimps, thieves and mountebanks of every sort.'[59] He even claimed that the end of money 'would soon cure us of the mania of displaying wit and making books'.[60] It is hard to imagine such well-read and enquiring minds as Babeuf and Germain agreeing with that.

Babeuf, however, had never shared Rousseau's hostility to luxury. In a letter to Dubois de Fosseux he enquired: 'Do we need to protest so loudly against luxury? Aren't we rather exaggerating the ills we attribute to it?' He went on to note that there was no problem of luxury in the countryside, and that in the towns it occupied people who might otherwise spend their money on buying land and doing further harm to country-dwellers.[61] Babeuf knew how to party. In a letter to his wife in

August 1790 he described how his supporters in a village called Tilloloy entertained him to a meal:

> Cordiality, openness and gaiety could be seen on every face . . . despite the moderate quality of the dishes, it was a true banquet, for the guests were free and equal men. We drank to the health of that freedom and equality which the inhabitants of Picardy will always want to enjoy.[62]

Far from being an economic pessimist, in a letter to Germain in 1795 Babeuf had insisted that: 'Neither arts, nor sciences, nor industry, would be endangered, far from it. They would receive an impulse in the direction of general utility, and would be transformed in their applications in such a way as to increase the sum of enjoyment of all.'[63]

For the most part, the proposals for the new society outlined by Buonarroti did not involve the rejection of the gains of modern civilization, but rather their transcendence into something better – though there were ambiguities which reflected disagreements between the conspirators and the fact that they had not had time to resolve the issues. Great towns were to disappear, but that did not mean a reversion to rural life with its economic and cultural limitations. Rather, they proposed to break down the distinction between town and country. France would be covered by a network of villages, linked by roads and canals for ease of rapid communication. The late eighteenth century was a period in which communications were developing rapidly – as Babeuf, who had spent his adolescence digging a canal, knew better than most. The palaces of the rich would disappear, but this would not mean the disappearance of architectural magnificence, which would live on in public buildings: stores, amphitheatres, circuses, aqueducts, bridges, canals, squares, archives, libraries and buildings for public assemblies.[64]

Babeuf could not foresee the technological developments that would transform human life after his death. But he welcomed technological advance. The *babouvistes* recognized that only in the framework of a planned economy could machinery be a boon to all:

> It is only in a system of community that the use of machines would be a true advantage for humanity, whose labours they would lessen, while increasing the abundance of necessary and agreeable things. Today, by suppressing a great quantity of manual labour, they take the bread out of the mouths of a mass of men, in the interests of a few greedy speculators whose profits they increase.[65]

One important technological advance of the 1790s was Chappe's sema-phore telegraph, which in 1794 was perfected to the point where it could send a message from Lille to Paris in less than an hour. In the *Draft Economic Decree* particular mention was made of the use of telegraphic lines in the new society to facilitate communications.[66]

The *babouvistes* knew of working-class opposition to mechanization. There had been machine-breaking at Rouen in 1789; elsewhere textile workers had opposed the introduction of spinning jennies and other machinery.[67] The conspirators took the position that the only solution lay in a planned economy. Charles Germain, in a letter to Babeuf in the summer of 1795, set out very clearly that industry could be best devel-oped in a socialist economy:

> Shall we destroy industry by organizing it, by administering it, by assign-ing a task to everyone, by not allowing anything useless to be under-taken, by constantly establishing a proportion between production and consumption, and putting everything in harmony . . . ?[68]

Babeuf's reply to Germain, already quoted (see Chapter 4), showed him to be not only a prophetic critic of the free market, but an advocate of the socialism of abundance.

11
Theory and Practice

If an equal society, based on democracy and plenty, was the goal, how was that goal to be reached? Rose argued that 'Babeuf began as a practical revolutionary and ended as a utopian dreamer'; and claimed that the conspiracy was: 'the most extreme reaction of traditional classes during the revolution against the challenge of accelerating capitalism, rather than . . . the harbinger of a new, progressive, socialist economic order.'[1] There is quite a lot of evidence to the contrary. Utopian dreamers were not seen as much of a threat, either before or after 1789, and they were not usually put to death. What gave Babeuf his specific place in the history of socialism was precisely his concern to unite theory and practice.

It would be wrong to transplant twentieth-century categories back onto Babeuf, but it is equally wrong to detach him from the complex pattern of class struggle in the course of the Revolution. To understand Babeuf's relation to class struggle in the French Revolution, it is necessary to consider his philosophical framework, in particular the way in which he had diverged from Rousseau. For Rousseau, human beings were naturally good but had been mysteriously corrupted by the forces of society. How that natural goodness could reassert itself was equally mysterious.

Babeuf, however, had learnt, probably from Helvétius, that human beings were governed by self-interest. In the *Prospectus* to the new series of the *Tribun du peuple*, published in the autumn of 1795, he wrote: 'We also know a bit about the elements that move human beings. Their interest is the best lever.'[2] The same theme was taken up in the secret directory's instructions to the military agents: 'It is a truth recognized long ago that men act vigorously only in their own interests; the general interest is made up of the sum of individual interests.'[3] If equality was to be achieved, the agency would have to be those who would benefit from equality, namely the poor and oppressed.

Babeuf was clearly groping towards a concept of class struggle, although often he saw it merely in terms of rich and poor. He defined the Revolution as 'a war declared between patricians and plebeians, between rich and poor'.[4] He linked this war of poor and rich directly to the pursuit of 'common happiness'.[5]

The question of Babeuf's perception of the potential agency of social transformation raises the vexed question of whether anything that could be described as a working class actually existed in Paris in the 1790s. Certainly wage labour was very widespread. Calculations first made by F. Braesch and revised by later historians suggest that somewhere in the region of half the population of Paris in the 1790s consisted of wage-workers and their dependants.[6] However, they did not constitute a homogeneous group. Many were domestic servants; many more worked in very small workplaces. But there were larger workplaces as well. One calculation is that the *average* number of workers per employer in Paris was 16.6.[7] Many workshops, notably in specialized luxury trades, were smaller than this, often with five workers or fewer, so there were a considerable number of workplaces with thirty or even fifty workers – quite large enough, as many twentieth-century workers can testify, for a sharp sense of opposition between worker and boss. Even larger units, beginning to resemble modern factories, were making their appearance. In Northern Paris there were a number of textile manufactories. And the events of the 1790s accelerated the process of proletarianization. The needs of war led to the creation of new forms of manufacture. The establishment of an Imprimerie Nationale replaced many small artisanal printshops with a large printing establishment employing wage labour and directly controlled by the government.[8]

Of course it is true, as Soboul insisted, that there was still a very substantial artisan sector, in which the journeymen ate and slept under their master's roof. The mentality of this sector, strongly attached to private property, and in which the lines between wage-earners and independent craftsmen were blurred, was extremely important in defining the politics of the Parisian *sans-culottes*. But it was not the whole picture.

Recent studies of journeymen have shown that the sheer numbers were such that most journeymen could never become masters. They often remained journeymen for many years, even their whole lives, frequently changing employers. Only a minority lived with their masters, and many were married with families. Those who failed to become masters often moved into domestic service, the armed forces or other employment.[9] As Robert Darnton concluded after a study of journeymen in the printing industry: 'Journeymen and masters may have lived together as members of a happy family at sometime somewhere in Europe, but not in the printing houses of eighteenth-century France . . . '[10]

Moreover a focus on the artisan/journeyman milieu may betray a bias involving both skill and gender. Skilled artisans were literate and well-organized and have left extensive records for subsequent historians, but they were not the only workers. As Michael Sonenscher has pointed out, one of the fundamental divisions in the eighteenth-century urban economy was 'between those who made things and those who moved them'.[11] Alongside the skilled artisans existed a great mass of unskilled workers: porters, dockers, water-carriers, those who did menial and unskilled tasks in manufacturing workshops. Haim Burstin has shown that 'a mass of workers were fluctuating in a precarious balance on the threshold of unemployment'; the boundary-line between these wage-workers and the large body of indigent poor was often difficult to decipher.[12]

Many of these unskilled workers were women. Women were excluded from most skilled trades and professions, and were generally considered unfit to exercise political rights; but that does not mean they were thought too ladylike to do heavy manual work. As Olwen Hufton has shown: 'Nothing was too menial. They carried soil, heavy vegetables to and from market, water, wood – anything. In the large cities, they found employment as rag sorters, cinder sifters, refuse collectors, assistants to masons and bricklayers.'[13] Generally their wages were between a third and a half of men's earnings; their role remains obscure because women were not included in employment statistics.[14]

But did this mass of wage-workers constitute a class? In defining a class both objective and subjective factors must be considered. That a large mass of wage-workers existed is not in doubt; what may be questioned is the extent to which they perceived themselves as a group having common interests. The boundary-lines between small masters and journeymen at one end of the scale, and between unskilled workers and the indigent poor at the other, were often blurred. Wage-workers often identified themselves as *sans-culottes* rather than as proletarians. But if they had shared interests in issues like food prices, they also had specific interests in wages. Throughout the Revolution there were strikes as well as bread riots. The predominance of small workplaces made organization more difficult but not impossible; it would not have been necessary for the Le Chapelier law to ban workers' organizations if nobody had been trying to organize. Recent work by Raymonde Monnier[15] and Haim Burstin shows the slow and contradictory emergence of a working class in the revolutionary period. The *babouvistes* had some implantation in this nascent working class; documents from the conspiracy show reports of support among unskilled workers, notably market porters and dockers.[16]

However, it is not necessary to prove that the working class exercised a significant impact on the course of the revolution. Certainly it was not a contender for power; it is of interest because it was a class with a future. In Guérin's image, it was an embryonic working class. But embryos kick vigorously in the womb, even though they are as yet incapable of independent existence. If they did not kick in the womb, they would not develop the muscles to walk when the time came.

A language of class and class struggle did not as yet exist for Babeuf, but behind some of his formulations the notions of labour and exploitation were clearly visible. He identified two diametrically opposed tendencies among supporters of the republic:

> One wants the republic of a million, which was always the enemy, the dominator, the extortionist, the oppressor, the leech of the twenty-four million others; the million which has revelled for centuries in idleness, at the expense of our sweat and labour; the other party wants the republic for these twenty-four million, who have laid the foundations and cemented them with their blood, who nourish and support the fatherland, supply all its needs, and defend it and die for its safety and its glory.[17]

Babeuf was one of the first to use the term *prolétaire* (proletarian), and while it would obviously be wrong to assume he was using it in the Marxist sense, it clearly had connotations of the propertyless who had no source of income but their labour. In his history Buonarroti declared that the 'proletarians' were the 'only true supporters of equality'.[18]

Likewise, the word *ouvrier* (worker) was commonly used in the late eighteenth century to mean anyone who worked with their hands, whether self-employed or wage-earning. But in some cases Babeuf seems to be using the word in the narrower sense of wage-earner. Thus in the introduction to the *Perpetual Land-Register*, where he referred to *ouvriers* suffering from reduced wages and unemployment, he was clearly thinking primarily of wage-workers.[19]

In dealing with the problems of the poor, Babeuf repeatedly referred to wages, seeing wage labour as the typical form of oppression. Thus when addressing soldiers he wrote: 'Returning to our beggar fathers, we have to expect to be beggars like them! To crawl like them under the insolent domination of the rich! To be their slaves! To work, for a miserable wage, from the first to the last hour.'[20] Though many of the soldiers addressed were in fact probably the children of peasants, the image evoked was of a wage-labourer.

There was no extended economic or sociological analysis to back up Babeuf's picture of class struggle. But he was clearly grappling with the issues. In a letter of July 1795 to Germain he wrote of:

> the plot whereby they succeed in getting a multitude of hands to work, without those whose hands do the work being able to obtain the products, which are destined from the outset to be amassed in great heaps in the hands of criminal speculators, who, after having concerted to constantly reduce the workers' wages, agree, either amongst themselves or together with the distributors of what they have accumulated, the merchants, their fellow-thieves, to fix the prices of everything, so that these prices are only within the reach of the rich, or of members of their league, that is, those who like them are in a position to misuse means of accumulating currency and to take possession of everything.

In short, the producers do not earn enough to buy what they themselves have made. He went on to ask:

> Why do the first agents, those who do the creative work, the essential work, derive from it incomparably less advantages than those who come later, than the merchants, for example, who, in my eyes, only do very secondary work, that of distribution?[21]

Here we have the beginnings of a theory of exploitation.

Victor Dalin discovered a manuscript of Babeuf's entitled 'The low price of wages ruins the bulk of the nation', in which he argued that low wages kept down the level of consumption, and as a result reinforced poverty.[22] Again Babeuf was grappling with the problem of exploitation and putting wage labour at the centre of the picture.

The conspirators did not attempt to base themselves exclusively or even primarily on the embryonic proletariat; to have done so would have meant turning their backs on potential allies and so limiting themselves to mere propaganda. But the documents of the conspiracy (see Chapter 4) show that considerable attention was given to wage-earners and to the state of consciousness and possible conflicts in workplaces, especially by Juste Moroy, the agent of the twelfth *arrondissement*, who at Vendôme described his territory as 'composed entirely of the working class, the most precious in society'.[23]

Confronted with the reality of class struggle within the revolutionary process, Babeuf also had to deal with the question of ideology. Time and again Babeuf's writings return to the power of ideology, or as he called it, opinion:

> Everything can be done by public opinion, and when you succeed in directing it towards a particular system, you are sure of making this system prevail, for the opinion of the people, as has been well said, is its strength, and the strength of the people is everything.[24]

For Babeuf 'opinion is the queen of the world'; the agents of the conspiracy were informed that 'it is through opinion that everything can be moved'.[25] He pondered on the problems of manufactured public opinion (*opinion factice*). In the *Perpetual Land-Register* he noted how the people was maintained in inertia by glamour (*prestiges*) and a 'horde of grotesque and barbarous machinations'. He claimed in the same text that 'prejudices, the offspring of ignorance, have always been the cause of the misfortunes of the human race'.[26]

Babeuf shrewdly observed some of the mechanisms used by ideology to hold people in submission. Thus he noted the process whereby the social order was made to seem permanent by assimilating it to nature: 'It seems to the rich . . . that by striving to make the poor believe that their condition is inevitable in nature, they have found the best barrier against the actions of the latter.'[27] Likewise he observed that the strength of ideology was that it contained a partial truth, and that its impact was greatest when it was able to manipulate a virtue; discussing the raising of troops for the Vendée, he wrote: 'They always give the most respectable motives when they want to set the people in motion, because they know it has virtues, that it never starts moving except for what it believes to be justice.'[28]

Babeuf was strongly hostile to the role of religion in society. He publicly repudiated Catholicism in 1790 and became, like Maréchal, an atheist. He was vigorously anti-clerical and used the word 'priest' as a synonym for 'charlatan' or 'impostor'.[29] The role given to religion in the projected future society was obviously a compromise, involving belief in God and immortality of the soul but rejection of revelation (Buonarroti came very close to Voltaire in arguing that it was socially desirable that people should believe in an 'infallible judge of their thoughts and secret actions').[30] But J.-M. Schiappa has argued that the religious policy of the *babouvistes* can be summed up in the three principles of *laïcité* (separation of state and school from church), militant anticlericialism and tolerance.[31]

Babeuf's preoccupation with ideology led him to give great importance to education. As Dommanget pointed out, education was a constant concern throughout his life.[32] In the *Perpetual Land-Register* he contrasted an educated people with the people as it exists today: 'The latter is coarse, superstitious, stupid and lacking in energy; the former will be enlightened, industrious, active and patriotic.' He lamented the poor standards of education in France; he claimed that it often happened that a school-master was appointed who could not read and write.[33]

Babeuf's recognition of the power of ideology raised crucial problems about the transition to an equal society. If the people were profoundly warped by the ideology of the old order, how could they assume the task of creating a new one? Tønnesson has written of Babeuf having both a 'maximum' and a 'minimum' programme, a long-term objective and a set of minimum demands.[34] It is a useful comparison, but it does not go far enough. What Babeuf was looking for was a means to bridge the gap between the two, demands which would fit the immediate experience of the Paris poor, but would lead forward logically to 'common happiness', what in the twentieth century have been known as 'transitional demands'.

In many ways the demand for the 1793 Constitution fitted the bill. This demand was not an invention of the *babouvistes*; it had been raised by the inhabitants of such traditionally militant faubourgs as Saint-Antoine and Saint-Marceau. It was a demand that looked realistic; the Constitution had been voted for only three years earlier, and working people remembered clearly that they had eaten better under Robespierre than under the Directory. At the same time it was a demand that called the whole social order into question, as the Directory clearly recognized by making its advocacy a capital offence. For despite its recognition of the principle of property, the Constitution could be read in such a way as to point towards a social order based on true equality. The term the Equals used for such demands was *acheminement* (step towards).

Buonarroti explained the proposal that immediately after the insurrection, the property of *émigrés* and enemies of the people would be distributed to soldiers and the poor:

> It would be wrong to consider the promise of a great distribution of property as contrary to the spirit of community which we aimed to achieve. The main point was to succeed, and the secret directory did not adopt its declaration of insurrection lightly, having felt that in order to achieve its aim, it needed neither too much reserve, which might have discouraged its true friends, nor too much haste, which would have swollen the number of its enemies.
>
> By the promise of distribution, the secret directory was winning the attention and upholding the hopes of the working class, without alienating those who, while hating the new aristocracy, did not for all that love true equality.[35]

But even if the people could be mobilized by such demands, there were other difficulties about the transition to 'common happiness'. Buonarroti summed up the problem:

> The experience of the French Revolution and more specifically the disturbances and vicissitudes of the National Convention have, it seems to me, sufficiently demonstrated that a people whose opinions were formed in a regime of inequality and despotism is quite unsuitable, at the beginning of a regenerating revolution, to indicate by its votes the men who have the responsibility of guiding it and carrying it through. This difficult task can belong only to wise and courageous citizens who, deeply enamoured of the fatherland and humanity, having long investigated the causes of public ills, have freed themselves from prejudices and common vices, have advanced the enlightenment of their contemporaries, and despising gold and popular signs of greatness, have staked their happiness on making themselves immortal by ensuring the triumph of equality. Perhaps it is necessary, at the birth of a political revolution, even out of respect for the true sovereignty of the people, to be less concerned about winning the votes of the nation than about making supreme authority fall

into wisely and strongly revolutionary hands in a manner that is as little arbitrary as possible.[36]

The Equals did not bequeath us a short, simple answer to this question. Among the documents quoted at the Vendôme trial was one which stated:

> we must ensure that power, removed from the hands of the rogues who now hold it, should pass into the hands of pure, true, absolute democrats, men of the people, those who are supremely its friends. How can we make this power pass to them? This is the difficulty which has held us up and which is still holding us up . . . [37]

This problem of transition was central to Babeuf's thought, and marked a clear break between him and his utopian predecessors and followers. The unity of theory and practice was a central preoccupation from the outset: 'it is only practice which can perfect theory' he wrote in a letter of 1787.[38]

Babeuf always insisted that there was a unity of means and ends. As he told the Vendôme court: 'Whoever wills the end wills the means. To achieve an end, it is essential to overcome all obstacles to it.'[39] In the autumn of 1794 he wrote: 'All means of defeating evil people are good, providing you succeed.'[40]

Babeuf's continued wrestling with the problem can be seen in his attitude to violence. By use of selective quotation Babeuf can be made into a pacifist or a psychopath; he was neither, but tried to establish that violence is profoundly regrettable but necessary, and that the question of its use is a tactical one. Buonarroti tells how two officers of the Police Legion offered to assassinate the five members of the Directory, but the conspirators refused because such an act would be useless in a situation where the other circumstances making success possible were not present.[41]

The Equals recognized that their complete economic programme could not be implemented immediately. Buonarroti tells us that the plan was that initially the rich should not be stripped of their property, but that they would be denied abundance, pleasure and respect; meanwhile the industrious man would be guaranteed 'honest, permanent prosperity'. This, he claimed, would soon open the eyes of those misled by prejudice and routine.[42]

This still left the question of who would carry through the transition. There were clear divisions within the secret directory on this question. Apparently Darthé first argued the necessity of a 'provisional revolutionary government', modelled on the rule of the Committee of Public Safety in 1793–4.[43] Buonarroti was close to this position. Darthé and Debon proposed a one-man dictatorship, but this was rejected by the rest of the secret directory.[44] Maréchal argued against the need for any period of transition.[45] Babeuf was probably tom between these positions. He doubtless saw that Maréchal's position was impracticable; yet Babeuf's constant advocacy of mass participation and democratic accountability did not fit well with the idea of a temporary dictatorship substituting itself for the people until the people was 'ready'.

What guarantee could there be that the 'provisional' dictatorship would not become a permanent one? One was the claim that the dictatorship would be of very short duration. One of the documents seized at Babeuf's arrest, and probably written by Babeuf himself, stated that it was impossible to form primary assemblies immediately because they would fall under royalist control, so the secret directory would act as government of the republic for three months during which time 'opinion' would be raised to a higher level, and then elections based on the 1793 Constitution would be held.[46] In fact the difficult questions of transition were still unresolved when the conspiracy was brought to an end.[47] But it is also possible to accuse Babeuf of over-optimism in fixing so short a timescale. The grip of old ideas and old habits, which Babeuf had understood so well, would scarcely evaporate in three months. This was the Babeuf who in 1793 had written that he believed 'general happiness on earth' could be established within a year.[48] It was the Babeuf of whom Buonarroti wrote: 'No-one has taken less account of the time necessary to operate such changes in the feelings and habits of men.'[49]

The other guarantee was the frequently repeated claim that the dictatorship would be exercised by men of proven virtue, who would not seek any personal gain. But virtue is in the eye of the beholder.

Yet there was also a recognition that even when elections were felt to be feasible, it would not be possible to simply leave everything to spontaneity. It was intended that the secret directory would remain in existence, and would keep a close watch on the workings of the elected assembly. The conspiracy itself was therefore to play a key role in the process of transition. But what sort of an organization was the conspiracy? The standard view of both friends and foes is to see Babeuf as a forerunner of Blanqui and Lenin. In fact he had relatively little in common with Blanqui, and if he anticipated Lenin in some respects, it is because the historical Lenin was very different from the Cold War caricature. Indeed Babeuf's conspiracy was very different even from the secret societies in which Buonarroti was involved in the early nineteenth century, which had rituals and catechisms and were generally much closer to freemasonry than the conspiracy of 1796.[50] The conspiracy is said to have been elitist and putschist; the truth is rather more complex.

Babeuf adopted the organizational form of a conspiracy because he saw conspiracies around him, and believed that the only way to counter them was to play the same game. The first document to the revolutionary agents explained that when the people were free, no-one had the right to act politically without consulting them. But when the people were in chains, then it was vital that 'the most intrepid, the most capable of dedicating themselves, those who believe themselves possessed to the highest degree of energy, ardour and strength' should take on the 'glorious title of conspirators for liberty' in order to save their fellow-citizens.[51]

An effective insurrection needed timing; it could not be left to spontaneity, and indeed spontaneity might have to be held back in order that the right moment was seized: 'The people will rise only as a whole and only when it hears the voice of its true liberators, whose signal it will recognize by unmistakable indications.'[52] In order to achieve this, a tightly centralized organization was necessary. As Babeuf told his accusers at Vendôme, it was impossible that the whole people should recognize the need for insurrection simultaneously: 'Someone has to begin.'[53]

Babeuf was facing a tough and repressive regime; he himself had been in jail several times and knew that revolutions are not organized from a prison cell. Therefore it was vital to build a centralized and clandestine organization. Lenin (or for that matter Blanqui) faced similar repression and had similar experiences; they drew similar conclusions, and did not need to learn organizational structures from Babeuf.

To see only this side of Babeuf's organization is to give a very distorted picture. If the conspiracy was to escape repression, it had to be clandestine; but if it was to mobilize and inspire the masses, it had to be as open as possible. The contradiction was in reality, and it was one to which there was no simple solution. The conspirators had to aim for as much clandestinity as necessary, and as much openness as possible. As the first circular to the agents pointed out, no harm could come from it being known that the secret directory existed; indeed, news of its existence might encourage the 'unhappy majority'; but the exposure of the leading personnel would destroy 'the combined set of ramifications leading from a single centre' as well as spreading demoralization among the citizens.[54] Later, the secret directory warned Moroy of the dangers of excessive clandestinity and urged him to 'show a great confidence in the goodness of your cause, and your air of conviction will easily make many recruits'.[55]

Dommanget criticized the conspirators for inadequate security measures. While he may have been right on detailed points, especially the failure to set up an alternative leadership in case of arrests, it is also true that no organization can grow without taking risks. Perfect security can be maintained only at the price of total isolation. It is easy to be wise after the event, but too much wisdom before the event can lead to paralysis.

The conspiracy was tightly centralized, but it was not monolithic. Within the central group of conspirators there were significant divergences on such questions as the evaluation of Robespierre, the nature of the transition and the role of women. The role of the agents was not simply to serve as a transmission belt between the leadership and the masses. On the contrary, the documents seized at Babeuf's arrest reveal clearly that there was a genuine two-way communication between the centre and the agents. Certainly the centre provided a regular flow of propaganda to be distributed, but the agents were also feeding in an uninterrupted supply of information. Some of this was of a purely technical nature (whereabouts of gun-shops and so on), but most of it was to do with the level of activity and state of consciousness among the masses. One of their main tasks was to 'take note of the daily thermometer of the public mind'.[56]

The conspiracy was centralized at the top, but at the base the aim was to build as many small groups as possible, generally meeting in supporters' homes, and largely unknown one to the other. By the nature of things the centre could scarcely monitor the activity of all these groups (the seized documents give little information about them beyond the fact of their existence), so the scope for rank-and-file initiative was considerable.

In its methods of working, the conspiracy seems to have foreshadowed activities that have characterized revolutionary groupings in many different contexts over the succeeding two centuries. They developed forms of mass propaganda, especially the use of fly-posting. They aimed to break down the barriers between party and masses by building up a periphery of contacts and supporters, by using such methods as visiting contacts in their own home. Above all, they gave prime importance to the distribution of revolutionary newspapers. Despite the repression, the open circulation of the press continued. In number 40 of the *Tribun du peuple* Babeuf made a passionate defence of the necessity for a revolutionary press:

> Moreover, a remnant of fear, rather than of shame, leads our dominators to constantly wrap all their plots up in shadows of disguise, so that their regular outrages are not usually grasped and appreciated at first sight in their full meaning and with all that they entail, by the majority of minds, who are still trusting, simple and good; therefore it is essential that a popular interpreter should constantly put them in a position to judge the eternal crimes of our oppressors in all their reality and extent.[57]

In this insistence on the key organizing role of the revolutionary press Babeuf was indeed anticipating the Lenin of *What is to be done?*, though this is not the parallel commonly made.

Ultimately Babeuf's theory derived from his concept of the role of the masses in the struggle. For Babeuf, the organization was an instrument of the people, not something that substituted itself for the people. The secret directory had drawn up a speech to be made to the people in the event of a victorious uprising; this contained the following sentence; 'Sovereign people! if we betray you, if after this our words too were to be the forerunners of our perfidy and our crimes, then in the name of the fatherland and liberty, do not let us finish them: immediately condemn us and punish us!'[58] So for Babeuf it must ultimately be the people, not the party, which decided. But this did not resolve the problems outlined above. Centuries of oppression and ignorance had instilled the people with habits which made it hard for them to recognize their own rights and their own entitlement to liberty. The classic Enlightenment remedy had been education; and as we have seen, Babeuf gave great importance to the role of education in the process of human emancipation. But education alone would not solve the problems. Firstly, it would take a long time, and secondly, it presupposed the existence of an elite who would do the educating.

Babeuf, on the other hand, belonged to the tradition of what Hal Draper called 'socialism-from-below'.[59] Thus he told the people they could not defeat their enemies by surprise, but only by open force:

> Away with that pusillanimity which would make us believe that we cannot do anything by ourselves, and that we always need rulers with us. Rulers only make revolutions in order to go on ruling. At last we want to make one to ensure for ever the happiness of the people by true democracy.[60]

This was echoed time and again in *babouviste* writings; the revolutionary agents were told:

> Make the people understand that they will never do anything great, that they will never make revolutions for themselves, for their true happiness, except when there are no rulers involved in any way in their movement; they must not be so distrustful of their own resources, and they must convince themselves that they, the people, are sufficient to be able to carry out a great undertaking. Thus, in the one we are preparing, take care to set aside everything which is not of the people . . . [61]

Already he had told his readers that 'press freedom is not decreed, it is conquered', and that the people 'can expect nothing except from itself to save its rights'.[62] Such statements stand unambiguously in the same tradition as Marx's insistence that 'the emancipation of the working classes must be conquered by the working classes themselves'.[63]

Babeuf has often been compared to his near contemporary Robert Owen, to whom Buonarroti was sympathetic in his later years.[64] The comparison is entirely in Babeuf's favour. Owen stood in the Enlightenment tradition of emancipation through education; he saw human beings as the product of environmental moulding. He had no faith in working-class self-activity and stated that workers were 'too ignorant and inexperienced to find a remedy to the existing evils'.[65] It was precisely of Owen that Marx was thinking in the third thesis on Feuerbach when he wrote:

> The materialist doctrine that men are products of circumstances and upbringing, and that, therefore, changed men are products of other circumstances and changed upbringing, forgets that it is men who change circumstances and that the educator must himself be educated. Hence

this doctrine is bound to divide society into two parts, one of which is superior to society . . . [66]

Babeuf had far greater faith in popular self-activity than did Owen, but he still had no adequate solution for the problem of how those warped by the ideological legacy of oppression could change. He had seen the Revolution, and all the rapid changes of consciousness that it involved; but he tended to regard such transformations of ideas as mere fickleness: 'of thirty thousand who adored Lafayette and his horse, not one could be found after his fall.'[67]

Marx's answer was that 'the coincidence of the changing of circumstances and of human activity can be conceived and rationally understood only as revolutionising practice.'[68] In other words, the oppressed transform themselves in process of changing the world. It is a truth which has been confirmed in many revolutions and social struggles over the last century and a half. Babeuf's failure to reach this point meant that he often seemed to oscillate between extreme libertarianism and extreme authoritarianism.

Yet if Babeuf is open to criticism from later socialists, that does not in any way lessen the importance of his achievement, which in the context of his time was a remarkable one. If socialism is about human selfemancipation, then it must be about learning from past struggles in order to make future struggles more successful. In such a learning process, the experience of Babeuf was an important stage, and it has all too often been ignored or marginalized. Hopefully this study will make a small contribution to restoring Babeuf to his rightful place in the history of socialism for English-speaking readers. It is the final kick that breaks down the door, but it can only do so if the door has been weakened by previous blows.

Appendix

A) EXTRACT FROM BABEUF'S LETTER OF JUNE 1786 TO DUBOIS DE FOSSEUX[1]

I should be greatly obliged, Sir, if you could obtain for me Dr Taranget's speech. The summary you give of it in the extract from your two public sessions makes me very anxious to have a fuller knowledge of what the famous professor's sleepless nights have produced. There is no subject in itself more interesting than the *natural and philosophical history of woman*; but the study of woman will always be incomplete when it is isolated from that of man: the doctor can observe one sex or the other separately, his concern is above all the physical phenomena which characterize each of them, and illnesses and crises are the main lessons. But there is something else to consider: the girl, even from earliest childhood, develops under influences which are too foreign to her nature for all her qualities and all the richness of her being not to be considerably reduced and all too often perverted. She grows with obstacles of every sort, her education moulds her from the earliest age for the domination of a master to whom she will have to yield everything and always; even in her most innocent games she is forbidden everything which could enable her to achieve the degree of health and skill which she is capable of acquiring. She is obliged, out of respect for a false modesty, to weaken herself physically and morally. We sacrifice and transform woman, enervate her in order to make her our slave. We envy the aptitudes of her organs, and we suppress her finest faculties by not allowing her to exercise them. No sciences for her, no skill, nothing serious, nothing considered; everything is frivolity and futility; everything is dissipation, or wretchedness – and yet woman still often rises, by her talents, by her courage, by her virtues, by her reason, above this atmosphere of oppression in which we strive to keep her.

I greatly regret that Dr Taranget declares himself as lightly as he does about woman's destiny, and I must say, he shocked me by declaring that the immediate product of her organization is the *temperament*, from which results, according to him, *weakness* and *fickleness*, two roots from which are composed the moral qualities, the qualities of mind, modified at the same source. – To explain everything by temperament, to reduce everything to temperament, may be all right for a doctor, but, if I may say so, it isn't appropriate for a philosopher or a scientist. To conclude from the temperament what kind of mind women have, is to attribute to temperament a meaning it doesn't have, or rather which it wouldn't have, if we hadn't taken measures to leave dormant everything in women which is not temperament. I don't understand on the basis of what observations Dr Taranget can attribute the birth of feelings such as *love, friendship*, and *pity*, to the appearance of puberty. – What, until then would the girl not have loved any of her female companions; would she not have felt anything for her father, her mother, her sisters, her brothers, nor for any of their friends! until then, would she have felt no sympathy for anyone's sufferings! Friendship and pity are feelings of affection which don't wait for the great revolution of puberty to appear: we are born with feelings of sympathy for almost everything that lives. Children love each other; however young they may be, they have a preference for someone, great or small; a very little girl who is not moved by seeing someone else's tears flow, or by hearing groans of pain, such a girl would be an exception.

Friendship and pity belong to all ages; but at a tender age friendship is a sort of general benevolence, the little girl and the little boy tend to love all those who approach them: the little *marquise* loves the little peasant girl, or perhaps the little peasant boy; she loves the daughter or son of her gardener; she loves her wet-nurse's children. The feeling of fraternity is innate to the human heart, and to get rid of it education has to stifle it. To begin with we feel we are all brothers; but soon in the name of two inequalities which nature did not create and does not recognize, namely rank and wealth, nobles are inspired with harshness and arrogant airs, and the rich are inculcated with the arithmetic of the most squalid interests. To those who are neither noble nor rich respect and submission are imposed; they are left their sheep-skins while the others are clad in wolf-skins. All are weaned from the sweet honey of fraternity.

The great majority are told with threats: *be Abel*, stay humble and benign; crawl, flatter, adore, that is your lot – the minority of nobles and rich are told *be Cain*: oppress, starve, kill, slaughter. That's the end of fraternity; in the same species we observe two instincts which inevitably become hostile to each other. – It's the end of friendship between the unequal, it doesn't survive the final prescriptions of an education whose main aim is to subordinate its principle to the satisfactions of vanity; the little *marquise* having become a great lady forgets her former friend the peasant girl, she kicks away her wet-nurse's son or daughter, she would not dare to fail to blush at a familiarity which used to be of the most agreeable sort. – It's also an end to friendship between those who are unequal, or considered to be so according to the opinion of the world: friendship is no longer anything but an affair of choice or convention and interest. It's a final very slight remnant of fraternity. – Friendship and pity are inborn dispositions, more marked in childhood than at any other time of life; without an unnatural education, they would develop into fraternity; in both sexes they precede puberty; the younger the blood, the more powerful they are, but they have nothing to do with puberty. Puberty is the precursor only of *love*, an imperious passion which will not cease to be a misfortune for many people until the day it becomes the principle and the law of marriage! Is it not cruel for individuals of both sexes to be reduced, as all too often happens, to doing violence to their strongest feelings out of deference to an inequality of conditions which destroys morals and all private happiness? When resignation replaces a shamefully repressed love, there is nothing but maternity which can attenuate the repulsion and sometimes cause it to be forgotten; the woman who has become a mother is then sublime in her dignity and abnegation, for the accomplishment of the duties of her new state converts her to loving the husband that she previously abhorred. A summary doesn't take account of everything, but while being ignorant of the details that must have been omitted, I am very much inclined, I should even say I feel entitled, to suspect that Dr Taranget has taken his subject from too narrow a point of view, and I consider that any *natural and philosophical history of woman* should lead to the conclusion that with regard to love and devotion woman is worth at least as much as man, and that without doubt the same would be true for science and the arts, if she received an education appropriate to her faculties. A woman generally has more acute senses than a man; she has more subtlety, more tact, more delicacy, better judgement, more presence of mind; she is physically weaker than man, but what does strength mean for her; from the moment that gun-powder and fire-arms were invented, strength even for men already lost much of its value; the superiority of giants was destroyed; there began to be one inequality less in the world, and the same will happen at each stage in the progress of humanity until all inequalities have disappeared. I think that progress is simply levelling. If you go back to the root of the family trees of our great houses, what you find at the origin is generally a warrior whose entire merit consisted in the immense superiority of his physical strength; that was the source of his nobility; but his descendants have not inherited it, and the superiority, by virtue of which we call him noble, no longer exists; the distinction is purely fictitious; it is one of the distinctions which are fatal to fraternity, which the faith of the ignorant still respects, but which no longer stands up to the reasoning of the phi-losopher or the investigations of the scientist.

The claimed superiority of man over woman and the despotic author-ity he asserts over her have the same origin as the domination of nobility, in both cases there is usurpation of rights and consecration of a preju-dice which led our fathers to make physical strength into a cult. – Let's abolish this profane cult, the most profane of all when it is exercised to the detriment of justice, let's eradicate the last traces, and re-establish woman in her rights and in the freedom which belongs to her as it does to us; let us recognize that if she is less favoured than we are in respect of physical strength, on the other hand she is endowed with qualities which we lack and which would be a thousand times more prominent if instead of having been crushed or distorted by a false direction they could have been developed in their true meaning. Let us not demand from woman this strength which we boast of and which we have so misused. What would she do with that strength which is so rarely combined with great intelligence and which is nearly always incompatible with grace? Is she destined for the terrible efforts of war, for the rough work of the fields, for the crushing task of the stevedore? And first of all, if I am not pre-suming too much on the great progress of human reason which already assures me that you will read without irritation all the bold propositions that I am allowing myself to address to you, don't we have good reason to predict that in the more or less near future, war – this most stupid of plagues, since it is our own work – will have disappeared for ever? And when we observe the progress of the sciences, can't we see coming a time when the invention of new machines will make superfluous the deployment of great muscular strength?

In proposing to write the *natural history of woman* Dr Taranget has, in my opinion, started from the wrong place. He has studied woman burdened and weighed down, made stupid and servile, transformed almost entirely from the cradle onwards, so that the law of our wretched superiority should prevail. He has studied woman subordinated to such an extent that she does not dare to stand up by herself, or know how to do so; she is such a slave that she would be afraid to question her inferiority; she is so unthinking, we have to say blinded, that she is no longer even conscious of the advantages she could exploit in order to stand on an equal footing with man. Dr Taranget has envisaged woman still laid low by the traditions of physical strength, the respect of which is merely the religion of barbarism – he has not imagined her restored to her free will throughout her life dating from the day when the law, if she is not in the power of her husband, declares her to be fully capable of judgement; he has not made an impartial parallel between the constitution of the dominating sex and that of the dominated sex, and studied the differences between the organs of the one sex and the organs of the other which indicate the dispositions which are natural to each sex. Without entering into the detail of such comparisons, we can already say that there are common dispositions, equal dispositions, dispositions that are dissimilar in the results that enable them to be recognized. On both sides there is hearing, sight, touch, taste, smell with the organs by which they are exercised. On both sides there is the brain and the heart, intelligence and sympathy; the voice, speech and everything which serves expression. – Which affects the mind more, which charms more, the voice of a man or that of a woman, whether speaking or singing? Despite the powerful attraction of one sex for the other, women prefer a beautiful female voice to a beautiful male voice; despite the attraction of one sex for another, they are more generally struck by the beauty of a beautiful woman than by that of a handsome man, and on this point we are perfectly in agreement with them – beauty of voice, beauty of figure, these are two superiorities which we cannot challenge them on. Are they more sensitive, more sympathetic, more patient, more long-suffering than we are? Who could doubt it? In the two sexes faculties are equal in number, and if, taken one by one, they don't always correspond completely, overall they balance out. There is no faculty in man which can't be found in woman; in each case they are applied to the same objects, but in a different fashion for several of them. For everything which is in the field of the imagination, for everything which depends on feeling and the perfection of external senses, the faculties of man and those of woman tend to be stressed, to get stronger, to moderate according to sex, unless they have been diverted from their natural propensities, unless they have been falsified by education. – There are *male* and *female* faculties which ask to be trained, developed, cultivated, exercised and deployed according to the type that each belongs to.

In this respect female faculties are indisputably equal to male faculties, they are not inferior the one to the other, but as soon as they are mingled together, it becomes impossible to say with certainty what is woman's destiny, since the knowledge of this destiny can result only from the knowledge of the natural propensity of each of her faculties. There has not yet been, as far as I know, education for women. Everywhere male and female faculties have been treated and directed in the same way, while conceding, in terms of an arbitrary view that linked all superiorities to physical strength, that female faculties were quite simply less than male faculties. As a result of this error, the physically weaker sex was left at the disposal of the physically stronger sex. The education of woman, which should have been conceived in terms of her faculties, has only been a truncated sketch of that of man, or a general miniature of this education. In everything she has been given only overviews, not allowing her complete ideas; she has been given only a superficial knowledge. That is why in the arts, in literature, the small number of women involved (for whom, exceptionally, more has been done without it being done better) aim only to produce male works, in which they are necessarily as clumsy as the man who strives to become effeminate in order to produce female work. Woman would not have taken refuge in these sad imitations, if her genius had not been killed: then there would have been a women's literature, a women's poetry, a women's music, painting and sculpture, parallel and equal to male genius: woman's genius would have arisen with the character which is appropriate to her, and the two sexes could have admired and charmed each other reciprocally. How much happiness and enjoyment we should have gained!

Science is one, it is science or it is not science; it could not have a sex. It therefore belongs to the domain of common dispositions, completely identical in women and in men. These are neither male nor female.

Women could not be learned in a different fashion from men, and if they are less so, it is because few of them get the chance to study; their education is given them with excessive parsimony, the colleges are closed to them, teachers would scorn to give them instruction. The matadors of physical strength fear their sagacity. They condemn them to ignorance, in order to always have an excuse for dominating them. But despite this old conspiracy by half the human race, to keep the other half under the yoke, from time to time it is proved by striking examples, that once they are initiated into whatever branch of science it may be, women make as much progress as we do: is it a question of languages? they learn them quicker than we do; are not Madame *Le Masson de Goltz* and Mademoiselle de Mérian walking proof of their supreme aptitude for mathematics, for physics, for chemistry and for all the branches of natural science? Would they not hold one of the most distinguished ranks among the celebrities of all the royal academies of science? Where women have wielded the sceptre, have they proved to be less clever in politics than kings or the most famous ministers? for example Queen Elizabeth of England and many others. If they understand politics, then they would understand history all the more easily. – Don't we see every day women carrying through negotiations in which men, the most crafty men, would have failed? So they would excel in diplomacy – a good number of commercial establishments have prospered under female management – more than one husband has only regained his fortune or re-established his ruined business after putting it in the hands of his wife who is more intelligent and energetic than he is. – If in a well-administered household where good harmony reigns, it is, as the saying goes, the housewife who *wears the trousers*, what conclusion should we draw? That the woman has a better head, that is, more intelligence, character, order and economy than the husband. Households run in this fashion are not rare. How many women are the oracles of their husbands who would undertake nothing, would not make any decision of any importance without consulting them! How many women, if access to the bar were not forbidden them, would be more eloquent, above all more moving than the majority of the most famous colleagues of M. Gerbier. The care of a good nurse, or of any other very dedicated, very vigilant woman has saved more sick people than the treatment of our doctors. Women, daughters, wives, mothers, friends, possess to a high degree the medical instinct which is strengthened by all their solicitude; they see everything, they observe everything, nothing escapes them; the slightest change in the appearance of the face, in the habits of the body, in the temperature of the skin is a revelation for them. Confident attention and insight, this is what they bring to the patient's bedside. So they would be valuable doctors. Their patience is greater than ours; the same is true of their prudence, their foresight, their gentleness. They have also more manual skill; and if, in order to comfort and cure, the surgeon were not obliged to make blood flow and cut into living flesh, if he didn't need a vigour which they lack, they could not be surpassed in the difficult art of operations, since they would be expeditious in order to shorten the patient's pain.

In the division of professions, men have argued on the basis of their physical strength, the depth of their intelligence and proprieties which are badly justified by prejudice, in order to grab all the functions they wished to exercise: these have been declared forbidden to woman, and she has been declared incapable, so that she can be kept more surely dependent on him. But the more we delve into the natural history of woman, the more we shall be surprised that her rights, which are so clearly written, so firmly imprinted in the richness of her organism, could have been denied or even questioned for a single moment. However that may be, these rights have not perished; woman may have let them be forgotten during the long reign of physical strength, but they will revive and we shall be very happy to make them revive, and triumph, when truth laid bare at last makes us blush at the most repulsive and cowardly of our iniquities. What should emerge from a conscientious and enlightened study of woman, is that this half of the human race is destined to be the equal of the other; in the social machine, the importance of one sex is no less than that of the other. To admit inequality is to subscribe to a depravation of the species: any divergence from the norm in human conditions is a disturbance or the result of a disturbance; every return to the norm is a return to natural order. True civilization (and we should give this name only to what is not in contradiction with the law of our nature, but essentially derives from it) does not involve this state of coming and going, this permanent ebb and flow where in a constant agitation the norm is alternately sought and abandoned. True civilization stops and majestically assigns a norm, and there is marked the end of all wretchedness, of all groanings, of all sobs, of all grinding of teeth. There alone, when all are reassured as to their fate, is the aim of society accomplished, since unless it is to be a league hostile to the principles of justice, it must be instituted for the sole end of ensuring that the weak is no more unhappy than the strong, the wife no more unhappy than the husband, the mother than the father, the children than the parents, the sisters than the brothers, the younger children than the elder; the happiness of individuals, of families, of peoples, of sexes, can only be an effect of equalization: equalization perfects and destroys nothing but that which destroys. Sooner or later it will destroy the servitude of woman; it will proclaim her emancipation. – What would be the consequences of this emancipation, what new laws would become indispensable, so that it should only have beneficial consequences? These are questions that I am not in a position to answer; but we shall have to think about them one day.

B) ANALYSIS OF BABEUF'S DOCTRINE[2]

This was the most widely distributed piece of babouviste *propaganda; produced as a poster and leaflet, it was fly-posted throughout Paris on 9 April 1796.*[3] At Vendôme, Babeuf made it clear that while he had not written it, he approved it as the 'most faithful summary' of his ideas.[4] *The text published by Buonarroti is accompanied by a commentary based on discussions by the secret directory.*

1) Nature has given every man an equal right to enjoy all goods.
2) The aim of society is to defend this equality, often attacked by the strong and the wicked in the state of nature, and to increase common enjoyments by the cooperation of all.
3) Nature has imposed on everyone the obligation to work; no-one can avoid work without being guilty of a crime.
4) Work and enjoyment must be shared.
5) There is oppression when one person is exhausted by work and lacks everything, while another wallows in abundance without doing anything.
6) No-one can, without committing a crime, appropriate to his exclusive possession the fruits of the earth or of industry.
7) In a true society, there must be neither rich nor poor.
8) The rich who refuse to renounce their superfluity in favour of the poor are the enemies of the people.
9) No-one may, by the accumulation of all the resources, deprive another of the education necessary for his happiness: education must be common.

10) The aim of the Revolution is to destroy inequality and re-establish common happiness.

11) The Revolution is not finished, because the rich consume all the goods and monopolize power, while the poor work just like slaves, languishing in poverty and being as nothing in the state.

12) The Constitution of 1793 is the true law of the French, since the people has solemnly accepted it.

13) Every citizen is expected to re-establish and defend in the Constitution of 1793 the wishes and the happiness of the people.

14) All powers emanating from the alleged Constitution of 1795 are illegal and counter-revolutionary.

15) Those who have attacked the Constitution of 1793 are guilty of treason against the people.

C) MARÉCHAL'S MANIFESTO OF THE EQUALS[5]

True equality, final aim of the social art. (Condorcet)

People of France!

For fifteen centuries you have lived as slaves, and hence unhappily. For six years you have begun to breathe, in the expectation of independence, happiness and equality.

EQUALITY! the first wish of nature, the first need of man, and the principal bond of any legitimate association! People of France! you have not been more favoured than the other nations which vegetate on this unhappy globe! Always and everywhere the poor human species, prey to more or less skilful cannibals, has served as a toy to all ambitions and as fodder for all tyrannies. Always and everywhere men were lulled with fine words: never and nowhere did they achieve the reality along with the word. From time immemorial they have repeated to us hypocritically that *men are equal*; and from time immemorial the most degrading and the most monstrous inequality has weighed impudently on the human race. Since there have been civil societies, the finest attribute of man has been recognized without challenge, but has not been put into practice a single time: equality was no more than a beautiful and sterile fiction of the law. Today, when it is demanded by a stronger voice, they reply to us: 'Be silent, wretches! true equality is only an illusion; be content with conditional equality: you are all equal before the law. Scum, what more do you want?' What more do we want? Legislators, rulers, rich property-owners, it's your turn to listen.

We are all equal, aren't we. This principle remains unchallenged, since no-one but a madman could seriously claim that it is night when it is day.

Well! we claim that henceforth we shall live and die equal as we were born: we want true equality or death; that is what we must have.

And we shall have this true equality, no matter what the price. Woe betide those who stand between it and us! Woe betide anyone who resists such a declared will!

The French Revolution is only the forerunner of another revolution which will be greater and more impressive, and which will be the last.

The people has walked over the bodies of the priests and kings allied against it; it will be the same with the new tyrants, the new political hypocrites seated in the places of the old ones.

What do we need more than the equality of rights?

We need not only that equality inscribed in the declaration of the rights of man and the citizen, we want it amidst us, under the roofs of our houses. We will accept anything for its sake, *to make a clean sweep in order to hold on to it alone*. May all the arts perish, if necessary, providing true equality remains!

Legislators and rulers, who have neither genius nor good faith, rich property-owners lacking in compassion, you will try in vain to neutralize our sacred undertaking by saying: 'They are only reiterating that agrarian law demanded many times previously.'

Insulters, it is your turn to be silent, and, in the silence of confusion, listen to our claims dictated by nature and founded on justice.

The agrarian law or the division of land was the short-term wish of some unprincipled soldiers, or some tribes moved by instinct rather than by reason. We are aiming at something more sublime and more equitable, the COMMON GOOD or the COMMUNITY OF GOODS! No more individual property in land, *the land belongs to no-one*. We demand, we want the common enjoyment of the fruits of the earth: Those fruits belong to everyone.

We declare that we will no longer allow the great majority of men to work and sweat in the service of and for the good pleasure of a tiny minority.

For long enough and too long less than a million individuals have disposed of what belongs to more than twenty millions of their fellow-beings, their equals.

It is time to put an end to this great scandal which our grandchildren will refuse to believe! It is time for you to disappear, sickening distinctions between rich and poor, between great and small, between masters and servants, between *rulers and ruled*.

Let there be no more distinctions between men except those of age and sex. Since all have the same needs and the same faculties, then let there be a single education and a single nourishment for them all. They make do with one sun and one air for all: why should the same ration and the same quality of food not suffice for each of them?

But already the enemies of an order of things which is the most natural that can be imagined, declaim against us:

'Wreckers and malcontents,' they tell us, 'you want nothing but massacres and plunder.'

People of France,

We shall not waste your time replying to them; but we shall say to you: 'the sacred undertaking which we are organizing has no aim other than to put an end to civil dissension and public poverty.'

Never has a greater plan been conceived and put into practice. From time to time some men of genius, some wise men, have spoken of it in a low, trembling voice. None of them had the courage to speak the full truth.

The moment for great actions has come. The evil is at its peak; it covers the face of the earth. Chaos under the name of politics has reigned there for too many centuries. Let everything return to order and regain its place. At the sound of equality's voice, let the elements of justice and happiness be organized. The moment has come to found the REPUBLIC OF EQUALS, this great sanctuary open to all men. The days of general restitution have come. Suffering families, come and sit at the table laid by nature for all her children.

People of France,

So the purest of all glories was reserved for you! Yes it is you who must be the first to offer the world this moving sight.

Old habits and old prejudices will again try to block the establishment of the *Republic of Equals*. The organization of true equality, the only one which responds to all needs, without making victims, without costing sacrifices, will perhaps not please everybody at first. The egoist and the ambitious man will quiver with rage. Those who own property unjustly will complain that it is injustice. Exclusive enjoyments, solitary pleasures, personal comforts will cause sharp regrets to a few individuals who are indifferent to the sufferings of others. The lovers of absolute power, the vile henchmen of arbitrary authority, will find it hard to bend their heads below the level of true equality. Their short sight will find it hard to penetrate the impending future of common happiness; but what can a few thousand malcontents do against a mass of men who are all happy, and surprised at having sought for so long for a happiness which was already within their grasp?

The very day after this true revolution, they will say in astonishment: So! common happiness was so easy to achieve? We only had to wish it. Oh! why did we not wish it sooner? Did we have to be told so many times? If there is a single man on earth who is richer and more powerful than his fellows, than his equals, then the equilibrium is broken: crime and misfortune are on earth.

People of France,
By what mark then will you recognize henceforth the excellence of a Constitution? . . . That which is entirely based on true equality is the only one which can suit you and satisfy all your wishes.

The aristocratic charters of 1791 and 1795 fixed your chains instead of breaking them. That of 1793 was a great practical step towards true equality, no-one had ever come so close; but it did not yet touch the goal and did not deal with common happiness, although it solemnly consecrated the great principle of it.

People of France,
Open your eyes and your hearts to the fullness of felicity: recognize and proclaim with us the REPUBLIC OF EQUALS.

D) THE MANIFESTO OF THE PLEBEIANS[6]

We shall explain clearly what is *common happiness, the aim of society.*

We shall demonstrate that the fate of every man should not have got worse with the transition from the natural state to the social state.

We shall define property.

We shall prove that the soil belongs to no-one, but that it is everyone's.

We shall prove that everything that an individual takes possession of beyond what can nourish him, is a social theft.

We shall prove that the alleged right *to dispose of property* is an infamous genocidal outrage.

We shall prove that *heredity by families* is no less great a horror; that it isolates all the members of the association, and makes each household into a little republic, which cannot fail to conspire against the greater republic, thus consecrating inequality.

We shall prove that everything a member of the social body has *below* the satisfaction of his needs of every kind and of every day results from the despoiling of his natural individual property, carried out by those who appropriate common property.

And that, by the same logic, everything which a member of the social body has *above* the satisfaction of his needs of all kinds and of every day, is the result of a theft from the other associates, which necessarily deprives a greater or lesser number of their share in the common property.

That all the most subtle reasonings cannot prevail against these unchanging truths.

That the superiority of talents and industry is only an illusion and a specious deception, which has always unduly assisted the plots of conspirators against equality.

That the difference of value and merit in the products of human labour is based only on the opinion that some of them have attached to these products and have been able to make prevail.

That it is doubtless wrongly that this opinion has evaluated the day's labour of someone who makes a watch as twenty times greater than that of a day's labour ploughing furrows.

That it is, however, by means of this false estimation that the income of a watchmaker has put him in a position to acquire the patrimony of twenty ploughmen whom he has, by this means, expropriated.

That all proletarians have become such only by the result of the same combination in all the other relations of proportion, but all starting from the single basis of the difference in value established between things by the sole authority of opinion.

That it is absurd and unjust to claim a higher reward for the person whose task demands a higher degree of intelligence, and more application and mental tension; for that in no way extends the capacity of his stomach.

That no reason can allow anyone to claim a recompense exceeding the satisfaction of individual needs.

That the value of intelligence is also only a matter of opinion, and it should perhaps also be examined whether the value of purely natural and physical strength is not worth just as much.

That it is the intelligent who have given such a high price to the conceptions of their brains, and that, if it had been the strong who had settled things at the same time, they would doubtless have established that the merit of the hands was worth that of the head, and that the weariness of the whole body could be compared to that affecting only the ruminating part.

That if this equalization is not posited, we are giving the most intelligent and the most industrious a licence to grab, a document entitling them to strip with impunity those who are less so.

That it is thus that the equilibrium of prosperity is destroyed, overthrown in the social state, since nothing is more firmly proved than our great maxim: *that you only succeed in having too much by arranging for others not to have enough.*

That all our civil institutions, our reciprocal transactions, are only the acts of a permanent brigandage, permitted by absurd and barbarous laws, in the shadow of which we are occupied simply in despoiling each other.

That our society of rogues brings about, as a result of its atrocious primordial conventions, all the kinds of vices, crimes and misfortunes against which some men of goodwill have in vain united to make war on them, a war in which they cannot triumph because they do not attack the ill at its root, and they only apply palliatives drawn from the stock of false ideas of our organic depravity.

That it is clear from all that has preceded that all that is possessed by those who have more than their individual share in the goods of society is theft and usurpation.

That it is therefore just to take it back from them.

That even the man who would prove, by the effect of his natural strength alone, that he is capable of doing as much as four men, and who, as a result, would demand the remuneration of four men, would none the less be a conspirator against society, because he would upset the balance by this means alone, and thus destroy precious equality.

That wisdom imperiously orders all his fellows to repress such a man, to pursue him as a social scourge, to reduce him at least to being able to do no more than one man's job, so that he cannot demand more than one man's remuneration.

That it is only our species which has introduced this murderous madness of distinctions of merit and value, and therefore it is only we who know misfortune and deprivation.

That there must not exist any deprivation of things which nature gives to all, produces for all, except those that are the consequence of inevitable accidents of nature, and that in this case, these privations must be borne and shared equally by all.

That the productions of industry and genius also become the property of all, the possession of the entire association, from the very moment when the inventors and workers produce them; because they are only a compensation for the previous inventions of genius and industry, of which these inventors and these workers have taken advantage in their social life, and which have assisted them in their discoveries.

That since acquired knowledge is the property of all, it must be shared equally among all.

That it is a truth wrongly questioned by bad faith, prejudice and thoughtlessness to say that this equal sharing of knowledge among all would make all men more or less equal in capacity and even in talents.

That education is a monstrosity when it is unequal, when it is the exclusive patrimony of one part of the association; since then it becomes, in the hands of that part, a mass of devices, a store of weapons of all sorts, by means of which that part fights against the other part which is disarmed, and as a result easily succeeds in crushing it, in deceiving it, in stripping it and in enslaving it in the most shameful chains.

That there is no truth more important than that which we have already cited, and which a philosopher has proclaimed in these terms: *talk as long as you like about the best form of government, you will have achieved nothing as long as you have failed to destroy the seeds of greed and ambition.*

So it is necessary that social institutions achieve this goal, namely that they remove from every individual the hope of ever becoming richer, or more powerful, or more distinguished by his intelligence, than any of his equals.

That it is necessary, to make this more precise, to succeed in *controlling fate*; in making the fate of each co-associate independent of fortunate and unfortunate chances and circumstances; *to ensure to each and to his descendants, however numerous they may be, sufficiency but nothing but sufficiency*, and thus to close for everyone all the possible paths whereby they could ever obtain more than their individual share in the products of nature and labour.

That the only way of achieving this is to establish *common administration*; to suppress private property, to attach every man to the talent and the trade he knows; to oblige him to deposit the products in kind in the common store; and to establish a simple administration of distribution, an administration of supplies which, keeping a register of all individuals and all things, will divide the latter with the most scrupulous equality, and deliver them to the home of each citizen.

That this form of government, shown to be practicable by experience, since it is the one applied to the twelve hundred thousand men of our twelve armies (what is possible on a small scale is possible on a large scale), that this form of government is the only one from which can result a universal, unchanging, unmixed happiness; *common happiness, the aim of society*.

That this government will lead to the disappearance of boundary-marks, hedges, walls, door-locks, disputes, trials, thefts, murders, all crimes; of courts, prisons, gallows, penalties, the despair caused by all these calamities; of envy, jealousy, insatiability, pride, deception, duplicity, in short all vices; and moreover (and this is doubtless the essential point), the gnawing worm of general anxiety, which is specific and permanent for each of us, about our fate tomorrow, next month and next year, about our old age, our children and their children.

E) DRAFT ECONOMIC DECREE (FRAGMENT)[7]

1) A great national community will be established in the republic.
2) The national community takes possession of the following assets, namely:
   • Assets which, having been declared to be national, had not been sold on 9 *thermidor* Year II;
   • The assets of enemies of the Revolution, which by the decrees of 8 and 13 *ventôse* were made over to the poor;
   • Assets handed over to, or due to be handed over to, the republic as the result of judicial sentences;

- Buildings currently occupied for the public service;
- Assets belonging to the *communes* before the law of 10 June 1793;
- Assets assigned to almshouses and public educational institutions;
- Housing occupied by poor citizens, in accordance with the proclamation made to the French people on . . .
- The assets of those who make them over to the republic;
- Assets appropriated by those who have enriched themselves while exercising public functions;
- Land whose owners fail to cultivate it.

3) The right of inheritance *ab intestat* or by will is abolished; all property currently owned by individuals will be taken over by the national community on their deaths.

4) The children of a father who is still alive and who are not required by law to join the army will be considered as current owners.

5) Every French person of either sex who makes over all his or her property to the fatherland, and devotes his or her person and labour to it, is a member of the great national community.

6) Old people who have reached their sixtieth year, and invalids, if they are poor, are members by right of the national community.

7) Likewise young people brought up in national educational institutions are members of the national community.

8) The assets of the national community are exploited in common by all its able-bodied members.

9) The great national community maintains all its members in a state of equal and decent sufficiency: it provides them with all they need.

10) The republic urges loyal citizens to contribute to the success of reform by voluntarily making over their property to the community.

11) As of the . . . nobody may be a civilian or military official without being a member of the said community.

12) The great national community is administered by local governors chosen by its members, in accordance with the laws and under the direction of the supreme administration.

13) . . .

Common Labour

1) Every member of the national community owes to it the agricultural labour and the exercise of skills of which they are capable.

2) Exception is made for old people over sixty and invalids.

3) Citizens who, by voluntarily making over their property, become members of the national community, will not be required to undertake any laborious tasks if they have reached their fortieth year, and if they did not practise a craft before the publication of the present decree.

4) In each *commune* the citizens are divided into classes, one for each craft; each class is made up of all those who practise the same skill.

5) Each class has governors appointed by the members: these governors manage work, ensure that it is equally shared, carry out the instructions of the municipal administration, and set an example of enthusiasm and activity.

6) The law lays down for each season the length of the working day for members of the national community.

7) Attached to each municipal administration is a council of elders, delegated by each class of workers; this council advises the administration on all matters concerning the allocation, alleviation and improvement of labour.

8) The supreme administration will apply to the labour of the national community machinery and methods designed to reduce human effort.

9) The municipal administration keeps under constant supervision the condition of workers of every class and the jobs required of them; it reports on this regularly to the supreme administration.

10) The movement of workers from one *commune* to another may be ordered by the supreme administration, in the light of the resources and needs of the community.

11) The supreme administration imposes forced labour, under the supervision of designated *communes*, on individuals of both sexes whose lack of good citizenship, idleness, luxury and dissolute behaviour give a pernicious example to society. Their property is expropriated by the national community.

12) The governors of each class has placed in the stores of the national community the fruits of the earth and products of craft which can be preserved.

13) An inventory of these objects is regularly communicated to the supreme administration.

14) The governors attached to the agricultural class take care of the breeding and improvement of animals required for food, clothing, transport and the easing of human labour.

The Distribution and Use of the Property of the Community

1) No member of the community may possess anything other than what the law makes available through the agency of the governors.

2) The national community guarantees, from this time forth, to each of its members:
   - Healthy, comfortable and decently furnished accommodation;
   - Clothing for work and leisure, in wool or yam, in accordance with the national costume;
   - Laundry, lighting and heating;
   - A sufficient quantity of food – bread, meat, poultry, fish, eggs, butter or oil; wine and other drinks used in the different regions; vegetables, fruit, seasonings, and other objects, the combination of which constitutes a moderate and frugal comfort;
   - Medical assistance.

3) In each *commune* at certain fixed times, there will be communal meals which all members of the community will be required to attend.

4) The maintenance of public and military officials is equal to that of members of the national community.

5) Any member of the national community who receives a wage or keeps money is punished.

6) Members of the national community can receive the common ration only in the district where they live, except in the case of movements authorized by the administration.

7) The home of current citizens is in the *commune* where they live at the time of the publication of the present decree.

   The home of young people brought up in national educational institutions is in the *commune* where they were born.

8) In each *commune* there are governors with the responsibility of delivering to the homes of the members of the members of the national community the products of agriculture and the various crafts.

9) The law fixes the rules whereby this distribution is made.

10) ...

The Administration of the National Community

1) The national community is under the legal direction of the supreme administration of the state.

2) For the purpose of the administration of the community, the republic is divided into regions.

3) A region includes all the adjacent *départements* whose products are more or less the same.

4) In each region there is an intermediate administration, to which the administrations of the *départements* are subordinated.

5) Telegraphic lines accelerate communication between the administrations of the *départements* and the intermediate administrations, and between these and the supreme administration.

6) The supreme administration determines, in accordance with the law, the nature and proportion of the distributions to be made to the members of the community in each region.

7) In accordance with these decisions, the administrations of the *départements* inform the intermediate administrations of the deficit or surplus in their districts.

8) If possible the intermediate administrations makes up the deficit of one *département* with the surplus of another, orders the necessary issues and transport, and gives the supreme administration an account of their needs or their surplus.

9) The supreme administration supplies the needs of regions suffering from shortages from the surpluses of those who have too much, or by exchanges with foreign countries.

10) First of all, each year the supreme administration deducts one tenth of all the harvests of the community and deposits it in military stores.

11) It ensures that the republic's surplus is carefully preserved for years of scarcity.

Trade

1) All private trade with foreign nations is forbidden; goods coming from such trade are confiscated by the national community, and offenders are punished.

2) The republic provides the national community with goods which it lacks by exchanging its surplus agricultural and craft products for those of foreign nations.

3) To this end, convenient warehouses are established on the land and sea frontiers.

4) The supreme administration deals with foreigners through its agents: it deposits the surplus it wants to exchange in the warehouses where it receives the agreed goods from abroad.

5) The agents of the supreme administration in the trading warehouses are frequently changed; anyone betraying their trust is severely punished.

Transport

1) In each *commune* there are governors with the responsibility of administering the transport of communal goods from one *commune* to another.

2) Every *commune* is provided with adequate means of transport, by land or water.

3) Members of the national community are called on in rotation to direct and supervise the objects to be transported from one *commune* to another.

4) Every year the intermediate administrations make a certain number of young people from the *départements* under their jurisdiction responsible for transport to more remote places.

5) Citizens who are responsible for any form of transport are maintained in the *commune* where they happen to be.

6) The supreme administration arranges the transport from *commune* to *commune*, by the shortest route, and under the supervision of the lower administrations, of those objects with which it makes up the deficit of regions in need.

Taxes

1) Only individuals who do not participate in the national community pay taxes.

2) They are liable to the taxes previously established.

3) The taxes are paid in kind and deposited in the stores of the national community.

4) The total quota for taxpayers for the current year is twice what it was the previous year.

5) This total is divided up by *département* progressively on all taxpayers.

6) Non-participants in the community may be required, if necessary, to pay into the stores of the national community, to be set against coming taxes, their surplus of goods or manufactured objects.

Debts

1) The national debt is abolished for all French people.
2) The republic will refund to foreigners the capital on perpetual loans owed to them. In the meantime, it pays interest on these loans, as well as lifetime annuities settled on foreign heads.
3) The debts of any French person who becomes a member of the national community to another French person are wiped out.
4) The republic takes responsibility for debts owed by members of the community to foreigners.
5) Any evasion in this respect is punished with perpetual forced labour.

Money

1) The republic ceases to manufacture currency.
2) Coins made over to the national community will be used to buy goods it requires from foreign nations.
3) Any non-participant in the community who is convicted of offering coins to one of its members will be severely punished.
4) No gold or silver may be introduced into the republic.

Bibliographical Note

The following abbreviations are used in the endnotes for the principal sources referred to in the text:

a) Works of Babeuf
Oeuvres: V. Daline, A. Saitta & A. Soboul (eds), *Oeuvres de Babeuf: tome I* (Paris, 1977). [This is the first volume of the Collected Works, and goes up to 1789. This is the only volume to appear in French; complete works in Russian appeared in four volumes in Moscow, 1975–82.]

b) Journals edited by Babeuf
JLP: *Journal de la liberté de la presse* (September–October 1794).
TDP: *Le Tribun du peuple* (October 1794–April 1796) [the two above journals were reprinted in facsimile, Paris 1966.]

c) Compilations of Babeuf's writings
Advielle: V. Advielle, *Histoire de Gracchus Babeuf et du babouvisme* (Paris, 1884), two volumes. [Facsimile reprint, Paris 1990. The second volume contains Babeuf's main speech at Vendôme and correspondence with Dubois de Fosseux. The correspondence is paginated separately and referenced as IIb.]
Pages: M. Dommanget (ed.), *Pages choisies de Babeuf* (Paris, 1935).
Mazauric: C. Mazauric (ed.), *Babeuf: Ecrits* (Paris, 1988).

d) Contemporary sources
Pièces: Haute Cour de Justice, *Copie des pièces saisies dans le local que Baboeuf occupoit lors de son arrestation* (Paris, Year V – 1796-7). Two volumes. [Papers seized at the time of Babeuf's arrest. They are

arranged in *liasses* (bundles) and *pièces* (documents); thus 8/29 indicates bundle 8, document 29.]

Débats: *Débats du procès instruit par la Haute-Cour de Justice contre Drouet, Baboeuf et autres* (Paris, 1979). Four volumes; fresh pagination begins half-way through Volume IV. [The stenographic record of the Vendôme trial.]

Hésine: *Journal de la Haute-Cour de justice ou L'écho des hommes libres, vrais et sensibles*, par Hésine (Vendôme, 1796–7; facsimile reprint, Paris, 1966.) [A 73-issue journal reporting the trial by a supporter of Babeuf.]

Buonarroti: P. Buonarroti, *Conspiration pour l'égalité dite de Babeuf* (Paris, 1957), two volumes; first published Brussels, 1828.

e) Biographical and critical works

Dommanget: M. Dommanget, *Sur Babeuf et la conjuration des égaux* (Paris, 1970).

Rose: R. B. Rose, *Gracchus Babeuf* (London, 1978).

Legrand: R. Legrand, *Babeuf et ses compagnons de route* (Paris, 1981).

Daline: V. Daline, *Gracchus Babeuf* (Moscow, 1987). [French translation; Russian original published 1963.] This seminal work has not yet been published in English, hence all references to Dalin in the Notes give the French form of his name, Daline.

Schiappa: J.-M. Schiappa, *Gracchus Babeuf, avec les Égaux* (Paris, 1991).

f) Others

AHRF: *Annales historiques de la Révolution française*.

Présence: A. Maillard, C. Mazauric & E. Walter (eds), *Présence de Babeuf* (Paris, 1994). [Papers from the conference on Babeuf held in Amiens in December 1989.]

Other primary and secondary sources are given in full in the endnotes. Part Two contains a review of historical work on Babeuf. There is a full bibliography up to *c.* 1973 in Daline.

Notes

1 INTRODUCTION

1. *Birth of Our Power* (Harmondsworth, 1970), p. 151.
2. *Pièces*, 8/29.
3. Hésine, 73/4.
4. Legrand, p. 212.
5. Buonarroti, II: 44.
6. *Débats*, I: 117–18.
7. *Présence*, p. 42.
8. *Collected Works* (Moscow, 1964), XV: 385.
9. J. Degras (ed.), The Communist International (London, 1971), I: 47.
10. (London, 1911).
11. (London, 1947), pp. 18, 106.
12. Rose, pp. v, 337.
13. A. Callinicos, *Is there a Future for Marxism?* (London, 1982), p. 4.
14. E.P. Thompson, *The Making of the English Working Class* (Harmondsworth, 1980), p. 12.
15. *Socialist Worker*, 1 April 1989.
16. S. Bianchi, *La révolution culturelle de l'an II* (Paris, 1982), pp. 38–9.
17. E. Faure, *La disgrâce de Turgot* (Paris, 1961), pp. 62–3, 317.
18. Buonarroti, I: 91.

2 'BORN IN THE MUD'

1. Daline, p. 35.
2. G. Lecocq, *Un manifeste de Gracchus Babeuf* (Paris, 1885), p. 9.
3. 'Chartism', *Selected Writings* (Harmondsworth, 1986), p. 189.
4. G. Lefebvre, *Etudes sur la révolution française* (Paris, 1963), p. 416.
5. Daline, pp. 59, 61.
6. P. Goubert, 'Les techniques agricoles dans les pays picards aux XVIIe. et XVIIIe. siècles', *Revue d'histoire économique et sociale* XXXV/1 (1957), p. 32.
7. Rose, p. 56.
8. Dommanget, p. 51.

9.   Daline, p. 71.
10.   *Oeuvres*, p. 254.
11.   Lecocq, pp. 2–3.
12.   Daline, p. 35.
13.   Rose, p. 8.
14.   Legrand, pp. 422–3.
15.   Advielle, I: 10; *Présence*, p. 32.
16.   *Oeuvres*, p. 256.
17.   *Oeuvres*, pp. 256–7.
18.   *Oeuvres*, p. 257.
19.   *Oeuvres*, pp. 257–8.
20.   Daline, p. 53.
21.   E.J.M. Vignon, *Etudes historiques sur l'administration des voies publiques en France aux dix-septième et dix-huitième siècles* (Paris, 1862), II: 194–5.
22.   A. Young, *Travels in France and Italy* (London, 1915), pp. 87–8.
23.   H. Cavaillès, *La route française* (Paris, 1946), p. 166.
24.   J. Stephen Jeans, *Waterways and Water Transport* (London, 1890), pp. 448–9.
25.   C. Hadfield, *The Canal Age* (Newton Abbot, 1968), p. 176.
26.   *Présence*, p. 123; K. & M. Middell, *François-Noël Babeuf* (Berlin, 1988), p. 18.
27.   Vignon, II: 195.
28.   A. Pelletier, 'Babeuf feudiste', *AHRF* 179 (1965), pp. 29–65.
29.   Rose, pp. 12–14.
30.   C. Mazauric, *Babeuf et la conspiration pour l'égalité* (Paris, 1962), p. 79.
31.   Dommanget, p. 86.
32.   Dommanget, pp. 47–8.
33.   *Oeuvres*, pp. 251–2, 262–77; Rose, pp. 25–7; Daline, pp. 117–22.
34.   *TDP*, No. 29, p. 285.
35.   F.-N.-C. Babeuf, *Le Scrutateur des décrets* (Paris, 1966 reprint), No. 6, 1791, pp. 56–7.
36.   *Oeuvres*, p. 108.
37.   Rose, p. 4.
38.   *TDP*, No. 40, p. 264.
39.   Legrand, pp. 423–6.
40.   Rose, p. 14.
41.   *Oeuvres*, pp. 219, 248, 245.
42.   M. Grégoire-d'Essigny *fils*, *Histoire de la ville de Roye* (Noyon, 1818), p. 401.
43.   Cited in P. McGarr, 'The Great French Revolution', *International Socialism* 2/43 (1989), p. 97.
44.   Daline, p. 550.
45.   Daline, p. 145.
46.   Daline, p. 534.
47.   Dommanget, pp. 60–8.
48.   L.-N. Berthe, *Dubois de Fosseux* (Arras, 1969), pp. 20, 120, 182ff.
49.   Berthe, pp. 96, 104, 114–15.

50. *Oeuvres*, pp. 239, 172, 196, 162, 157.
51. J.-J. Rousseau, *Oeuvres complètes* (Paris, 1964), III: 351.
52. A. MacIntyre, *A Short History of Ethics* (London, 1967), p. 188.
53. *Présence*, p. 253.
54. See *inter alia* C. Mazauric, 'Le rousseauisme de Babeuf', *AHRF* 170 (1962), pp. 439–64.
55. *Oeuvres*, p. 139.
56. Daline, pp. 355, 597.
57. Mazauric, pp. 26, 151.
58. Mazauric, 'Le rousseauisme de Babeuf', p. 454.
59. *Oeuvres*, p. 163.
60. Daline, p. 293.
61. *Oeuvres*, p. 216.
62. Morelly, *Code de la nature* (Paris, 1970), pp. 47, 58.
63. Morelly, pp. 129–32, 151.
64. Morelly, p. 127.
65. N. Wagner, *Morelly: le méconnu des lumières* (Paris, 1978), pp. 259, 304, 340; see also R. Coë, 'La théorie morellienne et la pratique babouviste', *AHRF* 150 (1958), pp. 38–64.
66. M. Collignon, *L'avant-coureur du changement du monde entier* (reprinted Paris, 1966); the original pamphlet was dated London, 1786, doubtless to deceive a possible censor.
67. A. Ioanissian, 'Sur l'auteur de "L'avant-coureur du changement du monde entier"', *AHRF* 184 (1966), pp. 1–14.
68. Advielle, IIb pp. 120, 164, 169, 173, 175, 180.
69. *Oeuvres*, pp. 215–16.
70. Dommanget, pp. 44, 52.
71. *Oeuvres*, pp. 105–6, 115, 109.
72. Daline, pp. 80–81.
73. *Oeuvres*, pp. 83–4, 89, 114.
74. *Oeuvres*, pp. 92, 101.
75. See I. H. Birchall, 'Babeuf and the Oppression of Women', *British Journal for Eighteenth-Century Studies* (forthcoming).
76. *Oeuvres*, p. 117.
77. *Oeuvres*, p. 81.
78. *Oeuvres*, p. 206.
79. *Le cadastre perpétuel* (Versailles, 1789); *Oeuvres*, p. 365.
80. *Oeuvres*, p. 373.
81. *Oeuvres*, p. 376.

3 ADVANCING REVOLUTION

1. H. Lemoine, *Le Démolisseur de la Bastille* (Paris, 1930), pp. 7–20.
2. Schiappa, pp. 7–8.

3.   *La nouvelle distinction des ordres, par M de Mirabeau* (Paris, 1789), in *Oeuvres*, pp. 294–5.

4.   R. Legrand, *Babeuf en 1790* (Abbeville, 1972), p. 42.

5.   *Oeuvres*, pp. 339–40.

6.   *Oeuvres*, pp. 298, 349.

7.   *Oeuvres*, p. 341.

8.   Rose, p. 62.

9.   *Oeuvres*, pp. 322–3.

10.   *Oeuvres*, p. 310.

11.   *Oeuvres*, p. 304.

12.   *Oeuvres*, p. 317.

13.   *Journal de la confédération*, No. 1, p. 1 (1966 reprint).

14.   Legrand, pp. 97, 48.

15.   R.B. Rose, 'Tax Revolt and Popular Organization in Picardy 1789–1791', *Past and Present*, No. 43 (1969), pp. 92–108.

16.   Rose, p. 66.

17.   Legrand, p. 74.

18.   *Journal de la confédération*, No. 1, pp. 2–4.

19.   *TDP*, No. 29, p. 285.

20.   Daline, pp. 59–60.

21.   *Le Scrutateur des décrets*, pp. 7–9.

22.   *Le sourd ou L'auberge pleine*, in *Théâtre de Desforges* tome I (Paris, 1820).

23.   *Pages*, p. 135.

24.   J. Foucart, 'Les tapisseries de Montdidier et l'autodafé de 1793', *Bulletin trimestriel de la société des antiquaires de Picardie*, 1976/2, pp. 249–71.

25.   Daline, pp. 126–7.

26.   F. Gauthier, *Triomphe et mort du droit naturel en révolution* (Paris, 1992), p. 25.

27.   *Pages*, pp. 116–18.

28.   *Pages*, pp. 98–9.

29.   *Pages*, pp. 101–2.

30.   R. Cobb, 'Babeuf et les électeurs d'Abbeville', *AHRF* 165 (1961), pp. 392–3.

31.   R.B. Rose, 'The "Red Scare" of the 1790s: the French Revolution and the "Agrarian Law"', *Past and Present*, No. 103 (1984), pp. 113–30.

32.   *Présence*, pp. 114–18; A. Patoux, 'Le faux de Gracchus Babeuf', *Mémoire de la société académique des ciences, arts, belles-lettres, agriculture & industrie de Saint-Quentin*, XVI (1913), pp. 140–209.

33.   J. Godechot (ed.), *Les constitutions de la France depuis 1789* (Paris, 1970), pp. 80–1.

34.   A. Lehning, *De Buonarroti à Bakounine* (Paris, 1977), p. 297.

35.   A. Aulard, *Etudes et leçons sur la révolution française – quatrième série* (Paris, 1904), pp. 50–1.

36.   Cited Legrand, p. 130.

37.   Mazauric, p. 35.

38.   Legrand, pp. 121–2.

39. C. *Fournier (Américain) à Marat* (Paris, 1793).
40. Daline, p. 423.
41. Daline, p. 453.
42. Daline, p, 428.
43. Mazauric, pp. 209–10.
44. *TDP*, No. 29, p. 286; see also G. Babeuf, *La guerre de la Vendée et le système de dépopulation* (Paris, 1987; first edition 1794), pp. 134–6.
45. Legrand, pp. 208–11.
46. *Histoire de la révolution française* (Paris, 1952), II: 990.
47. K.D. Tønnesson, *La défaite des sans-culottes* (Paris/Oslo, 1959), p. 52.
48. *JLP*, No. 1, pp. 1–2.
49. *JLP*, No. 3, pp. 1–3; No. 2, p. 8; No. 4, p. 2.
50. *TDP*, No. 30, p. 290.
51. G. Babeuf, *Voyage des jacobins dans les quatre parties du monde* (Paris, 1794), p. 12.
52. *JLP*, No. 2, p. 2; No. 13, p. 1.
53. *JLP*, No. 12, pp. 7–8.
54. L. Madelin, *Fouché 1759–1820* (Paris, 1930), I: 184–8.
55. *TDP*, No. 30, p. 30; No. 35, pp. 56ff.
56. *La guerre de la Vendée*, pp. 169, 115, 142.
57. *JLP*, No. 1, pp. 2–5.
58. *TDP*, No. 31, p. 313.
59. *Les battus payent l'amende* (Paris, 1794), pp. 2–3.
60. *Voyage des jacobins*, p. 5.
61. *La guerre de la Vendée*, pp. 152, 160–1, 167.
62. *La guerre de la Vendée*, pp. 141, 121, 115.
63. *La guerre de la Vendée*, pp. 116, 90–1, 95–6.
64. *TDP*, No. 23, pp. 1–2.
65. *TDP*, No. 41, pp. 269–70.
66. *JLP*, No. 21, p. 8; *TDP*, No. 26, p. 8; No. 27, p. 231; No. 31, pp. 321–2; No. 27, p. 230; No. 30, p. 310; No. 32, p. 333.
67. *TDP*, No. 23, pp. 4–5.
68. M.-J. Chénier, *Caïus Gracchus* (Paris, 1793), p. 11.
69. Buonarroti, I: 70.
70. *TDP*, No. 28, p. 237.
71. *TDP*, No. 29, pp. 258–9; No. 31, p. 312.
72. *Pages*, pp. 173–4.
73. See F. Gendron, *La jeunesse sous thermidor* (Paris, 1983).
74. *TDP*, No. 30, p. 301.
75. Legrand, pp. 210–11, 214.
76. Legrand, pp. 194–5, 421.
77. Buonarroti, I: 58.
78. *Débats*, II: 166.
79. E. Tarlé, *Germinal et prairial* (Moscow, 1959), pp. 323–4.

4   THE CONSPIRACY

1. *TDP*, No. 35, p. 93.
2. Text in Buonarroti, I: 40–5.
3. *TDP*, No. 35, pp. 92–3.
4. Mazauric, *Babeuf et la conspiration*, pp. 152–3.
5. *TDP*, No. 34, p. 7.
6. Letter printed in Dommanget, pp. 310–19.
7. Mazauric, p. 258.
8. *TDP*, No. 35, p. 76.
9. Schiappa, pp. 104–6.
10. *L'Eclaireur*, No. 2, p. 11.
11. *TDP*, No. 38, p. 177.
12. *TDP*, No. 39, p. 201.
13. *TDP*, No. 42, p. 286.
14. *Débats*, II: 198.
15. *TDP*, No. 36, pp. 124–6.
16. *L'Eclaireur*, No. 4, p. 30.
17. See Lecocq.
18. *JLP*, No. 22, pp. 7–8.
19. 'Une lettre inédite de Babeuf en 1795', *Bulletin de l'association 'Les amis de Gracchus Babeuf'*, No. 1 (1994), pp. 8–10.
20. Buonarroti, I: 75.
21. Buonarroti, I: 88.
22. *JLP*, No. 13, p. 2.
23. D. Greer, *The Incidence of the Terror during the French Revolution* (Cambridge, Mass., 1935), pp. 73, 152–3.
24. See E. Eisenstein, *The First Professional Revolutionist* (Harvard, 1959).
25. *Débats*, III: 211–12.
26. M. Leroy, *Histoire des idées sociales en France* (Paris, 1946–), I: 213.
27. Lehning, pp. 76–7.
28. *Débats*, III: 217.
29. M. Dommanget, *Sylvain Maréchal* (Paris, 1950), pp. 123–9, 144–5.
30. Dommanget, *Sylvain Maréchal*, p. 78.
31. Maréchal, *Voyages de Pythagore*, VI: 151–2, cited Dommanget, p. 280.
32. Dommanget, *Sylvain Maréchal*, pp. 192–3.
33. *TDP*, No. 40, pp. 253–62.
34. Mazauric, p. 286.
35. Legrand, p. 388.
36. *Débats*, IV: 174–5.
37. *Débats*, III: 110.
38. *TDP*, No. 37, pp. 134–5.
39. Legrand, p. 314.
40. Published by Arthur Ranc as an appendix to his edition of Buonarroti's *Gracchus Babeuf et la conjuration des égaux* (Paris, 1869), pp. 202–3.

41. *TDP*, No. 27, p. 229.
42. *L'Eclaireur*, No. 2, pp. 13–14.
43. *Pièces*, 7/92, 21/16.
44. *Drouet, représentant du peuple au corps législatif* (Paris, 1796).
45. *TDP*, No. 39, p. 208; No. 40, pp. 241–2.
46. *Pièces*, 7/50.
47. Buonarroti, I: 99.
48. I.H. Birchall, 'The Babeuf Bicentenary: Conspiracy or Revolutionary Party?', *International Socialism* 2/72 (1996), pp. 77–93.
49. Buonarroti, II: 90.
50. *Pièces*, 14/19.
51. *Présence*, p. 219.
52. *Pièces*, 8/6.
53. *TDP*, 'Prospectus' (1795), p. 3.
54. Dommanget, p. 152.
55. *L'Eclaireur*, No. 5, p. 45.
56. *Pièces*, 15/59.
57. *Pièces*, 10/28, 22/17.
58. Buonarroti, II: 155.
59. *Pièces*, 7/90, 2/12.
60. *Pièces*, 17/2.
61. Rose, p. 231.
62. Rose, p. 243; *Débats*, III: 554.
63. Legrand, pp. 320–1.
64. I. Woloch, *Jacobin Legacy* (Princeton, 1970), p. 40.
65. *Pièces*, 10/20.
66. Buonarroti, I: 155–212.
67. Buonarroti, I: 99, II: 94–8.
68. Dommanget, *Sylvain Maréchal*, p. 314.
69. *Pièces*, 7/67.
70. *Débats*, II: 90–1, 102–3.
71. Buonarroti, II: 164–70.
72. *Pièces*, 22/4.
73. Buonarroti, II: 173.
74. *Pièces*, 22/14.
75. *Pièces*, 8/34–5.
76. Buonarroti, II: 167.
77. P. Riviale, *La conjuration* (Paris, 1994), p. 401.
78. Buonarroti, I: 145.
79. 'Personnel sectionnaire et personnel babouviste', *AHRF* 162 (1960), pp. 436–57.
80. 'De l'an III à l'an IX, les derniers sans-culottes', *AHRF* 257 (1984), pp. 386–406.
81. Rose, pp. 248–9.

82. *Pièces*, 10/20, 10/25, 10/18, 14/2.
83. Buonarroti, II: 183–4.
84. Haute-Cour de Justice, *Pièces lues dans le cours de l'exposé fait par l'accusateur national* (Paris, 1797), pp 29–31.
85. Buonarroti, II: 108.
86. *Pièces*, 7/25.
87. Buonarroti, II: 78–9.
88. *Pièces*, 20/6.
89. *Pièces*, 21/9.
90. Buonarroti, II: 193.
91. *Pièces*, 14/20.
92. Schiappa, pp. 135–46; J.-M. Schiappa, 'Aspects de l'implantation de la conjuration babouviste', *AHRF* 291 (1993), pp. 115–23.
93. *La guerre de Vendée*, p. 129.
94. R. M. Andrews, 'Réflexions sur la conjuration des égaux', *Annales: economies, sociétés, civilisations* 29/1 (1974), pp. 73–106.
95. R. C. Cobb, *The Police and the People* (Oxford, 1970), pp. 71–8, 166–7.
96. Buonarroti, I: 128, 139.

5   THE TRIAL

1. Buonarroti, II: 21.
2. Cobb, *The Police and the People*, p. 166.
3. Dommanget, *Sylvain Maréchal*, pp. 301–3.
4. Buonarroti, I: 225.
5. Legrand, pp. 261–3.
6. A. Aulard, *Paris pendant la réaction thermidorienne et sous le directoire*, tome III (Paris, 1899), pp. 203–4.
7. Legrand, pp. 320, 322–3.
8. Cochon, *Rapport au directoire exécutif* (Paris, 1796).
9. Buonarroti, I: 147; P. Bessand-Massenet, *Babeuf et le parti communiste en 1796* (Paris, 1926).
10. In J. Droz (ed.), *Histoire générale du socialisme*, tome I (Paris, 1972), p. 252.
11. Dommanget, *Babeuf*, p. 37.
12. Schiappa, p. 197.
13. J.-M. Schiappa, 'Deux inédits de la conspiration pour l'égalité', *AHRF* 264 (1986), pp. 217–30.
14. *Débats*, IV: 258.
15. Haute-Cour de Justice, *Exposé fait par les accusateurs nationaux* (Paris, 1797), p. 35.
16. H. Carnot, *Mémoires sur Lazare Carnot* (Paris, 1907), I: 39.
17. V. Daline, 'Napoléon et les babouvistes', *AHRF* 201 (1970), pp. 409–18.
18. *Histoire du XIXe siècle*, tome I (Paris, 1872), pp. xvi-xvii.
19. *Pages*, pp. 227, 298–303.
20. *Réponse de Drouet* (Paris, 1796).

21. G. Deville, *Thermidor et directoire* (Paris, 1904), p. 324.
22. Rose, pp. 288–91.
23. Hésine, No. 25, pp. 3–4.
24. Legrand, pp. 269, 278, 276.
25. Buonarroti, II: 20.
26. *Débats*, I: 196.
27. Advielle, II: 95, 175.
28. Buonarroti, II: 35–6.
29. *Débats*, IV: 255.
30. *Pièces*, 7/40–1.
31. Rose, p. 317.
32. Buonarroti, I: 19.
33. Rose, pp. 297, 305.
34. I.H. Birchall, 'The Vendôme Defence Strategy', *British Journal for Eighteenth-Century Studies* (forthcoming).
35. *Débats*, III: 176–202.
36. *Pièces*, 8/34.
37. *Débats*, I: 103; I: 236–40; I: 359–61; I: 387; II: 11–14.
38. *Débats*, I: 265; I: 323; II: 154; III: 140.
39. Hésine, No. 63, p. 3; No. 64, p. 1.
40. Advielle, II: 13.
41. Advielle, II: 43.
42. Advielle, II: 56, 58.
43. Advielle, II: 316, 322.
44. Hésine, No. 70, p. 3.
45. *Mémoires du comte Dufort de Cheverny* (Paris, 1909), II: 244.
46. *Débats*, V: 66–7; V: 114–16; Hésine, No. 73, pp. 1–3; Rose, p. 323.
47. *Débats*, V: 118–31.
48. Buonarroti, II: 43; Hésine, No. 73, p. 3; *Mémoires du comte Dufort de Cheverny*, pp. 265–6.
49. J.M. Cammett, *Antonio Gramsci and the Origins of Italian Communism* (Stanford, 1967), p. 182.
50. Legrand, p. 280.
51. Buonarroti, I: 99.
52. *Débats*, IV: 101.
53. Legrand, pp. 254–5.
54. *Mémoires du comte Dufort de Cheverny*, p. 267.
55. *Présence*, p. 188.
56. *Débats*, IV: 76.
57. Eisenstein, *The First Professional Revolutionist*, p. 30.
58. See I. Woloch, *Jacobin Legacy*.
59. Legrand, p. 349; Schiappa, p. 132.
60. Legrand, pp. 424, 427–31.
61. *History and Class Consciousness* (London, 1971), p. 43.

6   FIRST OPINIONS

1.   F. Furet in F. Furet & M. Ozouf (eds), *The French Revolution and the Creation of Modem Political Culture* (Oxford, 1989), III: 507.

2.   *Reflections on the Revolution in France* (London, 1964), pp. 58–60, 149, 218, 219, 76.

3.   *Correspondance inédite de Mallet du Pan avec la cour de Vienne (1794–1798)* (Paris, 1884), II: 92, 281–3.

4.   H. Balzac, *La comédie humaine* (Paris, 1977), VIII: 507, 649.

5.   *La comédie inhumaine* (Paris, 1965), p. 554.

6.   *The Quarterly Review*, XIV (June 1812), pp. 412–38.

7.   Southey (1812), pp. 419, 436.

8.   Southey (1812), pp. 418–19, 420, 438.

9.   *The Quarterly Review*, XLV/LXXXIX (April 1831), pp. 167–209.

10. Southey (1831), pp. 169, 186, 197.

11. Southey (1831), pp. 181, 175, 207–8.

12. Southey (1831), p. 177.

13. *Buonarroti's History of Babeuf's Conspiracy for Equality*, translated by Bronterre (London, 1836), p. 57.

14. Guizot, *L'histoire de France depuis 1789 jusqu'en 1848* (Paris, 1878), p. 382.

15. M. A. Thiers, *Histoire de la révolution française* (Paris, 1878), II: 347.

16. J. Michelet, *Histoire du XIXe siècle* (Paris, 1872–5), I: x.

17. J. Michelet, *Histoire de la révolution française*, II: 408, II: 530, I: 1011.

18. J. Michelet, *Histoire du XIXe siècle*, II: 146, II: 183.

19. J. Michelet, *Ma jeunesse* (Paris, 1884), pp. 9–11.

20. See F. Engels, 'The June Revolution', Marx & Engels, *Collected Works* (London, 1975–), VII: 157–64.

21. Dommanget, p. 299.

22. 'Autobiography: chapter 45', *The Penny Satirist*, 21 April 1838.

23. A. Saitta, *Filippo Buonarroti* (Rome, 1950–1), I: 6, II: 149.

24. Dommanget, p. 378.

25. Buonarroti, I: 21.

26. *Pages*, p. 14.

27. See A. Galante Garrone, *Buonarroti e Babeuf* (Turin, 1948).

28. J. B. O'Brien, *A Dissertation and Elegy on the Life and Death of the Immortal Maximilian Robespierre* (London, 1859), p. 7.

29. P. Buonarroti, *Observations sur Maximilien Robespierre*, (Chalon-sur-Saône, 1912), p. 6.

30. *Présence*, p. 317.

31. Cabet, *Histoire populaire de la révolution française* (Paris, 1839–40), IV: 328–34; see also Cabet, *Voyage en Icarie* (Paris, 1848), p. 515.

32. J. Grandjonc, *Communisme/Kommunismus/Communism* (Trier, 1989), I: 151.

33. P.-J.-B. Buchez & P.-C. Roux, *Histoire parlementaire de la révolution française*, tome XXXVII (Paris, 1838), pp. 152–68.

34. D. Guérin, *Proudhon oui et non* (Paris, 1978), pp. 123–7; see also *Présence*, pp. 281–4.
35. A. B. Spitzer, *The Revolutionary Theories of Louis Auguste Blanqui* (New York, 1957), pp. 126–7.
36. Lehning, p. 301.
37. 28 April, 1879; cited S. Bernstein, *Auguste Blanqui and the Art of Insurrection* (London, 1971), p. 45.
38. *The Works of Heinrich Heine*, VIII (London, 1893), p. 51.
39. G. Duveau, *1848: The Making of a Revolution* (London, 1967), pp. 211–12.
40. *Peace-Republicans' Manual*, p. 85.
41. *The Life and Character of Maximilian Robespierre* (London, 1838); *A Dissertation and Elegy on the Life and Death of the Immortal Maximilian Robespierre*.
42. Bronterre, *Buonarroti's History*, p. 69.
43. Bronterre, *Buonarroti's History*, p. 219.
44. A. Mathiez, *Etudes sur Robespierre*, (Paris, 1958), p. 252.
45. Marx & Engels, *Collected Works*, VI: 11.
46. W. Markov, 'L'affaire Babeuf vue de Hambourg (1796–1797)', *AHRF* 162 (1960), pp. 507–13.
47. H. Heine, *Religion and Philosophy in Germany* (Boston, 1959), p. 109.
48. L. Stein, *Der Socialismus und Communismus des heutigen Frankreichs* (Leipzig, 1842), pp. 362, 368.
49. J. H. Billington, *Fire in the Minds of Men* (London, 1980), p. 233.
50. M. Hess, *Philosophische und sozialistische Schriften* (Vaduz, 1980), pp. 199, 201, 205.
51. Grandjonc, I: 169.
52. *Collected Works*, IV: 119.
53. *Collected Works*, VI: 514.
54. *Collected Works*, VI: 576.
55. *Collected Works*, VI: 514.
56. *Collected Works*, XXV: 19.
57. *Collected Works*, XXV: 609–10.
58. (New York, 1977–90), I: 133.
59. 1966; reprinted (London, 1996).

7   1848 AND AFTER

1. T. J. Clark, *Image of the People* (London, 1973), p. 131.
2. *Baboeuf et le socialisme en 1796* (Paris, 1850).
3. *Pages*, p. 15.
4. Fleury, pp. 111, 193, 143.
5. Fleury, pp. 8, 7, 22, 73, 20–1, 342.
6. I. M. Zeitlin, *Liberty, Equality and Revolution in Alexis de Tocqueville* (Boston, 1971), p. 24.
7. A. de Tocqueville, *Oeuvres Complètes*, tome IX (Paris, 1866). p. 517.
8. *Souvenirs d'Alexis de Tocqueville* (Paris, 1942), pp. 120–1.

9. Tocqueville, *Oeuvres Complètes*, IX: 542–3, 546.
10. H. Taine, *Les Origines de la France contemporaine* (Paris, 1876–93), IV: 291–2, 576–7.
11. Advielle, I: ix.
12. Advielle, I: 181.
13. Advielle, I: 189.
14. Advielle, I: 436, 473.
15. Advielle, I: xvi, 438.
16. G. Dallas, *At the Heart of a Tiger* (London, 1993), pp. 292–7.
17. A. Casanova & C. Mazauric, *Vive la révolution 1789–1989* (Paris, 1989), p. 37.
18. Cited J. Godechot, *Un jury pour la révolution* (Paris, 1974), p. 245.
19. J. Jaurès, *Histoire socialiste de la révolution française* (Paris 1969–72), I: 66.
20. Cited H. Hirsch, *Jean Jaurès as Historian* (Wyoming, 1944), p. 112.
21. *Histoire socialiste*, I: 211.
22. *Histoire socialiste*, I: 62.
23. See Casanova & Mazauric, *Vive la révolution*, p. 108.
24. *Histoire socialiste*, VI: 97.
25. G. Deville, *Gracchus Babeuf und die Verschwörung der Gleichen* (Zürich, 1887).
26. *Thermidor et directoire*, pp. 289, 315.
27. A. Rosmer, *Moscou sous Lénine* (Paris, 1953), p. 143; D. Guérin, *Le feu du sang* (Paris, 1977), p. 133.
28. Jaurès, *Histoire socialiste*, VI: 97.
29. *The Great French Revolution* (London, 1909), pp. 491–2.
30. M. Leroy, *Histoire des idées sociales*, II: 56.
31. See contemporary press reports in *Bulletin de l'association 'Les amis de Gracchus Babeuf'*, No. 1 (1994), pp. 11–15.
32. *Babeuf: la doctrine des égaux* (Paris, 1906), pp. 6–7.
33. *Les hommes de la révolution: Gracchus Babeuf* (Paris, 1907), pp. 170, 180, 197.
34. (London, 1911); see I. H. Birchall, 'Morris, Bax and Babeuf', *Journal of the William Morris Society* XII/1 (1996), pp. 41–7.
35. *The Story of the French Revolution* (London, 1907), pp. v, 80.
36. *The Last Episode*, pp. 135, 250–1.

8 THE SHADOW OF OCTOBER

1. *Collected Works*, VI: 203, XXXVIII: 40, 44.
2. *Pages*, p. 10.
3. See I. Deutscher, *The Prophet Unarmed* (Oxford, 1970), p. 292.
4. *Présence*, p. 299.
5. C. Rakovsky, *Selected Writings on Opposition in the USSR 1923–30* (London, 1980), p. 133.
6. (New York, 1965), p. 88.
7. See Deutscher, p. 437.
8. See J.-M. Schiappa, '"L'image" de Gracchus Babeuf dans l'action et la pensée de Trotsky', *Présence*, pp. 293–304.

9. T. Cliff, *Trotsky: The Sword of the Revolution 1917–1923* (London, 1990), p. 277.
10. *La conspiration des égaux* (Moscow, 1987) – reprint of French translation, originally published under the title *La vie de Gracchus Babeuf* (Paris, 1929).
11. See I. Ehrenburg, *Truce* (London, 1963).
12. See H. Siegel, *Asthetische Theorie und künstlerische Praxis bei Il'ja Erenburg* (Tübingen, 1979), p. 199.
13. Siegel, p. 191.
14. Siegel, pp. 113, 148, 151.
15. Ehrenburg, *La conspiration*, pp. 152–3.
16. *La Dépêche de Toulouse*, 2 September 1902, cited G. Belloni, *Aulard historien de la révolution française* (Paris, 1949), p. 117.
17. A. Aulard, *Etudes et leçons IV*, p. 21.
18. A. Aulard, *Etudes et leçons IV*, pp. 60, 66–7.
19. Schiappa, p. 247.
20. J. Friguglietti, *Albert Mathiez: historien révolutionnaire* (Paris, 1974), pp. 158, 180.
21. 'La politique de Robespierre et le 9 thermidor expliqués par Buonarroti', *Annales révolutionnaires* 3/4 (1910), p. 513.
22. *Autour de Robespierre* (Paris, 1925), p. 246.
23. *Le directoire* (Paris, 1934), pp. 164, 172.
24. Friguglietti, p. 230.
25. *L'Université libre*, 23 September 1944; reprinted *AHRF* 198 (1969), pp. 570–3.
26. J. Dautry, 'Albert Mathiez', *AHRF* 168 (1962) p. 140.
27. *Etudes sur la révolution française*, pp. 59, 146–7, 411; preface to *Pages*, pp. x, xi.
28. G. Lefebvre, *Le directoire* (Paris, 1971), p. 33.
29. A. Galante Garrone, *Buonarroti e Babeuf*; A. Saitta, *Filippo Buonarroti*.
30. *Les sources françaises du socialisme scientifique* (Paris, 1948), p. 279.
31. No. 7 (1949), pp. 111–12.
32. Cited J.-L. Rouch, *Prolétaire en veston* (Treignac, 1984), pp. 85–6.
33. D. Desanti, *L'internationale communiste* (Paris, 1970), p. 183.
34. *Les sans-culottes* (Paris, 1969), pp. 13–15, 55.
35. *Cahiers du communisme* 29/2 (1952), pp. 203–10; *La Pensée*, No. 53 (1954), pp. 39–62; see O. Bétourné & A. Hartig, *Penser l'histoire de la révolution française* (Paris, 1989), pp. 79–81, 111–14.
36. *La Pensée*, No. 37 (July–August 1951), pp. 119–22.
37. 'Personnel sans-culotte et personnel babouviste', *AHRF* 162 (1960), pp. 436–57.
38. Advielle, II: 157; *Débats* III: 609.
39. 'Sur le personnel ci-devant sectionnaire sous le directoire', *AHRF* 189 (1967), pp. 381–4.
40. *Babeuf* (Paris, 1937), p. 257.
41. *Babeuf: Textes choisis* (Paris, 1950), p. 21.
42. *Cahiers du communisme* (June–July 1979), pp. 105–7.

43. *Babeuf et la conspiration pour l'egalité* (Paris, 1962); *Babeuf: Ecrits* (Paris, 1988).
44. Mazauric, *Babeuf et la conspiration*, pp. 201–2.
45. Mazauric, *Babeuf et la conspiration*, p. 235.
46. *TDP*, No. 42, p. 294; Mazauric, p. 295.
47. Mazauric, p. 44.
48. Mazauric, *Babeuf et la conspiration*, p. 183.
49. *Présence*, p. 160.
50. *Pages*, p. 118; Mazauric, pp. 194–201.
51. *Pages*, p. 105.
52. P. Broué, *Trotsky* (Paris, 1988), pp. 794, 801.
53. See Rouch.
54. L. Trotsky, *Writings: Supplement 1934–40* (New York, 1979), p. 679.
55. *Babeuf et la conjuration des égaux*, Paris, 1922; reprinted Paris, 1969.
56. Dommanget, pp. 145–73; originally published *Annales révolutionnaires*, May–August 1922.
57. Dommanget, p. 146.
58. Rouch, p. 36.
59. Dommanget, p. 159.
60. V. Serge, *Memoirs of a Revolutionary* (Oxford, 1967), p. 169.
61. Rouch, pp. 76–7.
62. M. Dommanget, *Saint-Just* (Paris, 1971), pp. 149–50.
63. Dommanget, p. 167.
64. Dommanget, *Babeuf*, p. 58.
65. Dommanget, p. 178.
66. Dommanget, *Saint-Just*, p. 150.
67. Dommanget, *Babeuf*, p. 25.
68. Dommanget, *Babeuf*, p. 51.
69. *La lutte de classes sous la première république*, revised edition, Paris, 1968.
70. D. Guérin, *La révolution française et nous* (Paris, 1976), p. 63.
71. Guérin, *La lutte de classes*, II: 389, 391.
72. Guérin, *La lutte de classes*, II: 402, 404.
73. *AHRF* XIX (1947), pp. 173–9.
74. See G. Rudé, 'Les ouvriers parisiens dans la révolution française', *La Pensée* XLVIII-XLIX (1953), pp. 108–9.
75. D. Guérin, *La révolution française et nous*, p. 101.
76. Guérin, *La lutte de classes*, II: 392; *Pièces*, 15/49; *Débats*, IV: 153.
77. Guérin, *La lutte de classes*, II: 492.
78. Guérin, *La lutte de classes*, I:101.
79. L. Trotsky, *The New Course* (Ann Arbor, 1965), p. 114–18.
80. M. Kun, 'Victor Daline – opposant', *Cahiers Léon Trotsky* No. 38 (1989), pp. 5–12; see also two obituaries by C. Mazauric: *AHRF* 263 (1986), pp. 87–90; *La Pensée* 249 (1986), pp. 85–9.
81. Daline, pp. 383–4.
82. Daline, pp. 79–82.

83. Daline, p. 126.
84. Daline, pp. 190–1.
85. See A. Crosland, *The Future of Socialism* (London, 1956), pp. 81–2.
86. E. Tierno Galván, *Baboeuf y los iguales* (Madrid, 1967).
87. (London, 1930).
88. Laski, pp. 6, 14, 23, 18.
89. *Socialist Thought: The Forerunners 1789–1850* (London, 1953), pp. 13, 19.

9   COLD WAR AND AFTER

1. Reprinted London, 1970.
2. J.L. Talmon, *The Myth of the Nation* (London 1981), p. 535.
3. J.L. Talmon, *Utopianism and Politics* (London, 1957), p. 7.
4. Talmon, *Origins*, p. 6.
5. Talmon, *Origins*, pp. 1–2, 188.
6. Talmon, *Origins*, p. 207.
7. Talmon, *Origins*, p. 249.
8. *Contrepoint*, No. 34 (1980), pp. 103–7.
9. P. Baccou et le Club de l'horloge, *Le grand tabou* (Paris, 1981), pp. 23, 25–6, 39–40.
10. J.-P. Apparu (ed.), *La droite aujourd'hui* (Paris, 1979), p. 273.
11. P. Chaunu, *Le grand déclassement* (Paris, 1989), pp. 45, 259.
12. *La guerre de Vendée*, p. 53.
13. (Cambridge, 1965).
14. Cobban, p. 147.
15. *La république du centre* (Paris, 1988), p. 44.
16. *La gauche et la révolution* (Paris, 1986), p. 12; see also Bétourné & Hartig, pp. 15–35, 184–201.
17. F. Furet & D. Richet, *La révolution française* (Paris, 1986), p. 345.
18. F. Furet & M. Ozouf, *Dictionnaire critique de la révolution française* (Paris, 1988), pp. 200–2; Legrand, p. 329.
19. Furet & Ozouf, *Dictionnaire critique*, pp. 201–2; Buonarroti, H: 105–6.
20. *Marx et la révolution française* (Paris, 1986), pp. 114–15.
21. Furet & Ozouf, *Dictionnaire critique*, pp. 204–5.
22. Furet & Richet, p. 347.
23. *Penser la révolution française*, pp. 11–130.
24. O. Le Cour Grandmaison, *Les citoyennetés en révolution* (Paris, 1992), p. 81.
25. *Ami des lois*, cited *Tribun du peuple*, No. 36, p. 111.
26. Legrand, p. 440.
27. Schiappa, pp. 183, 165, 170, 247–51.
28. *La conjuration*, pp. 13, 5–7, 447.
29. *La conjuration*, p. 87.
30. *Gracchus Babeuf et le communisme* (Brussels, 1926).
31. *Pages*, p. 16.
32. C. Lévi-Strauss & D. Eribon, *De près et de loin* (Paris, 1988), pp. 15–16.

33. See F. H. & C. C. Lapointe, *Claude Lévi-Strauss and his Critics* (New York, 1977), which claims its bibliography is 'as complete as is technically feasible'.
34. Lévi-Strauss, *Gracchus Babeuf*, p. 27.
35. W. Harich, *Kommunismus ohne Wachstum* (Hamburg, 1975), pp. 63, 184–6.
36. Printed text (Paris, 1984).
37. I am indebted for information to Ted Freeman of the University of Bristol.
38. Bassis, p. 73.

10   COMMON HAPPINESS

1. Grandjonc, I: 13, 96–8.
2. *L'Eclaireur*, No. 4, p. 38.
3. Advielle, II: 31.
4. *Etudes sur la révolution française*, p. 147.
5. Bax, *The Last Episode*, pp. 124, 146.
6. *Pages*, pp. 157–8.
7. *TDP*, No. 35, p. 101.
8. A. Soboul (ed.), *Textes choisis de l'Encyclopédie* (Paris, 1962), p. 86.
9. *Pages*, p. 108.
10. *TDP*, No. 35, pp. 102–3.
11. *TDP*, No. 35, p. 104.
12. M. Sonenscher, *The Hatters of Eighteenth-Century France* (Berkeley & Los Angeles, 1987), pp. 25–7; R. Darnton, *The Great Cat Massacre* (New York, 1984), p. 88.
13. Buonarroti, II: 101.
14. *Pages*, pp. 113–14.
15. Daline, p. 154.
16. Dommanget, *Saint-Just*, p. 125.
17. See Schiappa, p. 186.
18. *TDP*, No. 43, pp. 301–2.
19. J. Freeman, 'A Year of Grace', *New Politics* IV/1 (1965), p. 112.
20. G. Lefebvre, *La France sous le directoire* (Paris, 1977) p. 208.
21. *TDP*, No. 35, p. 92.
22. Mazauric, p. 258.
23. *TDP*, No. 35, p. 105.
24. Buonarroti, II: 102–3.
25. Buonarrotti, I: 156–224.
26. *Communist Manifesto* in *Collected Works*, VI: 506.
27. *L'Eclaireur*, No. 6, p. 9.
28. Talmon, *Origins*, p. 44.
29. Schiappa, pp. 51–2.
30. *Pages*, p. 111.
31. *JLP*, No. 19, p. 3.
32. *TDP*, No. 30, p. 291.
33. Haute-Cour de justice, *Pièces lues dans le cours de l'exposé*, p. 13.

34. Buonarroti, I: 171.
35. *Pages*, pp. 118–19.
36. Buonarroti, I: 192–6.
37. Buonarroti, I: 209–10, 215.
38. *Les battus payent l'amende*, p. 22.
39. Lecocq, p. 35.
40. Lecocq, p. 43.
41. Buonarroti, I: 76.
42. Lecocq, p. 39.
43. Lecocq, pp. 39–40.
44. K.D. Tønnesson, *La défaite des sans-culottes*, p. 239; O. Hufton, 'Women in Revolution 1789–1796', *Past and Present* 53 (1971), pp. 90–108.
45. Buonarroti, II: 205.
46. 'Beyond 1793: Babeuf, Louis Blanc and the Genealogy of "Social revolution"', in F. Furet & M. Ozouf, *The French Revolution* . . . , III, pp. 509–26.
47. 'Le pessimisme économique de Babeuf et l'histoire des utopies', *AHRF* 164 (1961), pp. 215–33.
48. Mazauric, p. 62.
49. Mazauric, *Babeuf et la conspiration*, pp. 163, 36, 230.
50. *Présence*, pp. 254–6.
51. *JLP*, No. 5, p. 2.
52. Advielle, II: 56.
53. Buonarroti, I: 158.
54. Buonarroti, II: 156; *L'Eclaireur*, No. 5, p. 49.
55. Buonarroti, II: 208.
56. *L'Eclaireur*, No. 3, p. 5, No. 4, p. 37.
57. Marx & Engels, *Collected Works*, X: 429.
58. Buonarroti, I: 25.
59. Buonarroti, I: 165.
60. Buonarroti, I: 207.
61. *Oeuvres*, p. 234.
62. Legrand, p. 68.
63. Mazauric, p. 264.
64. Buonarroti, I: 165–7.
65. Buonarroti, I: 159.
66. Buonarroti, II: 210.
67. Guérin, *La lutte de classes*, II: 383.
68. Dommanget, p. 312.

11 THEORY AND PRACTICE

1. Rose, pp. 336, 339.
2. *TDP*, 'Prospectus', p. 2.
3. Buonarroti, II: 116.
4. *TDP*, No. 34, p. 11.

5. *TDP*, No. 40, pp. 235–6.
6. G. Rudé, *The Crowd in the French Revolution* (Oxford, 1967), p. 17.
7. M. Slavin, *The French Revolution in Miniature* (Princeton, 1984), p. 40.
8. H. Burstin, 'Les citoyens de quarante sous', *AHRF* 251 (1983), p. 111.
9. M. Sonenscher, *Work and Wages* (Cambridge, 1989), p. 102; W. H. Sewell, *Work and Revolution in France* (Cambridge, 1980), p. 40.
10. *The Great Cat Massacre*, p. 82.
11. Sonenscher, *Work and Wages*, p. 102.
12. H. Burstin, 'Le faubourg Saint-Marcel à l'époque révolutionnaire', *AHRF* 231 (1978), p. 123.
13. O. Hufton, 'Women in Revolution', p. 92.
14. Bianchi, p. 36.
15. R. Monnier, 'Les classes laborieuses du faubourg Saint-Antoine', *AHRF* 235 (1979), pp. 119–24.
16. *Présence*, pp. 249–50; *Pièces*, 10/18, 20/6.
17. *TDP*, No. 29, p. 263.
18. Buonarroti, I: 145.
19. *Oeuvres*, p. 374; see Daline, pp. 148, 540.
20. *TDP*, No. 41, p. 277.
21. Mazauric, pp. 254–5.
22. Daline, p. 289.
23. *Débats*, III: 293.
24. *JLP*, No. 18, pp. 1–2.
25. *TDP*, No. 38, p. 164; *Pièces*, I: 198.
26. *Oeuvres*, pp. 375–6.
27. *TDP*, No. 34, p. 13.
28. *La guerre de la Vendée*, p. 105.
29. *JLP*, No. 5, p. 2.
30. Buonarroti, I: 186–7.
31. 'Religion et conspiration des égaux', *Bulletin de l'association 'Les amis de Gracchus Babeuf'*, No. 5 (1996), pp. 3–19.
32. 'Babeuf et l'éducation', Dommanget pp. 107–38.
33. *Oeuvres*, pp. 378–9.
34. K.D. Tønnesson, 'The Babouvists – From Utopian to Practical Socialism', *Past and Present* 22 (1962), pp. 65–6.
35. Buonarroti, I: 124–5.
36. Buonarroti, II: 111.
37. Haute-Cour de Justice, *Pièces lues dans le cours de l'exposé*, p. 73.
38. *Oeuvres*, p. 232.
39. Advielle, II: 33.
40. *JLP*, No. 14, p. 1.
41. Buonarroti, I: 130.
42. Buonarroti, I: 222.
43. Dommanget, p. 32.

44. Buonarroti, I: 113–14.
45. Dommanget, p. 234.
46. *Pièces*, 7/39.
47. Buonarroti, I: 152–3.
48. Legrand, p. 130.
49. *Encyclopédie nouvelle;* cited Advielle, I: 413.
50. Saitta, II: 61–84.
51. Buonarroti, II: 84–5.
52. *TDP*, No. 42, p. 291.
53. Hésine, No. 9, p. 4.
54. Buonarroti, II: 86.
55. *Pièces*, 14/19.
56. Buonarroti, II: 82.
57. *TDP*, No. 40, p. 230.
58. Buonarroti, II: 196.
59. Draper, *The Two Souls of Socialism*, p. 4.
60. *TDP*, No. 42, p. 294.
61. *Pièces*, 7/92.
62. *JLP*, No. 6, p. 1; *TDP*, No. 27, pp. 218–19.
63. 'General Rules of the IWMA', *Collected Works*, XXIII: 3.
64. Saitta, I: 66.
65. 'Address to the Chartists', cited D. McNally, *Against the Market* (London, 1993), p. 113.
66. *Collected Works*, V: 7.
67. *JLP*, No. 16, p. 5.
68. *Collected Works*, V: 7.

APPENDIX

1. *Oeuvres*, pp. 95–102.
2. Buonarroti, II: 99–107.
3. Schiappa, p. 123.
4. *Débats*, II: 371; Advielle, II: 32–3.
5. Buonarroti, pp. 94–8.
6. *TDP*, No. 35, pp. 102–6.
7. Buonarroti, II: 204–14.

Index

Names marked with an asterisk* were, or were accused of being, involved in Babeuf's conspiracy; dates of birth and death are given where known.

About Haymarket Books

Haymarket Books is a nonprofit, progressive book distributor and publisher, a project of the Center for Economic Research and Social Change. We believe that activists need to take ideas, history, and politics into the many struggles for social justice today. Learning the lessons of past victories, as well as defeats, can arm a new generation of fighters for a better world. As Karl Marx said, "The philosophers have merely interpreted the world; the point, however, is to change it."

We take inspiration and courage from our namesakes, the Haymarket Martyrs, who gave their lives fighting for a better world. Their 1886 struggle for the eight-hour day, which gave us May Day, the international workers' holiday, reminds workers around the world that ordinary people can organize and struggle for their own liberation. These struggles continue today across the globe-struggles against oppression, exploitation, hunger, and poverty.

It was August Spies, one of the Martyrs targeted for being an immigrant and an anarchist, who predicted the battles being fought to this day. "If you think that by hanging us you can stamp out the labor movement," Spies told the judge, "then hang us. Here you will tread upon a spark, but here, and there, and behind you, and in front of you, and everywhere, the flames will blaze up. It is a subterranean fire. You cannot put it out. The ground is on fire upon which you stand."

We could not succeed in our publishing efforts without the generous financial support of our readers. Many people contribute to our project through the Haymarket Sustainers program, where donors receive free books in return for their monetary support. If you would like to be a part of this program, please contact us at info@haymarketbooks.org.

Shop our full catalog online at www.haymarketbooks.org or call 773-583-7884.

Printed in the USA
CPSIA information can be obtained
at www.ICGtesting.com
JSHW022219140824
68134JS00018B/1142

9 781608 466054